Anna Ullrich

Anna Ullrich used her off-time during graduate school to learn HTML and Web design, eventually teaching at different universities while still working on her MFA and doing a wide variety of freelance creative work. After graduation, she spent five years working at Adobe Systems in Seattle in various jobs: writing user guides (including the After Effects 6.5 release) and tutorials, illustrating technical guides, and even providing technical support.

Anna studied photography at the University of Washington in Seattle, where she earned her BFA and was first introduced to digital imaging by the pioneering computer-based artist Paul Berger. She went on to earn her MFA in photography at the University of Notre Dame in Indiana, where she studied with Martina Lopez (another former photo student of Paul's), whose digital artwork emphasizes personal narratives.

Anna is an accomplished fine artist, best known for her frenzied, large-scale, two-dimensional digital montages. She recently exhibited a group of work in a show organized by FotoFest (**www.fotofest.org**) that traveled throughout the world, most recently to the Moscow Museum of Contemporary Art.

Anna is currently taking her artwork into new dimensions and works as a freelance artist and Web designer.

Acknowledgments

Many thanks and much gratitude to Christine Yarrow for introducing me to the folks at Peachpit Press and for appreciating me and my pottery collection. Thank you to James, Danielle, and Jason for their inspiring creativity and talent; I'm just riding on their coattails with this one. Thank you to the After Effects team for being the coolest and nicest team of people I ever worked with at Adobe. (Christine's easily the coolest individual at Adobe.) And special thanks to Tiffany Taylor and Rebecca Gulick at Peachpit for working with me and the constantly shifting schedule.

About the Contributors

Jason Croatto

Jason Croatto hails from New York State. He is a graduate of Rochester Institute of Technology in Rochester, New York. Jason moved to California after graduating in 2001; he currently resides and works in Los Angeles as an associate producer/ graphic designer for a production/promo house.

Danielle Heitmuller

A native of Connecticut, Danielle Heitmuller began her career as a traditional artist and landscape painter. A keen interest in art and entertainment took her to Rochester Institute of Technology in Rochester, New York, where she studied film and animation. While at RIT, she was first exposed to After Effects and began experimenting with it as a compositing tool for her own animated shorts.

After graduation, Danielle made her way west to the greater Los Angeles area, where she now resides and works as a freelance storyboard artist and motion graphics artist. Her work has included a number of interstitials for Bungalow 3 and the Fine Living Network, as well as a variety of independent projects. Danielle is currently working on an animated short using traditional techniques combined with digital compositing.

Table of Contents

Table of Contents

Table of Contents

Table of Contents

Introduction

Welcome to *Adobe After Effects 6.5 Magic!* Like the other books in New Riders' *Magic* series, the book you have in your grasp contains original, hands-on projects that are written for readers who already understand the basics. You can easily expand upon each project in this book using your own creative and innovative ideas. We provide a few suggestions at the end of each chapter that will help you experiment and enhance the projects to take them to the next level. All the techniques revealed within can be recycled into something new and unique over and over again simply by changing the content and tweaking some base values.

To make the most of this book, we hope you approach the projects here with a spirit of discovery and experimentation. Let them serve as a starting point for your own exciting new motion graphics ideas and After Effects creations!

How this book was written

This book was the brainchild of LA-based motion graphics pro and teacher, James Rankin. James said, "The original concept of this book was inspired by a comment from an audience member at one of my speaking engagements on After Effects. He said, 'I love these sessions. They're like a cookbook of recipes for people who do this for a living and used to have to figure it out from scratch.' Then he asked, 'Do you have a book out like this?' There wasn't one like it then, but thanks to the good people at New Riders, there is now."

The After Effects projects featured in this book were crafted by James Rankin and contributors Jason Croatto and Danielle Heitmuller. Jason designed the projects for chapters 8, "Animating with Illustrator"; 12, "Sonic Promo"; and 22, "Video Cubes." Danielle designed the projects for chapters 1, "Spinning Squares"; 2, "Falling Squares"; and 3, "Wall of Squares." And James designed the remaining chapters' projects.

Co-author Anna Ullrich expanded on the finished developed projects, in some cases generating simpler solutions for some tasks and restructuring others. She crafted the step-by-step language that will enable you to make quick and effective use of the wealth of creative ideas found in these pages.

Who this book is for

Even though this book targets experienced users of After Effects, we've tried to ensure that new users can also keep up with every project. Toward that objective, we use the same terminology that After Effects Help uses to name features and refer to user-interface elements. This way, you can easily locate related documentation in Help.

About this book and companion DVD

This book uses Adobe After Effects 6.5, and features that are specific only to that version are incorporated into many of the projects. Some projects also use features that are available only in the Professional version of After Effects 6.5, such as motion tracking and particular effects. (These features are noted in the book's text wherever relevant, so you aren't sent on a wild goose chase searching for a feature or reporting a bug that doesn't exist in the software or book.)

For your convenience, the book's companion DVD offers a 30-day tryout version of After Effects 6.5 Professional. Some projects use third-party effects (which were developed by other companies for After Effects and which must be installed into After Effects). Demo versions of those effects are also provided on the book's DVD; you'll find a 30-day demo version of Zaxwerks' 3D Invigorator Classic effect and a 14-day demo version of Boris FX's Continuum Complete collection of effects. Finally, the companion disc includes QuickTime movies of all the finished chapter projects and source materials you can use to complete each project yourself.

Let the fun begin!

CHAPTER 1 | Spinning Squares

In your work, you may often be asked to create something from nothing: no footage, perhaps just a logo and a few stills. In this chapter and the next two, we'll show how much you can do with so little by working with the multitalented and jack-of-all trades (in the right hands, of course) Solid layer in After Effects.

Starting with only a company logo, you can pick a color palette and graphic style that work within the client's persona. For this project, you have three product shots and the company logo to work with. By focusing on four main colors (orange, green, purple, and yellow), you can build an engaging sequence for each product shot by using different shades and tints of each particular color to distinguish each segment.

It Works Like This

Check out the **Ch1_Finished_Movie.mov** file in this chapter's folder on the book's DVD to see the 15-second advertisement you'll create in this project. The project uses solids to create interesting layouts from scratch and creates modular sequences that you can duplicate and easily modify to quickly build a cohesive presentation. You can take these skills and use them to create your own layouts out of solids or replace the solids with textures and other footage. The basic principles of this project are as follows:

1. Design interesting animations and layouts using nothing but solids.

2. Use solids to matte images of various sizes.

3. Use effects to transition from one sequence to another and to bring text onto the screen.

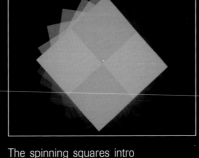

The spinning squares intro

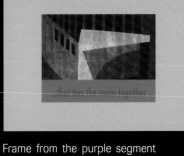

Frame from the purple segment

The block dissolve transition

Preparing to Work

To prepare for this project, do the following:

1 Start with a new project, and import the **Images** folder from this chapter's folder on the DVD. It contains the files **RainbowLamp. jpg**, **Sofa_01.jpg**, and **Rug.jpg**.

2 Create another folder named **Graphics**. Import **Style_Logo.psd** by using the Composition - Cropped Layers option (rather than Footage or Composition).

Import As Options: Do You Really Understand Them?

- *Footage*—You probably noticed long ago that when you import a layered file as footage, the file appears in After Effects either as if the layers have been flattened into one or with only a single layer that you pick. The layers are still there in the original source file, but you won't have access to the layers in After Effects. That's all well and good for some projects.

- *Composition*—When you choose this option for a layered file, the file is presented as a composition that contains an After Effects layer for each Photoshop layer. The composition has an associated folder in the Project window, which contains a footage item for each particular layer (handy!). In addition, any Photoshop layer that uses a Photoshop layer style is presented as a nested composition with a layer for each essential property in the layer style's effect. For example, a Photoshop layer that uses the Bevel and Emboss layer style will produce three layers in After Effects: a layer for the Photoshop layer, a layer for the style's shadow property, and a layer for the style's highlight property. This chapter's project takes advantage of this feature by animating a layer style contained in the logo.

- *Composition - Cropped Layers*—When you choose this option for a layered file, you get the same results you would for the Composition option, except for one crucial difference. The

---

Composition - Cropped Layers option defines the dimensions of each layer according to the actual content within the Photoshop layer; in contrast, the Composition option defines the dimensions of each layer according to the dimensions of the entire file. This may sound like the Composition option stretches any layers that have smaller dimensions than the entire file, but it doesn't.

Building the Intro

You'll start this project by building the first modular component. Once it's built, you can duplicate it and modify it to quickly create the second part of the spinning intro, lickety-split.

Spin and scale, part 1

You'll begin by creating a snappy intro out of nothing but some orange, square-shaped solids:

1 Create a new composition named Horizontal Zoom, and set its dimensions to 720 × 540, the Frame Rate to 29.97, and the Duration to 5;00 seconds.

2 Create a new solid (Layer > New > Solid) named and colored Dark Orange (RGB: 236, 82, 2), with the dimensions 720 × 720.

3 Press the S key to display the layer's Scale property, and then set it to 25, 25%.

4 Duplicate the Dark Orange layer.

5 Select both layers in the Timeline, press A to display their Anchor Point properties, and then set the property for each layer as follows:

Layer 1: 715, 715

Layer 2: 0, 0

You've just set the landing position for the squares. Now you'll animate them onto the screen:

1   Go to time 0;20, select both layers, and press P to display their Position properties.

2   Add Position keyframes for both layers with the value 360, 270.

3   Go back to time 0;05, and move the top layer off the screen to the right (Position: 920, 270).

4   Move the bottom layer off the screen to the left (Position: –210, 270).

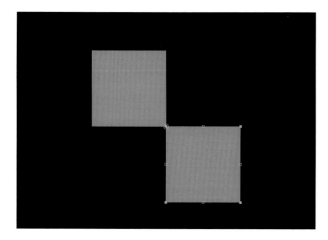

Both squares with new anchor points

Press the Home key and then the Spacebar to preview the animation. The squares should be offscreen to begin with and then slide in horizontally, pass each other, and stop kitty-corner to one another.

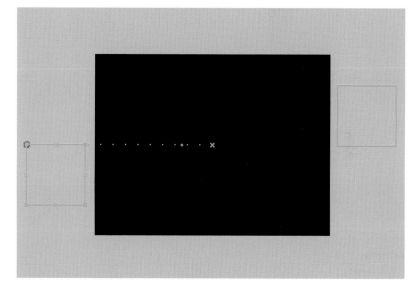

Composition with both squares offscreen on the gray pasteboard

To add a little more zip, let's make the squares spin after they pass each other:

1   Return to time 0;20, select both layers, and press the R key to display the Rotation property.

2   Add Rotation keyframes for both layers with the values 0 x +0.0.

3   Go to time 1;20, and change both layers' Rotation to –2 x +0.0. Now the squares rotate around the anchor point twice in a counterclockwise direction.

4   Press Shift+S to display the layers' Scale properties alongside Rotation. Click the stopwatch to add a Scale keyframe for both layers at time 1;20. (The Scale values should already be 25, 25% for both layers.)

5   Go to time 2;15, and change both layers' Scale to 50, 50%.

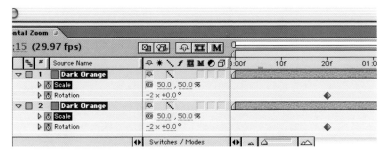

Timeline with Scale and Rotation keyframes revealed

Save and preview your work. The squares should slide in horizontally, pass each other, spin counterclockwise, and then scale outward. This is just half of the intro sequence.

Spin and scale, part 2

Next you'll modify a duplicate of the comp you just created in order to quickly create a vertical version of it:

1   Duplicate the Horizontal Zoom composition in the Project window, rename the duplicate Vertical Zoom, and then open it.

2   Rename and recolor both solids Mid Orange (RGB: 255, 107, 15).

3   Change each layer's Anchor Point property as follows:

> Layer 1: 715, 0
>
> Layer 2: 0, 715

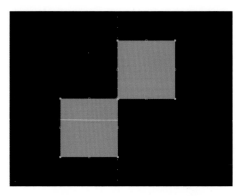

Squares in the Vertical Zoom comp with new anchor points

4   For each layer, move the Position keyframe at time 0;20 to time 0;15, and move the keyframe at time 0;05 to time 0;00.

5   Press Home to go to 0;00, and then change Layer 1's Position to 360, −200 and Layer 2's Position to 360, 740.

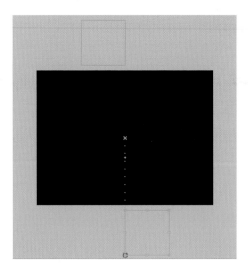

Both squares offscreen and on the gray pasteboard

That's it! The Rotation and Scale keyframes you need are already set up. Now the squares slide in from the top and bottom of the composition, pass each other, spin counterclockwise, and then scale outward.

Spin together

You're almost done with the opening animation. All that's left is to nest these two compositions in a third "parent" composition. First, you should organize the Project window:

1   Create a new folder called **Zooms**, and move the Horizontal Zoom and Vertical Zoom comps into it.

2   Select both Zoom compositions in the Project window, and drag them to the window's New Composition button. In the New Composition From Selection dialog, make sure Single Composition is selected, and click OK.

3   Rename the new comp *Intro* in the Project window.

Save and then preview your work. The squares should slide in from all four sides of the comp, form a square, spin counterclockwise, and then fill the comp window.

Building the Color Sequences

This project is created through a series of modular components. As you saw in the previous sections, you save lots of time by duplicating and altering sequences to create new sequences that create a cohesive whole. This process also lets you substitute different colors and content easily, without having to redo the entire project.

Orange sequence and a transition

Since you used orange squares in the intro, you'll use orange shades in the following sequence to create a smooth transition. If you want a more dramatic change, you can choose to use a different color for either section. Here are the steps:

1   Create a new composition named Orange Body, with dimensions of 720 × 540, Frame Rate 29.97, and Duration of 5;00 seconds.

2   Create a new solid named BG Orange, make it pale orange (RGB: 255, 194, 137), and make it comp size (click Make Comp Size in the Solid Footage Settings dialog).

3   Create a new solid named and colored Mid Orange (RGB: 255, 107, 15), and make it comp size too.

4   Set the Mid Orange layer's Scale to 60, 60%.

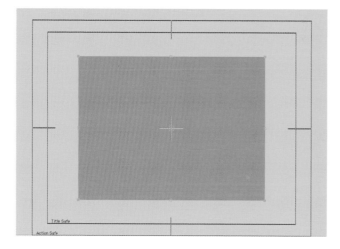

Orange body background and mid orange rectangle

The Transition effects in After Effects are generally used between scenes or to get an object on or off the screen. In this case, you'll use the Block Dissolve Transition effect to bring in an object:

1   Go to time 0;15, and apply Effect > Transition > Block Dissolve to the Mid Orange solid layer.

2   Set the effect's Block Width and Block Height properties to 20.0.

3   Set the Transition Completion property to 100%, and then click its stopwatch to create a keyframe for the property.

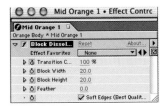

The settings for the Block Dissolve effect

4   Go to time 1;00, and change Transition Completion to 0%. Press Home and then the Spacebar to preview the transition.

Tip: Six of the seven Transition effects have a vital property named Transition Completion, which works like this: When the property is set to 100%, the layer is totally out of the scene; when the property is set to 0%, the layer is totally in the scene. Animate this property, and you've got yourself an instant slick transition.

5   Create a new solid named Pic Matte with dimensions of 432 × 324, using any color.

A matte is an easy way to set up a consistent size and position for any picture. No matter what picture you need to put in that spot, only the image area that lies within the matte's boundaries will display.

6   Position the Pic Matte layer at 360, 228.

7   Change its Scale to 100, 75%.

Positioning the blue photo matte

8   Add **RainbowLamp.jpg** to the Orange Body Timeline at time 1;00, and drag it under the Pic Matte layer.

9   Set the RainbowLamp layer's Track Matte to Alpha Matte "Pic Matte". Now the photo is matted by the Pic Matte layer.

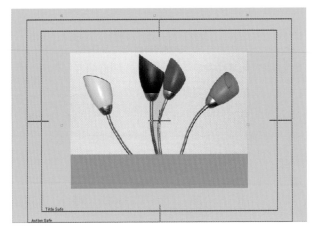

Adding a Track Matte to the picture

10 Set the RainbowLamp layer's Position to 350, 280 and its Scale to 84, 84%.

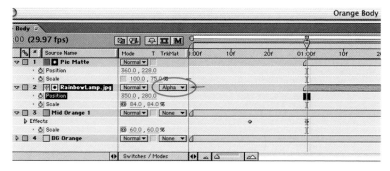

The Pic Matte and photo in the Timeline

11 Still at time 1;00, add a 0% Opacity keyframe to **RainbowLamp.jpg**.

12 Go to time 1;10, and change the Opacity to 100%.

You're almost there. The position of the image is now set. Now you'll add a little text to the spot and apply a different Transition effect to bring it on:

1 Create a new text layer at time 1;10 that displays the text *That little something…*. Use a really dark orange color (RGB: 214, 75, 3) and a font and text size that display the line of text within the orange rectangle beneath the image. (We used 40 for the Text Size, centered the text, and positioned it at 220, 410.)

2 Apply Effect > Transition > Linear Wipe to the text layer, and set the effect's Wipe Angle to 0 x +270.

3 Still at time 1;10, add a keyframe for 100% Transition Completion.

4 Go to time 1;20, and change Transition Completion to 0%.

Settings for the Linear Wipe effect

The sequence is nearly complete. Now you'll animate this section's opacity to create a transition to the next sequence:

1 Go to time 2;15, and select the text, matte, and photo layers.

2 Press T to display the layers' Opacity property, and then create a 100% Opacity keyframe for each layer.

3 Go to time 2;25, and change all three layers' Opacity to 0%.

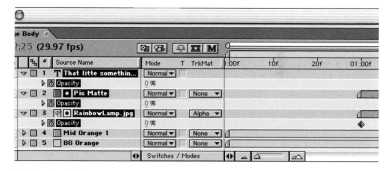

Adding the fade out

4 Go to time 2;23, select layer 4 (Mid Orange), and create a Scale keyframe at the current size, which should be 60%, 60%.

5 Go to 3;08, and change the layer's Scale to 100, 100%.

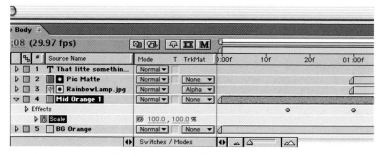

Creating the screen wipe by animating Scale

Save and preview your work. The Orange Body comp should scale and wipe the screen.

Green sequence

When we chose the palette for the Style Design Center spot, we decided to work with a different color for each product section and the closing spot featuring the client logo. Since you're working with modular components, you'll be able to easily modify the Orange Body comp to produce a green version for the next sequence:

1   Duplicate the Orange Body comp, rename it Green Body, and then open it.

2   Rename and recolor the Pale Orange layer to Pale Green (RGB: 185, 217, 161) and the Mid Orange layer to Mid Green (RGB: 67, 179, 63).

Changing the colors to make the green section

3   Select the RainbowLamp layer. Hold down Alt (Windows) or Option (Mac OS), and drag **Sofa_01.jpg** from the Project window onto **RainbowLamp.jpg** in the Timeline. This replaces the RainbowLamp image with the sofa image but retains the RainbowLamp layer's keyframes.

4   Scale the Sofa_01 layer to 68, 68%, and position it at 372, 300.

5   Change the Pic Matte layer's Position to 360, 310.

6   Change the text layer to display ...*extra special*..., change the text's color to a really dark green (RGB: 38, 106, 37), and position the layer at 255, 163.

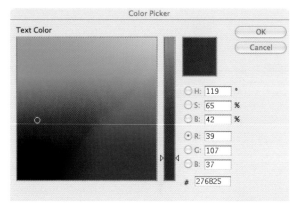

Changing the text's color

Save and preview your work. In just a few easy steps, you've designed the green sequence. You'll do the purple sequence using even fewer steps.

Purple sequence

Purple makes a nice third color choice because it's the complementary color to yellow, so the color transition between this section and the yellow-colored end tag really pops. Here are the steps:

1   Duplicate the Orange Body comp, and rename it Purple Body.

2   Rename and recolor the Pale Orange layer to Pale Purple (RGB: 187, 168, 255) and the Mid Orange layer to Mid Purple (RGB: 133, 79, 255).

3   Select the RainbowLamp layer. Hold down Alt (Windows) or Option (Mac OS) while dragging **Rug.jpg** from the Project window to replace the **RainbowLamp.jpg** layer in the Timeline and retain the layer's keyframes.

Leave the Position and Scale as they are.

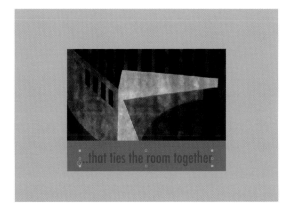

New colors for the purple section

4   Change the text layer to display *...that ties the room together*, change the text's color to a really dark purple (RGB: 85, 50, 168), and position the layer at 177, 410.

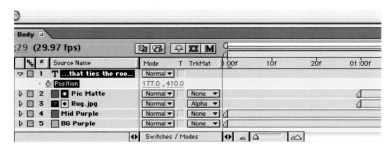

Changing the text for the purple section

Save and preview your work.

Creating the End Tag

The section that will close your project will be kept pretty simple to keep the focus on the client's brand, but simple can still be fun (i.e., animated!).

Animating the effects

The client has given you their company logo: a beveled script text on top of a flat sans serif font. You'll make the logo come alive by animating the type's bevel, which is courtesy of a layer style that was applied to the logo beforehand in Photoshop:

1   Create a new composition named End Tag with dimensions of 720 × 540, Frame Rate 29.97, and Duration 5;00 seconds.

2   Open the Layer Effects comp from the **Graphics** folder in the Project window.

The timeline for the Photoshop layer style

3   Go to time 0;10 in the Layer Effects comp, and select both the Bevel Highlight and the Bevel Shadow layers.

4   Apply Effect > Transition > Radial Wipe to both layers.

5   Add a 100% Transition Completion keyframe to each layer.

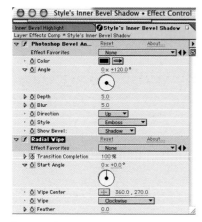

Settings for the Radial Wipe effect

6   Go to time 0;20, and change each layer's Transition Completion property to 0%.

The logo is now a lot more interesting. Let's add it to the End Tag comp:

1   Return to the End Tag comp. Create a new solid that's named and colored Pale Yellow (RGB: 252, 253, 162) and that's at comp size.

2   Go to time 0;10, and drag the Style_Logo comp to the Timeline.

3   Add a 0% Opacity keyframe to the StyleLogo layer.

4   Go to time 0;20, and change the layer's Opacity to 100%.

Adding the fade in to the End Tag sequence

Save your work.

Completing the Finished Spot

You finally have all the pieces required to complete the final spot. You just need to assemble them and add some dissolves to soften the transitions:

1   Create a new comp named Final_Squares1 that's 720 x 540 in size, with Frame Rate 29.97 and Duration 15;00 seconds.

In order to have really smooth transitions, you need to add a cross fade between sections by animating the Opacity of each.

2   Add the Intro to the Final_Squares1 Timeline at time 0;00.

3   Go to time 3;00, and add the Orange Body comp to the Timeline.

4   Insert a 0% Opacity keyframe for the Orange Body layer.

5   Go to time 3;15, and change the layer's Opacity to 100%.

Timeline for the final comp with the Intro and the orange section

The green section comes next:

1   Go to time 6;15, add the Green Body comp to the Timeline, and add a 0% Opacity keyframe to the layer.

2   Add a 100% Opacity keyframe to the Orange Body layer.

3   Go to time 6;25, and change the Orange Body layer's Opacity to 0%.

4 Go to time 7;00, and change the Green Body layer's Opacity to 100%.

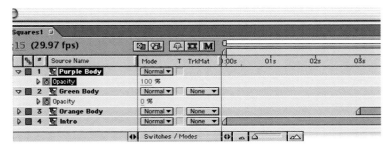

Adding the green section to the final comp

Now you add the purple section:

1 Go to time 10;00, add the Purple Body comp to the Timeline, and add a 0% Opacity keyframe to the layer.

2 Add a 100% Opacity keyframe to the Green Body layer.

3 Go to time 10;10, and change the Green Body layer's Opacity to 0%.

4 Go to time 10;15, and change the Purple Body layer's Opacity to 100%.

Adding the purple section to the final comp

The cross fade you'll create between the Purple Body comp and the End Tag comp is a little different than those you've created so far. The Purple Body takes exactly as long to fade out as the End Tag takes to fades in:

1 Go to time 13;15, add the End Tag comp to the Timeline, and add a 0% Opacity keyframe to the layer.

2 Add a 100% Opacity keyframe to the Purple Body layer.

3 Go to time 13;25, and change the Purple Body layer's Opacity to 0%.

4 Change the End Tag layer's Opacity to 100%.

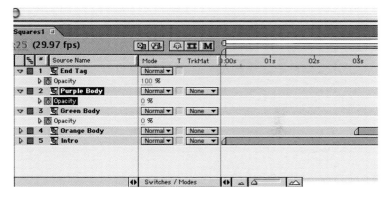

Adding the yellow End Tag section to the final comp

Save and preview your work.

Tip: If you wish to cut down on render time, close the Timeline before rendering so After Effects doesn't have to display what it's rendering.

Now Try This

Congratulations! By now you've learned how easy it is to create a visually engaging spot from scratch using the extremely versatile Solid layer:

- Since After Effects 6.5 treats solids like any other footage in the Project window, you can easily replace a solid with footage. Try replacing the Mid colored background layers with a moving texture or some footage.

- The mattes you've created allow you to put different items over the backdrop. Experiment by replacing the still image with video, or by adding an animated logo over the moving texture.

CHAPTER 2

Falling Squares

After Effects provides some great prebuilt effects for creating scene transitions, but there's only so much you can do with them (or anything prebuilt!) when you want to make something unique. This chapter shows you how to design a lively transition that's simply made of animated solids. The transition features solids radiating outward toward the viewer and then collapsing inward to reveal a layout that's falling into place.

In the previous chapter, you worked almost exclusively with 2D solids to create cool and interesting effects. You'll use those same techniques in this chapter but add a bit of 3D and some dynamic animations to the brew. And since this project relies on solids for its transitions and layout, you can easily transform the solids even further or swap out the solids for your own content to make the project your own.

It Works Like This

Open the **Ch2_Finished_Movie.mov** file from this chapter's folder on the DVD to see the spot you'll create. This project continues Chapter 1's theme of working with solids in place of video, animation, or other footage. In addition, you'll add some depth to the design by animating the solids in 3D space. The basic principles you'll use are as follows:

1. Use solids to create an enticing backdrop.

2. Matte images of various sizes using solids.

3. Create eye-catching transitions by animating solids.

4. Use Vector Paint to animate a Photoshop file's native effects.

Solids rotating through space

The transition of radiating squares

The green section of the product spotlight.

Preparing to Work

To prepare for this project, do the following:

1   Start with a new project, and create three folders named **Elements**, **Graphics**, and **Sections**.

2   Import the **Images** folder from this chapter's folder in the book's DVD. This folder contains the following files:

    • **Chair_02.jpg**

    • **Chandelier.jpg**

    • **Kitchen_02.jpg**

    • **Bedroom_01.jpg**

    • **Television.jpg**

3   Using the Import As option Composition - Cropped Layers, import the **Style_Logo.psd** file from the DVD into the Graphics folder.

Building the Transitions

The transitions you'll build in this chapter are inspired by retro designs of the 1960s and 70s. There's a positive madness for all things retro these days, which just so happens to work well with solids that are left in their "natural" state.

The orange transition

The idea behind the transitions is simple: a set of concentric squares that radiates out to wipe the screen and then comes back in to reveal a new scene. Simple, yes, but really snazzy, too!

You start with the squares:

1   Generate a new comp named Orange Squares in the **Elements** folder, with dimensions 720 × 540, Frame Rate 29.97, and Duration 4;00.

2   Create a new solid at 0;00 named Mid Orange (RGB: 255, 107, 15) with dimensions 720 × 720.

3   Create a 0% Scale keyframe.

4   Go to time 0;10, and change the Scale to 100%.

5   Duplicate the layer twice. Change the color of layer 1 to light orange (RGB: 255, 139, 52) and the color of layer 2 to dark orange (RGB: 236, 82, 2), and then rename both layers according to their new color.

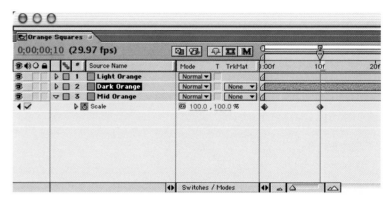

Adding the scale change and duplicating the layers

Right now the three squares scale simultaneously, but you only see the top light-orange layer. So, you'll stagger the In points of the layers to make the squares appear to radiate outward:

1   Select layer 2, and go to time 0;03.

2   Press [to bring the layer's In point to time 0;03.

3   Select layer 1, and go to time 0;06. Press [to bring the layer's In point to time 0;06.

4   Select all the layers, and copy them.

5   Go to time 0;09, and paste the new layers.

6   Press Shift while dragging the layers, and snap the first frame of the Mid Orange layer to the Current Time Indicator (CTI).

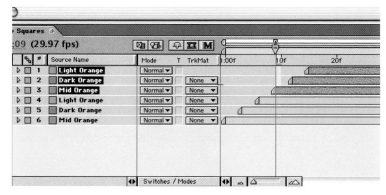

Duplicating the layers so there are six squares

Scaling squares

You should now have squares that radiate out from the center of the screen with a three-frame offset between each layer. Very cool. Of course, there's more to do! Now you'll make the squares collapse back inward:

1   Go to time 1;05, and insert a 100, 100% Scale keyframe for layer 1.

2   Go to time 1;15, and change the Scale to 0%.

3   Copy these two keyframes.

4   Go to time 1;08, and paste the keyframes on layer 2. Paste the keyframes again on the remaining layers at the following points in time:

> Layer 3: 1;11
>
> Layer 4: 1;14
>
> Layer 5: 1;17
>
> Layer 6: 1;20

The staggered Scale keyframes

The squares should now radiate out for 25 frames, hold for 10 frames, and then collapse into the center for 25 more frames.

Save your work, and preview the animation.

Generating the other transitions

You need to create the same transition in the other three colors chosen for this spot:

1   Duplicate the Orange Squares comp three times, and rename the copies Green Squares, Purple Squares, and Yellow Squares.

2   Open the Green Squares comp. Rename and recolor the orange squares to the corresponding green hue: Light Green (RGB: 79, 217, 74), Dark Green (RGB: 45, 126, 43), and Mid Green (RGB: 67, 179, 63).

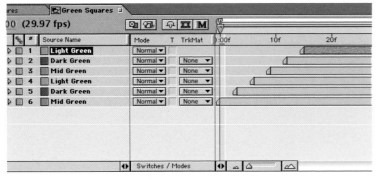

Changing the colors to shades of green

3   Repeat this process for the Purple Squares and Yellow Squares comps: Light Purple (RGB: 154, 127, 255), Dark Purple (RGB: 99, 58, 190), and Mid Purple (RGB: 133, 79, 255); and Light Yellow (RGB: 250, 253, 85), Dark Yellow (RGB: 187, 165, 57), and Mid Yellow (RGB: 199, 201, 67).

Save your work.

Building Backdrops

Now you have the transitions you need for the final. These bold graphics should reveal an impressive layout underneath. It's time to start exploring the 3D aspect of the project. Next you'll create the background elements for each section using nothing but our multi-talented friend the solid.

Fun with 3D

If you're getting tired of the flat solid, this is the part you've been waiting for. You'll give your solids a little more punch and depth by spinning them in three-dimensional space until they land in place in your layout:

1   Create a new composition named Moving BG Orange with dimensions 720 × 540, Frame Rate 29.97, and Duration 10;00.

2   Create a new solid named BG Square 1 with dimensions 720 × 720 in a mid orange color (RGB: 255, 107, 15).

3   Duplicate the layer.

4   Go to time 3;00, and insert a composition marker (Shift+1.) This marker lets you quickly return to this point in time by pressing the 1 key.

5   Turn on the 3D switch for each layer in the Timelines's Switches column.

6   Set the Position of BG Square 1 to 360, 270, 88, and add a Position keyframe.

7   Set BG Square 1's Scale to 48, 48%, and add a Scale keyframe.

8   Set the Position of BG Square 2 to 596, 32, 88, and add a Position keyframe.

9   Set BG Square 2's Scale to 18, 18%, and add a Scale keyframe.

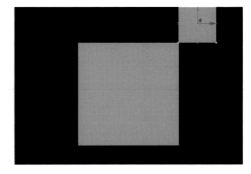

Creating the 3D squares background

You've positioned the squares where you want them to land after they spin in space. Working backward, now you need to make them spin in to place:

1   Go to time 0;00, and create the following keyframes for the BG Square 1 layer:

Position: 360, 270, 0 (animating the solid's position on the Z-axis from 0 to 88 makes the solid appear to move away from the viewer)

Scale: 110, 110, 110

Orientation: 0, 0, 0

X Rotation: 0 x +0.0

2   Still at time 0;00, create the following keyframes for the BG Square 2 layer:

Position: 592, 38, 0

Scale: 50, 50, 50

Orientation: 0, 0, 0

Y Rotation: 0 x +0.0

3   Press 1 on the keyboard to return to time 3;00.

4   Add the following keyframes for the BG Square 1 layer:

Orientation: 0, 0, 270

X Rotation: 2 x +180

5   Add the following keyframes for the BG Square 2 layer:

Orientation: 0, 0, 270

Y Rotation: 1 x +180

Adding the Rotation and Position keyframes

Save your work, and then preview the animation. The orange solids fill the entire Comp window and then rotate away from the viewer and stop spinning.

Creating the backdrop in multiple colors

Naturally, you need this fabulous backdrop in different colors for each sequence. Duplicate the Moving BG Orange comp twice. Rename the new comps Moving BG Green and Moving BG Purple. You could leave the squares where they are and change only their colors. However, the finished spot will be more eye-catching if you alter each background slightly.

Green

For the green sequence, leave the large solid where it is, and make the small solid land at the lower-left corner of the large solid instead of at the upper right:

1   Open the Moving BG Green comp, and change the color of both solids to a mid green (RGB: 67, 179, 63).

2   At time 0;00, change BG Square 2's Position to 80, 530, 0.

3   Press 1 to go to time 3;00, and then change the Position of BG Square 2 to 121.3, 508.7, 88.

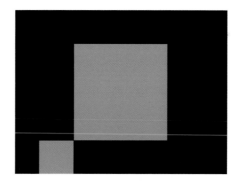

New layout for the green background

Purple

For the purple sequence, make the small solid land at the upper-left corner of the large solid:

1   Open the Moving BG Purple comp.

2   Change the color of both solids to a mid purple (RGB: 133, 79, 255).

3   At time 0;00, change BG Square 2's Position to 70, 4, 0.

4   Press 1 to go to time 3;00, and then change the Position of BG Square 2 to 123.3, 33.5, 88.

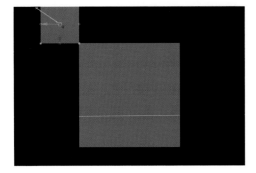

New layout for the purple background

Save your work.

Building the Sections

Are you ready to start engineering the final masterpiece? All the elements you'll use to build the main body sections of the final are now complete; you just need to put them together. You'll create a polished stage on which your client's ever-important product information will shine.

The orange section

First you'll create a mellow background and position your backdrop:

1   Create a new composition named Section1_Orange in the **Sections** folder, with dimensions 720 × 540, Frame Rate 29.97, and Duration 10;00.

2   Add the Orange Squares comp at time 0;00.

3   Go to time 0;28, and create a new solid named BG Orange that's comp size and pale orange (RGB: 255, 194, 137).

4   Drag the solid layer under the Orange Squares comp in the Timeline.

5   Go to time 1;00. Drag the Moving BG Orange comp to the Timeline, and position it so it's layer 2.

6   Change its Position to 346, 325.

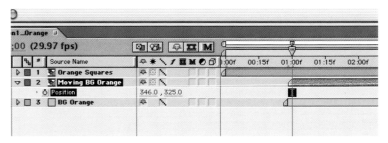

Beginning to build the orange section

The spot will look more professional and work much better if the transitions interact with the elements they're revealing. The setup doesn't have to be elaborate—you'll simply tweak the transition's position so the transition interacts with the backdrop:

1   Go to time 1;29, and add a Position keyframe of 560, 100 to the Orange Squares layer. Doing so lines up the final radiating orange square with the small orange solid's resting position.

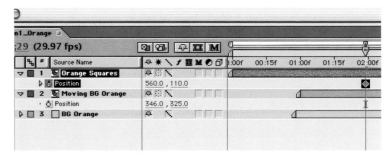

Adding the Position keyframes to the transition

2 Return to time 0;00, and change the Position of the Orange Squares layer to 78, 476. Now the orange squares radiate outward starting from the lower-left corner of the composition.

3 Go to time 0;25. You should tweak the Orange Squares layer's position so that it covers the entire comp during the transition to the Moving BG Orange comp. Add a Position keyframe of 360, 270, and then copy the keyframe.

4 To hold the Orange Squares layer in that position during the transition, go to time 1;06 and paste the keyframe you copied.

5 Scrub the frames between the two keyframes you just created. You'll notice that the Orange Squares composition moves around even though the two keyframes have the same coordinates. To fix this, select the keyframe at time 0;25, and choose Animation > Toggle Hold Keyframe.

Timeline with the Hold keyframe

Play back what you have so far, and note how the Orange Squares comp crops the squares as they scale outward. To fix this, turn on the Collapse Transformations switch for the Orange Squares comp layer. Now the layers aren't confined by the dimensions of the Orange Squares composition.

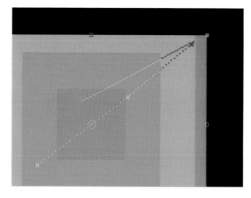

The scaling squares are cropped by the nested comp's dimensions.

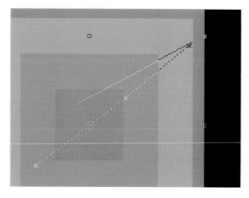

The Collapse Transformations switch reveals the layers entirely.

Matting a photo

Next, let's begin adding the client's product photos:

1   Go to time 4;00, and add a composition marker (Shift+2).

2   Create a new solid called Pic Matte that has dimensions of 720 × 720 and is any color. (Since you'll be using this solid as a track matte to frame and crop the product photos, the color doesn't matter as long as it's different from the mid orange color so you can see it in the Comp window as you work.)

3   Set the Scale (44.1, 31.5) and Position (346, 278) of the Pic Matte so it takes up the top two thirds of the larger orange square.

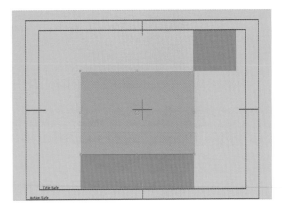

Adding the Pic Matte

4   Add the **Bedroom_01.jpg** file to the Timeline, under the Pic Matte layer. Notice that the image fills the entire composition.

5   Change the Bedroom_01 layer's Track Matte to Alpha Matte "Pic Matte". The image is cropped to the Pic Matte layer's dimensions.

6   Change the Position of the Bedroom_01 layer to 360, 260 and the Scale to 65, 65%.

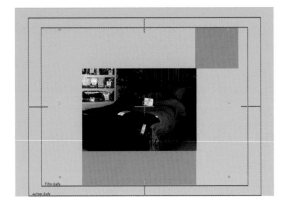

Adding the Track Matte to the picture

7   Add a 0% Opacity keyframe.

8   Go to time 4;10, and change the Opacity to 100%. Now the product image fades in after the orange squares land in place.

Adding text

The images are all in place, but they're only half of your visual symphony. Let's bring in another movement: text. You'll start with an element that will remain consistent throughout the project:

1   Press 2 on the keyboard to return to time 4;00.

2   Create a new horizontal text layer that displays the word *STYLE* in a dark orange color (RGB: 214, 75, 3). (For the other text properties, we used Futura Condensed Medium, size 92 pixels, and centered.)

3 Move forward in the Timeline so you can see the photo. Move the text so it's centered in the mid orange area under the photo. (We used Position 344, 475.)

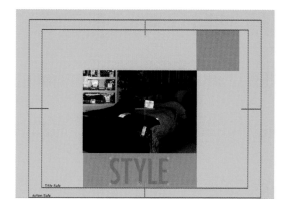

Creating the STYLE text element

Next, you'll create a horizontal graphic element to serve as a backdrop for text you'll place above the photo:

1 Press 2 to return to time 4;00.

2 Create a new solid layer named Horizontal Bar that has dimensions 720 × 110 and is colored a pale orange (RGB: 255, 232, 206).

3 Position the Horizontal Bar at 436, 110 so its bottom edge lies along the top edge of the big square.

4 In the Timeline, drag the Horizontal Bar layer so it's just above the BG Orange layer.

5 Apply the Linear Wipe effect (Effect > Transition > Linear Wipe) to the Horizontal Bar layer.

6 Set the effect's Wipe Angle to 0 x +270.

7 Add a Transition Completion keyframe of 100%.

8 Go to time 4;10, and change the Transition Completion property to 30%. Now the solid slides in from left to right.

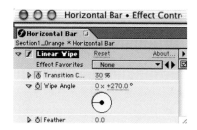

Settings for the Linear Wipe effect

Now you'll create a vertical version of the backdrop you just created, for the left side of the photo:

1 Copy the Horizontal Bar, and then paste it at time 4;02.

2 Rename the duplicate solid to Vertical Bar, and change its dimensions to 110 × 540 and its color to RGB 255, 232, 206.

3 Position the Vertical Bar at 129, 326 so its right edge lies along the left edge of the big square.

4 Change the Vertical Bar's current Wipe Angle keyframe to 0 x +0.0.

5 Go to the Vertical Bar's next keyframe at time 4;12, and change the Transition Completion to 21%.

Adding the color bars

Now that you have your backdrops, you can add the last two text elements. The first is a vertical element that scrolls on the screen and then fades to a lighter color:

1   Create a new horizontal text layer that displays *STYLE* in a dark orange color (RGB: 214, 75, 3). (For the other text properties, we used Futura Condensed Medium, size 92 pixels, and centered.)

2   At time 4;13, add a vertical text layer that displays *PERSONAL* in a dark orange color (RGB: 214, 75, 3). (For the other text properties, we used Futura Condensed Medium, size 36 pixels.)

3   Position the text so the top of the *P* is about even with the top of the picture (about 133, 310).

4   Apply a Linear Wipe effect (Effect > Transition > Linear Wipe).

5   Set the Wipe Angle to 0 x +0.0.

6   Create a 100% Transition Completion keyframe.

7   Go forward 15 frames by pressing Ctrl+G (Windows) or Command+G (Mac OS) and entering +15 in the dialog.

8   Change the Transition Completion to 0%.

9   Go to time 5;08, and add a 100% Opacity keyframe.

10   Go forward 15 frames, and change the Opacity to 50%.

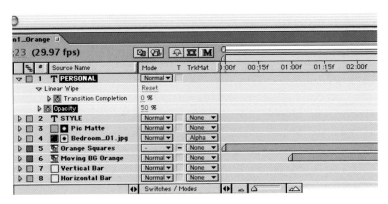

Fading down on the text

The final text element is horizontal and lies above the photo. It also scrolls on and fades out:

1   Go to time 5;08, and create a horizontal text layer that displays *EXPRESSION* in a dark orange color (RGB: 214, 75, 3). (For the other text properties, we used Futura Condensed Medium, size 36 pixels.)

2   Position the layer at 330, 127.

3   Apply a Linear Wipe effect (Effect > Transition > Linear Wipe) to the layer.

4   Set the Wipe angle to 0 x +270.

5   Create a 100% Transition Completion keyframe.

6   Go forward 15 frames, and change the Transition Completion to 0%.

7   Go to time 6;03, and add an Opacity keyframe at 100%.

8   Move forward 15 frames to time 6;18, and change the Opacity to 50%.

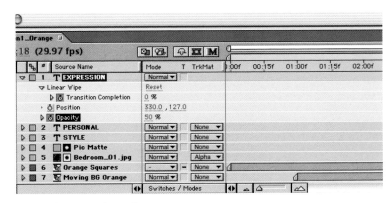

Adding the second text layer

The orange section is now complete. Save and preview your work.

Creating the green section

Once again, you'll use the duplicate-and-modify technique to create the other sections. You've probably already guessed that, since the 3D moving squares background is laid out differently, it will require you to make some adjustments to placement. Let's forge ahead into green territory:

1   Duplicate the Section1_Orange comp, and rename the duplicate Section2_Green. Open the Section2_Green comp.

2   Delete the Moving BG Orange layer, and replace it with the Moving BG Green composition.

3   Select the Orange Squares layer, and then hold down Alt (Windows) or Option (Mac OS) while dragging the Green Squares comp onto the Orange Squares layer.

4   At time 0;00, change the Position keyframe of the Green Squares layer to 560, 110.

5   At time 1;29, change the Position to 132, 426.

The keyframes at time 0;25 and time 1;06 remain at 360, 270 to effectively wipe the screen.

6   Rename the BG Orange layer to BG Green, and change its color to a pale green (RGB: 185, 217, 161). (Leave the remaining settings alone.)

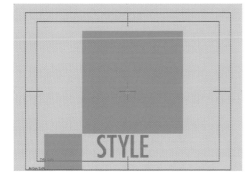

Changing the small square's position for the green layout

In order to add more visual interest, you'll move the picture matte relative to the background:

1   Press 2 to go to time 4;00.

2   Reposition the Pic Matte layer to 375, 289, and then duplicate it.

3   Select the Bedroom_01 layer, and hold down Alt (Windows) or Option (Mac OS) while dragging the **Chandelier.jpg** image to replace the Bedroom_01 image in the Timeline. The Chandelier image inherits the keyframes and position in time.

4   Scale **Chandelier.jpg** to 55, 55%, and Position it at 372, 295.

5   Go to time 5;13, and add a 100% Opacity keyframe to the layer.

6   Go forward 15 frames, and change the Opacity to 0%.

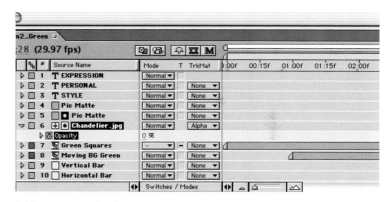

Adding a cross dissolve

To get more bang for the buck out of this section, add a second picture that will cross-fade with the other image:

1   Go to time 5;13, and add **Kitchen_02.jpg** to the Timeline.

2   Drag the layer under the topmost Pic Matte layer.

3   Set Kitchen_02's Track Matte to Alpha Matte "Pic Matte".

4   Set its Scale to 41, 41% and its Position to 376, 270.

5   Add a 0% Opacity keyframe to Kitchen_02.

6 Go forward 15 frames, and change the Opacity to 100%.

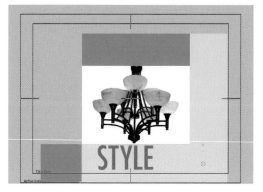

Adding a second image to the composition

If you preview the composition from time 4;00 to 6;00, the chandelier photo should fade out while the kitchen image fades in at the same location.

Next, you need to move the vertical and horizontal bars to match the rest of this layout:

1 Go to time 4;00.

2 Select the Vertical Bar layer, and press the [key to bring the layer's In point to the current time.

3 Change the color of the Vertical Bar and Horizontal Bar solids to RGB 215, 254, 188.

4 Move the Vertical Bar to Position 589, 353, and move the Horizontal Bar to 572, 458.

5 Press U to reveal all keyframes for the Horizontal Bar layer, and then change the layer's final Transition Completion keyframe to 40%.

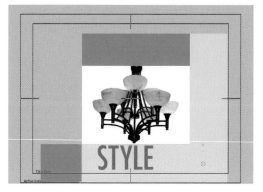

Moving the color bars to fit with the green layout

Of course, you need to change the text elements. You'll also change the timing of the linear wipe so it looks better with the length of the shorter words:

1 Select the STYLE text layer, and change the color to a really dark green (RGB: 38, 106, 37).

2 Change the layer's Position to 375, 165, so the text is centered in the green space above the picture.

3 Go to time 4;13, select the EXPRESSION text layer, and press [to move the layer's In point to the current time.

4 Change the text to say *LIGHT*, and change the color to a really dark green (RGB: 38, 106, 37).

5 Position the text at 375.5, 465.5 so it's centered under the picture.

6 Press U to reveal the text layer's keyframes.

7   Go to time 5;03, and select the final Transition Completion keyframe and both Opacity keyframes.

8   Drag the selected keyframes, and press Shift to snap the Transition Completion keyframe to the CTI. Doing so increases the duration of the linear wipe to 20 frames to account for the shorter word (and shifts the opacity fade-out).

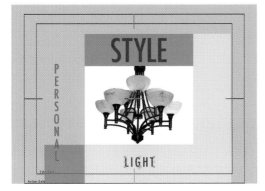

Changing the text

9   Change the PERSONAL text layer to say *SPACE*, and change its color to darkest green (RGB: 38, 106, 37).

10 Position the layer at 589, 288 so it lies to the left of the photo.

11 Go to time 5;18. With the SPACE layer still selected, press [to move the layer's In point to the current time.

12 Go to time 6;18, and press U to reveal the layer's keyframes.

13 Select the last three keys, and drag to the CTI. (Drag and then press Shift to snap the final Transition Completion keyframe to the CTI.)

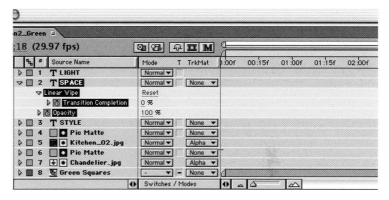

Altering the linear wipe to work with the new text

Save your work, and close the composition.

The purple section

You're almost finished with the main sequences: You just need to take care of your friend Purple. Although the layout of the purple moving squares background is more similar to the original orange section, you want to reuse the photo cross fade you created in the green section:

1   Duplicate the Section2_Green comp, and rename it Section3_Purple. Open the Section3_Purple composition.

2   Select the Green Squares layer. To replace this layer but retain its keyframes, press Alt (Windows) or Option (Mac OS) as you drag the Purple Squares composition from the Project window onto the Green Squares layer.

3   At time 0;00, change the Position keyframe on the Purple Squares layer to 154, 456.

4   At time 1;29, change the Position keyframe to 124, 110.

Leave the keyframes at time 0;25 and time 1;06, because they hold the transition.

5   Select the Moving BG Green layer. Hold down Alt (Windows) or Option (Mac OS), and drag the Moving BG Purple composition onto it to replace it.

6   Move the Moving BG Purple layer to Position 355, 326.

7   Change the BG Green layer's name to BG Purple, and change the color to pale purple (RGB: 187, 168, 255).

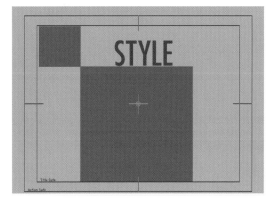

Changing the layout and colors for the purple section

The Vertical Bar and Horizontal Bar must be moved, sized, and colored to match the new layout:

1   Go to time 4;10. Change the color of the Vertical Bar layer to RGB 214, 209, 255 and its dimensions to 116 × 540.

2   Move the layer to Position 137, 329.

3   Change the Horizontal Bar layer's color to 214, 209, 255 and its dimensions to 720 × 115.

4   Move the layer to Position 442, 113.

The pictures must also be replaced, and you need to move the matte in relation to the new backdrop:

1   Select the Chandelier layer, and then hold down Alt (Windows) or Option (Mac OS) while dragging **Chair_02.jpg** onto the layer in the Timeline.

2   Change the Scale to 60, 60% and the Position to 421, 310.

3   Select both Pic Matte layers, and set their Positions to 355, 280.

4   Select the Kitchen_02 layer, and then hold down Alt (Windows) or Option (Mac OS) while dragging **Television.jpg** onto it in the Timeline.

5   Change the layer's Scale to 50, 50%, and move it to Position 360, 271.

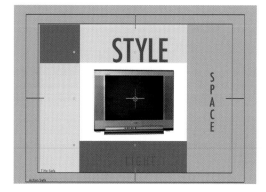

Adjusting the mattes and pics to work with the new layout

Naturally, the text elements also need to change for the purple section:

1   Change the STYLE text layer's color to darkest purple (RGB: 85, 60, 168).

2   Move the layer to Position 354, 477 so it's below the photo.

3   Change the SPACE text layer to read *FORM*.

4. Change the layer's color to darkest purple (RGB: 85, 60, 168).

5. Set the layer's Position to 138, 298.

6. Change the LIGHT text layer to read *FUNCTION*.

7. Change the color to a really dark purple (RGB: 85, 60, 168), and set the Position to 353.5, 126.5.

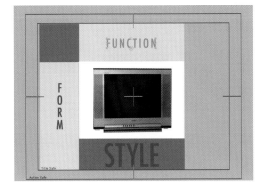

Changing the text for the purple section

For some variety, swap the In points of the FUNCTION and FORM layers:

1. Go to the In point of the FORM layer (time 5;18), and set a new composition marker (Shift+3).

2. Go to the In point of the FUNCTION layer (time 4;13).

3. Select the FORM layer, and press the [key to move the In point to the current time.

4. Press 3 to return to the composition marker at time 5;18.

5. Select the FUNCTION layer, and press [to move its In point.

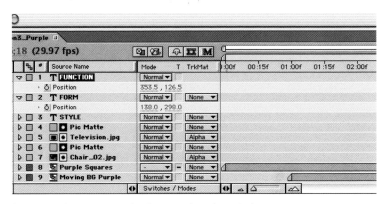

Switching the timing on the horizontal and vertical text

Looks good—but it's a little too boxed in comparison to the green and orange sections, which use the small square solid to break up the square shape the other elements create. Never fear, though; there is a simple solution:

- At time 4;10, set the Transition Completion keyframes for both the Horizontal Bar and the Vertical Bar layers to 0% so the solids extend beyond the screen.

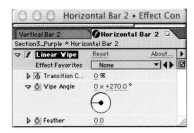

Settings for the Linear Wipe effect

Save your work, and close the composition.

The yellow section

You're almost finished creating your sections. Now you'll add the logo with a new twist on the end tag that you created in the previous chapter.

Create a new composition named Section4_Yellow in the **Sections** folder, with dimensions 720 × 540, Frame Rate 29.97, and Duration 10;00. Although you could copy and replace the footage you need and delete the rest, it's just as fast to build this comp from scratch:

1   Drag the Yellow Squares composition to the Timeline at time 0;00, and then turn on the Collapse Transformations switch.

2   At time 0;00, create a Position keyframe of 132, 114.

3   At time 0;25, change the Position to 360, 270.

4   Go forward three frames to time 0;28. Create a new solid named Yellow BG that's comp size and pale yellow (RGB: 252, 253, 162).

5   Drag the Yellow BG layer under the Yellow Squares layer in the Timeline.

6   Go to time 2;00, and add the Style_Logo composition above the other two layers in the Timeline.

7   Insert a 0% Opacity keyframe.

8   Go to time 2;10, and change the Opacity to 100%.

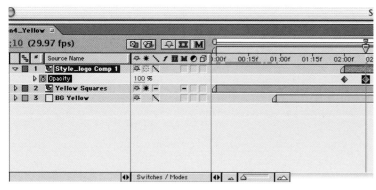

Beginning to build the yellow section

Save and preview your work.

Fun with Vector Paint

As you did in Chapter 1 ("Spinning Squares"), you'll animate the text's layer style in the Photoshop file to create more visual interest. This time you'll use the Vector Paint effect instead of the Radial Wipe effect used in the Chapter 1 project:

1   Open the Layer Effects comp in the **Style_logo Comp 2** folder in the Project window.

2   Go to time 0;10 in the Layer Effects comp Timeline.

3   Select both the Bevel Highlight and the Bevel Shadow layers.

4   Choose Effect > Paint > Vector Paint.

5   Set the following Vector Paint effect properties for both layers:

Brush Setting Radius: 15

Playback Mode: Animate Strokes

Playback Speed: 1.00

Composite Paint: As Matte

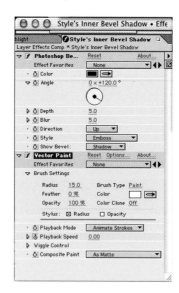

Settings for the Vector Paint effect

6 Add a keyframe for Playback Speed to the Bevel Shadow layer.

7 Paint over the letters of *STYLE* in the Composition window as if you were writing them on the screen. Don't worry if it looks messy; just be sure you cover the entire area of each letter.

8 Go to time 1;00, and set the playback speed to 50.00.

9 Copy both keyframes, go to time 0;10, and paste the keys on the Bevel Highlight layer.

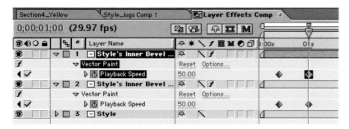

Timeline with Vector Paint keyframes

Save and preview your work. As you can see, the bevel appears to be painted on by invisible hands.

Completing the end tag

Now you'll add the company's Web address and animate the text's tracking so the text expands onto the screen:

1 Return to the Section4_Yellow comp, and go to time 3;00.

2 Create a new text layer that says *www.styledesigncenter.com*.

3 Position the layer so it's centered below the logo.

4 Add a 0% Opacity keyframe.

5 Go forward 15 frames to time 3;15, and change the Opacity to 100%.

6 Press the J key to go back to time 3;00.

7 Display the text properties for the layer, and then choose Animate > Tracking in the Timeline.

The Animate menu in the Timeline

8 Add a Tracking Amount keyframe, and set it to −20 to squish the letters together.

9 Go to time 3;15, and change the Tracking Amount to 5.

Save and preview your work. After the bevel effect covers the logo, the Web address expands outward to the comp edges.

Finishing Touches

You're undoubtedly ready to see all this hard work in action. Now you can assemble the final spot with each of the sections. This will take practically no time at all:

- Create a new composition named Squares2_Final with dimensions 720 × 540, Frame Rate 29.97, and Duration 30:00.

- At time 0;00, add Section1_Orange to the Timeline.

- Go to time 7;00, and add Section2_Green to the Timeline.

- Go to time 14;15, and add Section3_Purple to the Timeline.

• Go to time 22;00, and add Section4_Yellow to the Timeline.

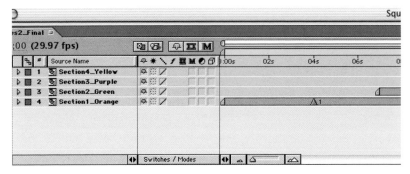

The finished Timeline

Now Try This

Well done: You've finished your second spot for the Style Design Center. By adding 3D space to the solids, you can really grab the viewer's attention and create a slick, hip, graphic look that has a sense of depth.

• To add a little more snap, try using Vector Paint to paint the whole word *STYLE* in the logo comp instead of just the bevel effects.

• For those who really like a challenge, play with shrinking the Square 1 on the Moving BG. Then add the smaller square on each point. Replace the smaller solids and the images with video clips. Now you have one large screen displaying video, surrounded by four smaller screens simultaneously showing clips.

| **Wall of Squares**

Like the projects in Chapters 1 and 2, this project works with modular sequences built with solids. The most prominent of these sequences is a checkerboard-patterned background and transition you'll present in four variations. The checkerboard pattern you'll create is made from solids that could easily be swapped with other files to create textures or to make a wall of images or video.

A checkerboard pattern is one of those things that never seems to go out of style. The checkerboards you'll build in this project dazzle the eye by glittering into and out of each segment. Solids that you'll animate in 3D space then add some dimension on top of the checkerboard by falling into place in the final product layout.

It Works Like This

Check out the **Ch3_Finished_Movie.mov** file in this chapter's folder on the book's DVD. This project uses solids to create dynamic backgrounds and eye-catching 3D animations, and to position and frame product shots. As in the first two chapters, the project depends on modular components to help speed up production. Even better, we provide you with rendered movies for some of the components. The main aspects of this project are as follows:

1. Using solids to create an animated pattern.

2. Using solids to matte pictures of different sizes.

3. Animating 3D solids to create a falling dominoes effect.

4. Animating a nested comp to create a swinging garage-door effect.

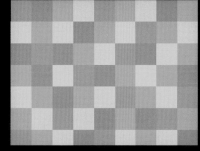

Animated orange checkerboard made of solids

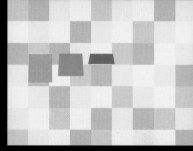

Yellow section with flipping blocks of color

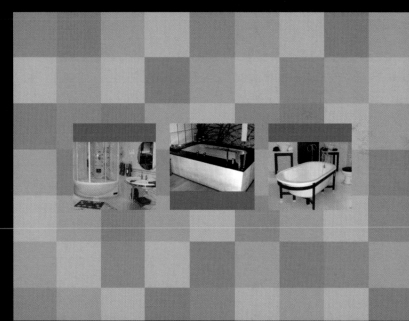

Purple section with matted pictures

Preparing to Work

To prepare for this project, do the following:

1   Start with a new project.

2   Import the **Images** folder from the Chapter 3 folder on the DVD.

3   Create a folder named **Graphics**, and import the **Style_Logo.psd** file by using the Footage and Merged Layers options.

Building the Background

To create the backgrounds, we randomly placed 80 × 80 solids in four different shades of one color family and then pre-comped the individual colors. If you wish, you can do the same until you're happy with the checkerboard design. Otherwise, we've provided you with a chart of the colors and the solids' positions.

Here are the steps:

1   Create a new composition named Orange Squares BG, with dimensions 720 × 540, Frame Rate 29.97, and Duration 10;00 seconds.

2   To arrange the square pattern more easily, turn on the composition grid (View > Show Grid) and the Snap To Grid option in the same menu.

3   The quickest way to reproduce our pattern is to start with an 80 × 80 solid and duplicate it as many times as specified for that particular color in the table. Then select all the layers of that color, press the P key to display their Position properties, and enter the Position values specified in the table.

Tip: Once you've selected a position value in the Timeline, you can quickly navigate to the other layers' Position fields by pressing the Tab key (forward) or Shift+Tab (backward).

Squares' Positions

	Pale Orange (RGB: 255, 194, 137)	Light Orange (RGB: 255, 139, 52)	Mid Orange (RGB: 255, 107, 15)	Dark Orange (RGB: 236, 82, 2)
Layer 1	200, 120	520, 520	360, 520	200, 200
Layer 2	40, 360	40, 440	200, 440	680, 280
Layer 3	200, 280	680, 440	440, 360	520, 200
Layer 4	200, 520	680, 40	360, 40	280, 520
Layer 5	280, 440	520, 360	120, 200	520, 440
Layer 6	600, 520	280, 360	520, 120	600, 40
Layer 7	600, 360	680, 200	440, 200	120, 280
Layer 8	600, 200	120, 120	40, 520	200, 360
Layer 9	280, 40	360, 120	600, 440	40, 200
Layer 10	440, 120	200, 40	40, 40	120, 40
Layer 11	360, 200	40, 280	680, 360	680, 520
Layer 12	120, 440	120, 520	280, 280	360, 440
Layer 13	360, 360	440, 440	440, 40	360, 280
Layer 14	440, 520	120, 360	N/A	280, 120
Layer 15	520, 280	280, 200	N/A	N/A
Layer 16	680, 120	600, 120	N/A	N/A
Layer 17	40, 120	440, 40	N/A	N/A
Layer 18	520, 40	600, 280	N/A	N/A
Layer 19	N/A	440, 280	N/A	N/A

4 When you're done positioning solids of a particular color, pre-comp (Layer > Pre-compose) those layers, and name them according to their color: Pale Orange Squares, Light Orange Squares, Mid Orange Squares, and Dark Orange Squares.

Tip: Lock each pre-comp in the Timeline until you've finished creating the others.

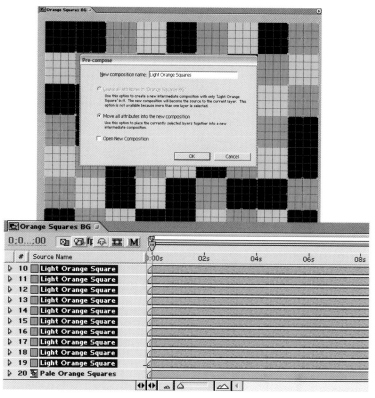

Pre-comping the light orange solids

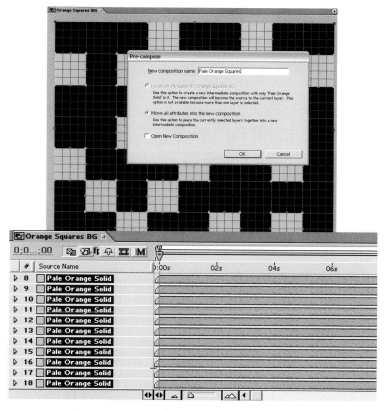

Pre-comping the pale orange solids

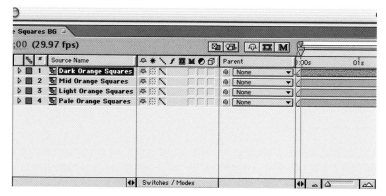

The Orange Squares BG Timeline

Save your work.

Mixing it up

Now you'll add a little variety by making the squares fade in and out at different times. By subdividing and animating the different colors, you can create a gradual transition to your checkerboard background:

1   Open the Pale Orange Squares comp, and select the first 10 layers.

2   Pre-comp these layers (Layer > Pre-compose) into a new composition named XL Phase 1.

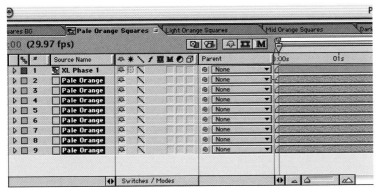

Dividing the layers into two comps

3   Pre-comp the remaining pale orange layers into a new composition named XL Phase 2.

4   Select both comp layers, and add 0% Opacity keyframes to them.

5   Go to time 1;00, and change the Opacity for both layers to 100%.

6   Go to time 0;10, select only XL Phase 2, and press the [key to move the layer's In point to the current time.

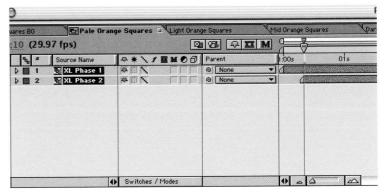

Offsetting the start time of the checkerboard phases

Repeat this process with the remaining comps:

1   Open the Light Orange Squares composition, and pre-comp the first 11 layers into a new composition named L Phase 1.

2   Select the remaining layers, and pre-comp them (Layer > Pre-compose) into a new composition named L Phase 2.

3   Select both layers, and add 0% Opacity keyframes to them.

4   Go to time 1;00, and change the Opacity of both layers to 100%.

5   Go to time 0;10, select only the L Phase 2 layer, and press the [key to move the In point to the current time.

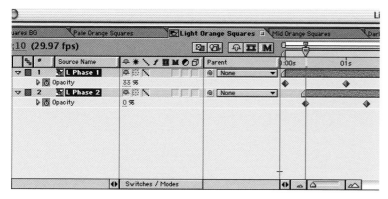

Adding a fade-in to the checkerboard phases

6   Open the Mid Orange Squares composition, and pre-comp the first six layers into a new composition named M Phase 1.

7   Select the remaining layers, and pre-comp them into a new composition named M Phase 2.

8   Select both layers, and add 0% Opacity keyframes to them.

9   Go to time 1;00, and change the Opacity for both layers to 100%.

10 Go to time 0;10, select M Phase 2, and press [to move the layer's In point.

What the fade-in will look like

11 Open the Dark Orange Squares composition, and pre-comp the first seven layers into a new comp named D Phase 1.

12 Pre-comp the remaining layers into a comp named D Phase 2.

13 Select both layers, and add 0 % Opacity keyframes to them.

14 Go to time 1;00, and change both layers' Opacity to 100%.

15 Go to time 0;10, select only the D Phase 2 layer, and press the [key to move the layer's In point.

Save your work.

Adding a little more spice

Now you'll double the effect of the fade-ins by staggering the In points of the comp layers:

1   Select all the layers, and add a 0% Opacity keyframe to each one.

2   Go to time 1;00, and change the Opacity of all layers to 100%.

3   Go to time 0;05, select the Pale Orange Squares layer, and press [to move the In point.

4   Go to time 0;10, select the Dark Orange Squares layer, and press [.

5   Go to time 0;15, select the Mid Orange Squares layer, and press [.

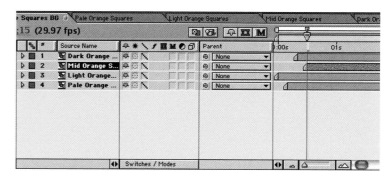

Offsetting the start time of the different color squares

Save and preview your work: The squares should fade in at various times. Now, close all the compositions.

The Other Backgrounds

Although the process in the previous section took some time, it creates a really nice background with a lot of movement. Based on what you've done in earlier exercises, you could easily replace the footage to create the same background in green, purple, and yellow. However, in the interest of time, the remaining backgrounds are included as QuickTime Movies on the DVD. You can access them as follows:

1   In the Project window, create a new folder named **Squares BG**.

2   Move the Orange Squares BG composition into the folder.

3   Import the following files from the DVD into the Squares BG folder:

- **Green Squares BG.mov**
- **Purple Squares BG.mov**
- **Yellow Squares BG.mov**

Getting organized

This project contains a lot of items, so let's take the time to organize the Project window now:

1   Create a new folder named **Orange Squares**, and move the Pale Orange Squares, Light Orange Squares, Mid Orange Squares, and Dark Orange Squares comps into it.

2   Create a new folder named **Phases** within the Orange Squares folder, and move the various Phases compositions into it.

An organized Project window is easier to work with

Building More Elements

Next, you'll create a 3D element in black and white that you can use as a matte for any color solid. It's a fun little flip that will showcase the client's products.

The first step

1   In the Project window, create a folder named **Flips**.

2   In the **Flips** folder, add a new composition named Horizontal Flip that has dimensions 720 × 540, Frame Rate 29.97, and Duration 10;00 seconds.

3 Create a new solid named Flip_Square that has dimensions 150 × 150 and is colored white (RGB: 255, 255, 255).

Note: Normally, you wouldn't use pure white for broadcast. However, this will be a matte, so it won't be visible.

---

4 Turn on this layer's 3D switch in the Timeline.

5 Set up a four-comp view (Window > Workspace > Four Comp Views) so you can see the solid rotate in space.

6 Set the layer's Anchor Point to 0, 75, 0 and its Position to 360, 270, 0.

7 Go to time 0;10, and add a keyframe for Y Rotation with a value of 0 x +0.0.

8 Press Home to go to time 0;00, and then change the Y Rotation to 0 x +90.

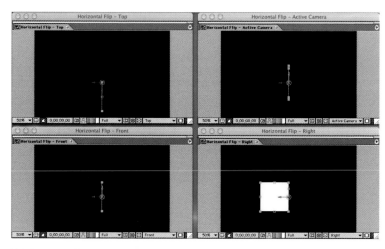

Working in 3D space to make the flip

Save and preview your work. You can then return to the default one-comp view (Window > Workspace > 1 Comp View).

A chorus line

The results so far don't seem all that impressive. You'll make the project more interesting by duplicating your comp and then repositioning the layers to create a line of flipping squares:

1 Create a new composition named Line Flip that has dimensions 720 × 540, Frame Rate 29.97, and Duration 10;00 seconds.

2 Add the Horizontal Flip comp to the Timeline at 0;00, and then duplicate it twice.

3 Go to time 1;00 so you can see the squares as you work. Set the following positions:

> Layer 1: 460, 270
>
> Layer 2: 285, 270
>
> Layer 3: 110, 270

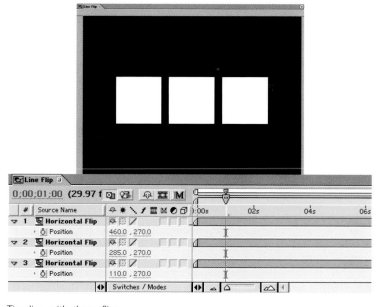

Timeline with three flips

Now the squares flip simultaneously; but to get the domino effect, you need to stagger their In points:

1   Go to time 0;03, select layer 2, and press [to move its In point.

2   Go to time 0;06, select layer 1, and press [.

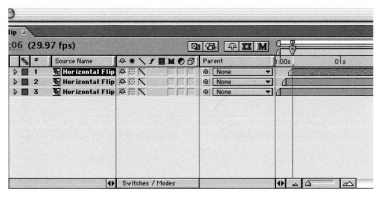

Staggering the In points of the layers to time the flips like falling dominoes

Save and preview your work.

Building the Sections

By now you're undoubtedly ready to get going with the sections. Once you see all the pieces working together, you'll be delighted with the effect. Let's use the components and begin building the orange section.

Act 1: orange

1   Create a new composition named 1_Orange that is—you guessed it—720 × 540, with Frame Rate 29.97 and Duration 10;00 seconds.

2   Add the Orange Squares BG comp to the Timeline at 0;00.

3   Go to time 2;00, and create a new pale orange solid (RGB: 255, 194, 137) that's comp size and named Pale Orange BG.

4   Drag the new solid under the Squares BG layer in the Timeline.

5   Add a 100% Opacity keyframe (Windows: Alt+Shift+T; Mac OS: Option+Shift+T) to the Squares BG layer.

6   Go forward 10 frames, and add a 50% Opacity keyframe.

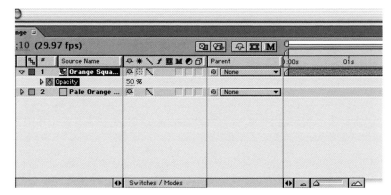

Fading down the Orange Squares BG comp, and adding a solid underneath to warm it up

This approach enables the Squares BG layer to act as a transition and all your hard work to be appreciated. It also tones down the squares enough that they form a suitable backdrop for the products being displayed.

Next you'll use the line flip you just created to matte a solid:

1   Go to time 2;10, and add the Line Flip comp to the Timeline.

2   Create a new solid named Dark Orange that is comp size and dark orange (RGB: 236, 82, 2).

3   In the Timeline, drag the solid under the Line Flip layer.

4   Set the Dark Orange layer's Track Matte to Alpha Matte "Line Flip".

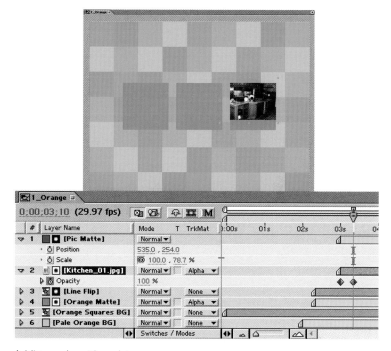

Assigning a Track Matte to the solid

Naturally, you'll use your multi-tasking friend the solid to create mattes. Let's add the picture mattes and the images you need:

1   Go to time 3;00. Create a new solid named Pic Matte in any color, with dimensions 150 × 150.

2   Set its Position to 535, 254 and its Scale to 100, 78.7%.

3   Add the **Kitchen_01.jpg** file under the Pic Matte layer in the Timeline.

4   Set the Kitchen_01 layer's Position to 522, 250 and its Scale to 53, 53%.

5   Set the Kitchen_01 layer's Track Matte to Alpha Matte "Pic Matte".

6   Add a 0% Opacity keyframe at time 3;00.

7   Go to time 3;10, and change the layer's Opacity to 100%.

Adding and matting pictures

Of course, you have three squares, so you need two more mattes and pictures:

1   Duplicate the Pic Matte layer, and set its Position to 360, 286.

2   Go to time 3;05, and press the [key to move the layer's In point.

3   Add **Kitchen_04.jpg** under the new Pic Matte layer in the Timeline.

4   Set Kitchen_04's Position to 360, 270 and its Scale to 64, 64%.

5   Set Kitchen_04's Track Matte to the new Pic Matte layer.

6   Add a 0% Opacity keyframe.

7   Go forward 10 frames, and change the Opacity to 100%.

Varying the placement of the images within the squares

One down, one to go:

1   Duplicate a Pic Matte layer, and move the duplicate to Position 185, 254.

2   Go to time 3;10, and press the [key to move the layer's In point.

3   Add **Kitchen_03.jpg** under the Pic Matte layer in the Timeline.

4   Change **Kitchen_03.jpg**'s Position to 186, 257 and its Scale to 35, 35%.

5   Set its Track Matte to Alpha Matte "Pic Matte".

6   Add a 0% Opacity keyframe.

7   Move forward 10 frames, and change the Opacity to 100%.

The final placement of the pictures in the orange composition

Save and preview your work. You'll notice that the flips go from left to right, and then the products come on from right to left. Once again, this technique keeps the viewer's eye moving. This is also why you alternate the photo positions inside the solids. Position and timing help make the viewer look where and when you want them to look. Behold, the power of design!

Act 2: green

As you've done before, you'll duplicate this composition and make a few alterations to create the green and purple versions. Recycling comps saves a lot of time and make you more efficient:

1   Duplicate the 1_Orange composition, and name the duplicate 2_Green.

2   Open the 2_Green comp, and select the Orange Squares BG layer.

3   Hold down Alt (Windows) or Option (Mac OS) while dragging **Green Squares BG.mov** from the Project window onto the Orange Squares BG layer in the Timeline. Green Squares BG replaces the Orange Squares BG layer and inherits its keyframes and position.

4   Rename the Pale Orange solid to Pale Green, and change its color to RGB 185, 217, 161.

5   Rename the Dark Orange solid to Dark Green, and change its color to RGB 45, 126, 43.

To mix things up a bit, let's replace the photos and reposition the mattes slightly to make them vertical:

1   Select Kitchen_01 in the Timeline, and then hold down Alt (Windows) or Option (Mac OS) while dragging **Wardrobe_01.jpg** onto the Kitchen_01 layer.

2   Change Wardrobe_01's Position to 550, 251 and its Scale to 60, 60%.

3   Change its Pic Matte (above it in the Timeline) to Position 550, 270 and the Scale to 80, 100%.

4   Select Kitchen_04 in the Timeline, and then hold down Alt (Windows) or Option (Mac OS) while dragging **Wardrobe_02.jpg** onto it.

5   Change Wardrobe_02's Position to 362, 300 and its Scale to 73, 73%.

6   Change the Pic Matte layer's Position to 360, 270 and Scale to 80, 100%.

7   Select Kitchen_03 in the Timeline, and then hold down Alt (Windows) or Option (Mac OS) while dragging **Wardrobe_03.jpg** onto it.

8   Change the Wardrobe_03 layer's Position to 158, 270 and its Scale to 66, 66%.

9   Change its Pic Matte layer's Position to 170, 270 and Scale to 80, 100%.

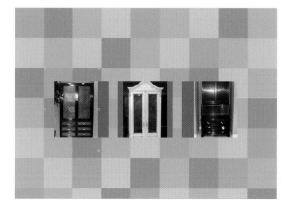

The final picture placement for the green section

Save and preview your work.

Act 3: purple

The green section is complete. See how fast you can go once you have the basic framework laid out? In a snap, you can create the purple section:

1   Duplicate the 1_Orange composition in the Project window.

2   Rename the duplicate 3_Purple, and then open it.

3   Select the Orange Squares BG layer in the Timeline, and then hold down Alt (Windows) or Option (Mac OS) while dragging **Purple Squares BG.mov** onto it.

4   Rename and recolor the Pale Orange solid to Pale Purple (RGB: 187, 168, 255).

5   Rename and recolor the Dark Orange solid to Dark Purple (RGB: 99, 58, 190).

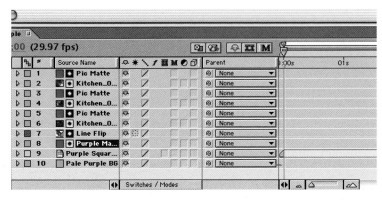

Timeline for the purple section with all the colors modified

This time, you'll leave the photo mattes horizontal, but you'll alternate their position within the solids:

1   Select the Kitchen_01 layer in the Timeline, and then hold down Alt (Windows) or Option (Mac OS) while dragging the **Bath_03.jpg** file onto it.

2   Set the Bath_03 layer's Position to 566, 282 and its Scale to 53, 53%.

3   Move its Pic Matte to 535, 286.

4   Select the Kitchen_04 layer in the Timeline, and then hold down Alt (Windows) or Option (Mac OS) while dragging the **Bath_04.jpg** file onto it.

5   Change Bath_04's Position to 360, 270 and its Scale to 57, 57%.

6   Change the Position of its Pic Matte to 360, 254.

7   Select the Kitchen_03 layer in the Timeline, and then hold down Alt (Windows) or Option (Mac OS) while dragging **ShortBath_03.jpg** onto it.

8   Change the ShortBath_03 layer's Position to 255, 290 and its Scale to 97, 97%.

9   Change the Position of its Pic Matte to 185, 286.

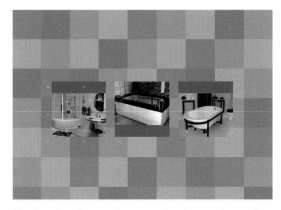

Altering the picture placement for the purple section

Save and preview your work.

The Big Finale

Now you need to create the yellow section with the end tag. Instead of animating the logo's bevel effect, as you did in Chapters 1 and 2, you'll animate the entire logo and some other elements in 3D space.

Creating a kick line

Let's create a vertical domino effect for the end tag. You'll use it later as a backdrop for some text:

1   Create a new composition named Vertical Flip in the **Flips** folder, with dimensions 720 × 540, Frame Rate 29.97, and Duration 10;00 seconds.

2   Create a new solid named Flip_Rectangle that has dimensions 125 × 150 and is colored white (RGB: 255, 255, 255).

3   Turn on the layer's 3D switch.

4   Switch to four-comp view (Window > Workspace > Four Comp Views) so you can see the solid's flip from various angles.

5   Move the solid's Anchor Point to 62.5, 0, 0 so you can flip the solid along its top edge.

6   Go to time 0;10, and add an X Rotation keyframe of 0 x +0.0.

7   Press Home to return to time 0;00, and change the X Rotation value to 0x −90.

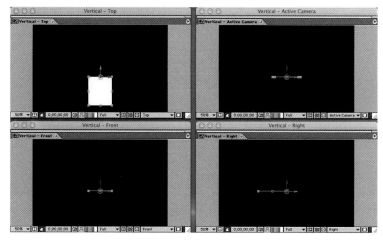

Working in 3D space to make the vertical flip

Save and preview your work. The solid should appear to swing vertically into view.

Next, you need to create a line of these solids:

1   Return to the one-comp view (Window > Workspace > One Comp View).

2   Create a new composition named Vertical Line Flip with dimensions 720 × 540, Frame Rate 29.97, and Duration 10;00 seconds.

3   Add Vertical Flip to the Timeline at 0;00.

4   Change its Position to 126, 200 and its Scale to 70, 70, 70%.

5   Create a new comp-size solid that is named and colored Mid Orange (RGB: 255, 107, 15).

6   Drag the Mid Orange layer under the Vertical Flip layer in the Timeline.

7   Set the Track Matte of the Mid Orange layer to Alpha Matte "Vertical Flip".

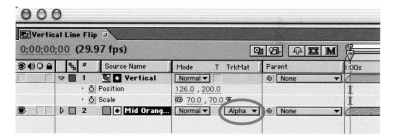

Assigning a Track Matte to the solid

You'll duplicate these layers to create additional flips in different colors with staggered In points:

1   Duplicate the Vertical Flip and Mid Orange layers.

2   Rename and recolor the Mid Orange duplicate to Mid Green (RGB: 67, 179, 63).

3   Select the Mid Green layer and the Vertical Flip layer above it, go to time 0;03, and press [to move the duplicate layers' In points.

4   Change the Position of the Vertical Flip layer to 243, 200.

5   Duplicate the Mid Green layer and the Vertical Flip layer above it.

6   Rename and recolor the duplicate Mid Green to Mid Purple (RGB: 133, 79, 255).

7   With the Mid Purple and Vertical Flip layers selected, go to time 0;06 and press [to move both layers' In points.

8   Change the Vertical Flip layer's Position to 360, 200.

9   Duplicate the Mid Green and Mid Orange layers, along with the Vertical Flip layer above each layer.

10 Select just the new Mid Green layer and the Vertical Flip layer above it, go to time 0;09, and press [to move their In points.

11 Change the Position of the Vertical Flip layer above the new Mid Green layer to 478, 200.

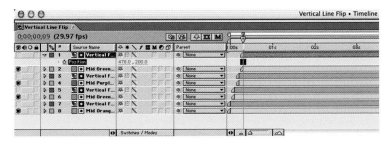

Duplicating and moving the green flip

12 Go to time 0;12, select the newest Mid Orange layer and the Vertical Flip layer above it, and press [to move their In points.

13 Change the Position of the Vertical Flip layer above the new Mid Orange layer to 596, 200.

Save and preview your work. The solids should swing into view from left to right.

One last song and dance

Now that these components are complete, you can begin to create the yellow section. You're almost there!

1   Create a new composition named 4_Yellow with dimensions 720 × 540, Frame Rate 29.97, and Duration 10;00 seconds.

2   Add the **Yellow Squares BG.mov** comp to the Timeline at 0;00.

3   Go to time 2;00, and add a 100% Opacity keyframe to the Yellow Squares BG layer.

4   Go to time 2;10, and change the layer's Opacity to 50%.

5   Create a new comp-size solid that is named and colored Pale Yellow (RGB: 252, 253, 162).

6   Drag the Pale Yellow layer under the Yellow Squares BG layer in the Timeline.

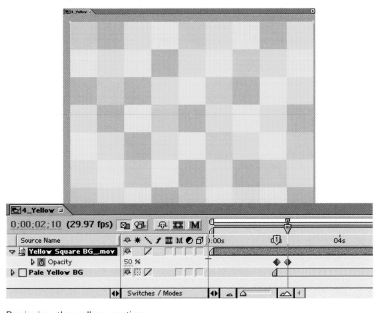

Beginning the yellow section

You need to tone down the background and add your new flips. You'll also drop the saturation once the boxes flip on, so they will match the intensity of the rest of the composition. Otherwise, they will distract from the text that's resting on them:

1 Go to time 2;00, and add Vertical Line Flip to the Timeline.

2 Go to time 2:20, and apply Effect > Adjust > Hue/Saturation to the Vertical Line Flip layer.

3 Click the Channel Range stopwatch to create a keyframe for it.

4 Go to time 3:00, and change the Master Saturation to –38.

Animating saturation using the Hue/Saturation effect

Now you can use the flip boxes as a backdrop for the letters in the word *STYLE*:

1 Create a new text layer for each letter in the word *STYLE*. Our text properties include Futura Condensed Medium, size 105, and color pale yellow (RGB: 252, 253, 162).

2 Position each text layer in the center of a rectangle:

  S: Position 105, 292

  T: Position 225, 292

  Y: Position 340, 292

  L: Position 460, 292

  E: Position 575, 292

Placement of the letters on the color blocks

3 Select all the text layers you just created, press T to display their Opacity, and create a 0% Opacity keyframe for each layer.

4 Go to time 3;10, and change the Opacity for each text layer to 100%.

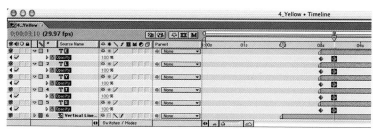

Adding a fade-in to the letters

Save and preview your work.

Bringing down the curtain

Finally, you need to add the logo to the spot. You'll work in another 3D flip, but this one will come in like a swinging garage door closing over the entire Comp window. This approach switches things around with the logo but stays consistent with the rest of the spot:

1 Create a new composition named 3D Logo with dimensions 720 × 540, Frame Rate 29.97, and Duration 10;00 seconds.

2 Add the Pale Yellow BG solid from the Solids folder to the Timeline.

3 Add **Style_Logo.psd** on top of the Pale Yellow BG layer in the Timeline.

4 Return to the 4_Yellow comp, go to time 4;00, and add a composition marker (Shift+1).

5 Add the 3D Logo to the Timeline, and turn on its 3D switch.

6 Set both its Anchor Point and Position properties to 360, 0, 0.

7 Create an X Rotation keyframe of 0 x -90.

8 Go to time 4;20, and change the layer's X Rotation to 0 x +0.0.

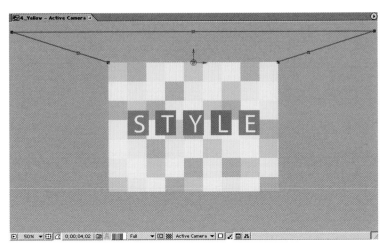

The 3D Logo layer at the top of its swing

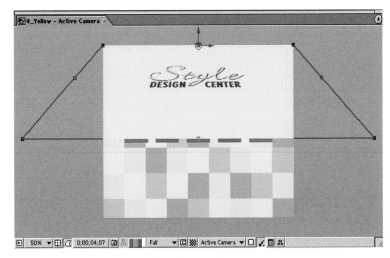

The 3D Logo layer midway through its swing

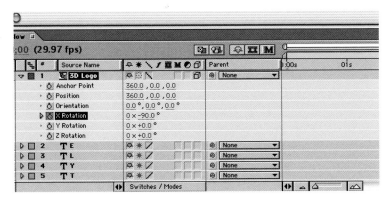

Creating a garage-door effect for the logo

Save and preview your work.

I know you've been waiting for it. Finally, you can assemble the completed spot:

1   Create a new composition named Squares3_Final with dimensions 720 × 540, Frame Rate 29.97, and Duration 30;00 seconds.

2   Add 1_Orange to the Timeline at 0;00.

3   Go to time 7;00, and add the 2_Green comp to the Timeline.

4   Go to time 14;00, and add the 3_Purple comp to the Timeline.

5   Go to time 21;00, and add the 4_Yellow comp to the timely Timeline.

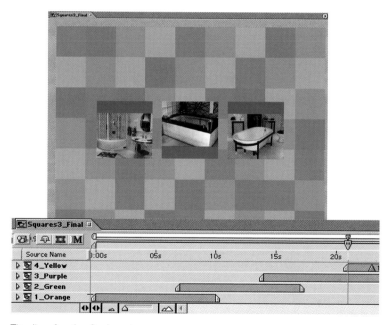

Timeline for the final spot

Now Try This

Admire your work! We hope that through the exercises in these first three chapters, you've gained a new respect for the Solid layer in After Effects. If you use these ideas and techniques as a jumping-off point, there's no limit to what you can do with solids. Let your imagination take you where it will. Here are a couple of options to get you going:

- Replace every square of a particular color in the backgrounds with a video clip, to create a wall of televisions.

- Use the vertical and horizontal flips as dominoes to spell words or create an image or shape.

CHAPTER 4 | Designing Title Effects

You don't need to search in any particular area for ideas for titles and credits; if you keep your eyes and mind open, ideas can be found everywhere from movie trailers to cereal boxes to the night sky. You can also get ideas by first designing something you might consider conventional and then working to transform it from there. That's what you'll do with the project in this chapter.

One common approach to bringing text onto the screen is to have it fade in as a blur and then come into focus once the text reaches its final destination. You'll use that approach as the basis for the main title in this chapter's project. But you'll customize the technique by using shooting stars and light flashes to introduce each section of the title.

It Works Like This

Check out the **Ch4_Finished_Movie.mov** file on the DVD to see the text effects you'll create in this chapter. You'll animate the text onto the screen with a blurred motion, revealing one section at a time with light bursts. Here are the project's basic steps:

1. Create a background blur for the title.

2. Divide the title into sections by using masks, and then animate each mask's opacity.

3. Use the Lens Flare effect on a solid to create flashes that reveal each section of the title.

4. Create "comets" by animating a masked and feathered solid.

A comet-like solid and light flash introducing sections of the title

The blurred title, fully revealed

The title comes into focus

Preparing to Work

To prepare for this project, do the following:

1   Start with a new project, and import the **BackgroundMovie.mov** file from this chapter's folder on the book's DVD.

2   Save your project as Ch 4 Title Effects.

Creating the Title

This movie is built within a single composition, which you'll create now:

1   Create a new comp named Master Comp, using the Medium, 320 × 240 preset, with Frame Rate 30 and Duration 10;00 seconds.

2   Select the Title-Action Safe button at the bottom of the Comp window.

3   Click the Horizontal Type tool in the Tools palette, and set the following properties in the Character and Paragraph palettes:

> Fill Color: white
>
> Stroke Color: None
>
> Font Family: Myriad
>
> Font style: Roman
>
> Font size: 40 pixels
>
> Tracking: −50
>
> Centered text

Your text will be big enough to be read easily, but these settings leave enough room around the title so that a background and other animated elements can also be viewed.

4   Press Ctrl+Alt+Shift+T (Windows) or Opt+Command+T (Mac OS) to create a new text layer in the center of the Comp window. Then, type the title LA HI-RISE.

5   Select the layer in the Timeline, and press the up arrow key several times to nudge the layer upward to make room for a second line of text underneath.

We used all caps so that the tall letters keep the high-rise theme of the title and project.

The title

Dividing the Title

You may have noticed that in After Effects, there are several ways to accomplish the same result. When you're deciding which technique is best, it often comes down to personal preference and work style. Sometimes the best technique is the one that can be most easily revised when your client wants you to tweak things here and there.

The objective in the next few steps is to reveal sections of the LA HI-RISE title at different times. One way to accomplish this is to duplicate the text layer and apply a separate mask to each text layer while staggering the start time for each layer. You can also create a separate text layer for each group of letters and then animate the layers separately. In this project you'll use only one layer to do this, because it takes fewer system resources and allows previews to play back more quickly:

1   Go to time 1;00, and use the Rectangular Mask tool to draw a mask around the letter *L* in the Master Comp window.

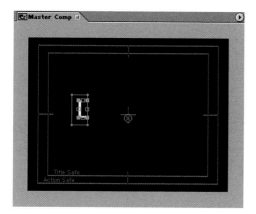

Masking the letter *L*

2   Continue using the Rectangular Mask tool to create masks for the letter *A*, the letters *HI*, the hyphen with the letters *RI*, and the letters *SE*, for a total of five masks. When you're placing the masks, be sure you cover each letter or set of letters completely and don't overlap the adjoining letters. To get a closer look at your masks and letters, press Ctrl (Windows) or Command (Mac OS) and the plus–sign key (+) to increase the magnification of the Composition window.

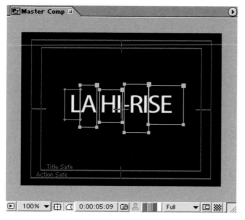

Masking the title

3   To make each mask easier to identify in the Timeline, click the mask's name, press Enter or Return, and then type the letter or letters that are masked. Repeat this for each mask.

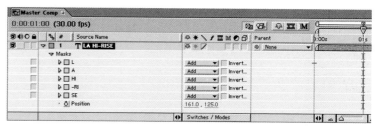

The renamed masks in the Timeline

Animating the Masks

Now you'll animate the Mask Opacity of each mask and reveal the letters at different times:

1   Select all the masks, and press TT to display each mask's Mask Opacity property.

2   Go to time 1;00, and set a 0% Mask Opacity keyframe for mask L.

3   Go forward one frame to time 1;01, and change the Mask Opacity value to 100%.

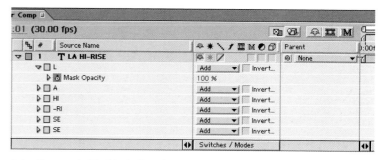

Animating mask L's Mask Opacity

4   Select both Mask Opacity keyframes, and copy them.

5   Go forward 19 frames to time 1;20, select mask SE, and paste the keyframes.

6   Go forward 20 frames to time 2;10, select mask HI, and paste the keyframes.

7   Go forward 20 frames to time 3;00, select mask A, and paste the keyframes.

8   Go forward 20 frames to time 3;20, select mask –RI, and paste the keyframes.

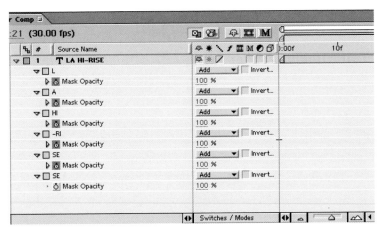

All the Mask Opacity keyframes in place

Press Home and then the spacebar to preview the animation. You should see the masked sections of the title appear at different times.

Creating the Title Blur

It's time to duplicate the text layer and use it to create the blurred title that appears before the main title comes into focus:

1   Select the LA HI-RISE layer, and duplicate it.

2   Select the lower LA HI-RISE layer in the Timeline, apply Effect > Blur & Sharpen > Fast Blur, and set Blurriness to 10. (No keyframe is needed.)

3   To make the topmost text layer appear after the blurred version fades in, go to time 3;20 and add a 0% Opacity keyframe to the top layer.

4   Press Alt + [(Windows) or Opt + [(Mac OS) to trim the layer's In point and leave its keyframe at the current point in time. (If you press only [, the keyframe moves to time 7;20, which you don't want to happen.)

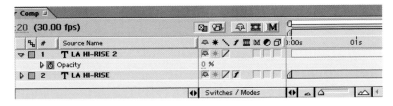

Trimming layer 1 without moving its keyframe

5   Go to time 5;00, and change the layer's Opacity to 100%.

If you preview the animation, the blurred letters should fade in at different times. Then the sharp version of the title should quickly fade in on top of the blurred letters.

Adding Flashes of Light

You'll create light flashes by animating the Lens Flare effect (available only in the Professional version of After Effects). First, you'll create a Flare Center keyframe over each portion of the title at the same time each portion is revealed. Then, you'll move the flare forward a bit in time so that viewers see the flash just before they see the title come into view.

Note: If you have the Standard version of After Effects (and so don't have the Lens Flare effect), you may be able to create similar results by importing a Photoshop file that uses the Photoshop Lens Flare filter. It won't be nearly as easy to work with as the After Effects effect, but it's worth a try.

---

1   Go to time 0:00, and create a new comp-size solid named Light Flash that's colored black (RGB: 0, 0, 0).

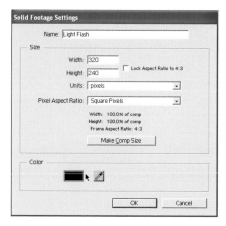

Settings for the Light Flash solid

2   Apply Effect > Render > Lens Flare to the solid. It's a bit too brilliant right now, but you'll tone it down later.

3   Display the Modes column in the Timeline, and set the Light Flash layer's mode to Screen. Doing so lets you reveal the text layers behind the black solid in the next steps.

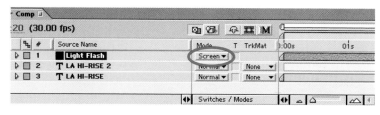

Blending the Light Flash layer with the title

4   Go to time 1;01, and create a keyframe for the effect's Flare Center property. Press U to reveal the Light Flash layer's keyframes in the Timeline.

5   Reposition the Flare Center so that it lies right over the blurred *L* in the Comp window. The light will act as a reveal for the blurred text layer later in the project.

6   Go to time 1;21, and drag the icon in the Flare Center over the next portion of the title (the letters *SE*) that's revealed in the Comp window. Be sure to drag the circled + (plus sign) at the center of the flare; otherwise, a keyframe isn't created when you reposition the lens flare.

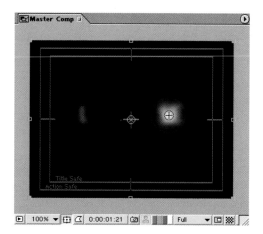

Animating the lens flare's center

7   Repeat step 6 at times 2;11 (letters *HI*), 3;01 (*A*), and 3;21 (*-RI*).

Next, we'll show you an easy way to offset the time of all five Flare Center keyframes:

1   Go to time 0;26, and click the Flare Center property name to *select* all of its keyframes.

2   Hold down your mouse pointer on the first keyframe, press Shift, and drag to snap the first keyframe to the Current Time Indicator (CTI). Reposition all the keyframes accordingly.

If you preview the comp at this point, the lens flare should glide back and forth over the title. The masked sections of the title fade in right after the lens flare passes over a section.

Now you'll make the lens flare stay put over each set of letters until the next set appears, instead of gliding between the letters:

1   Make certain that all your Flare Center keyframes are selected.

2   Choose Animation > Toggle Hold Keyframe. This option prevents interpolation between the keyframes so the property's value doesn't change until the next keyframe.

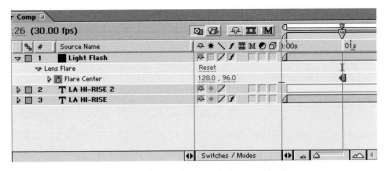

Setting the Flare Center keyframes' interpolation to Hold

Animating the Flare Brightness

Next, you'll animate the flare's brightness so that it fades in and out when it reveals each section of the title:

1   Go to time 0;26, and add a keyframe to the Lens Flare effect for 0% Flare Brightness.

2   Move forward five frames to time 1;01, and change the Flare Brightness to 85%.

3   Move forward five more frames to time 1;06, and change Flare Brightness back to 0%. These keyframes make the first flare fade in and out.

4   Click the Flare Brightness property name to select all three keyframes. Copy them, and then paste them at the same point in time as each Flare Center keyframe (1;16, 2;06, 2;26, and 3;16).

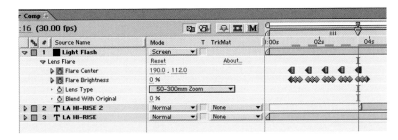

Pasting the Flare Brightness keyframes

At this point, your lens flare should fade in to reveal each portion of the title and then fade out.

Creating the Comets

You have your light flashes; now you need to add the shooting-star or comet effect that coincides with each light flash. Each comet is made by animating a solid that's shaped by feathered masks:

1   Go to time 0;26, and create a white solid layer named White Line that's 200 × 50. The final line won't be nearly that large, but this size gives you room to feather the layer masks you'll add next.

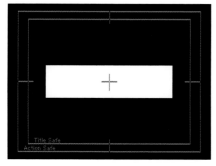

Creating the first White Line solid layer

2   Use the Rectangular Mask tool (Q) to create a thin straight line within the solid. Be sure areas of the solid surround all four sides of the mask for feathering.

3   Press F on the keyboard to display the Mask Feather property in the Timeline, and set its value to 3, 3.

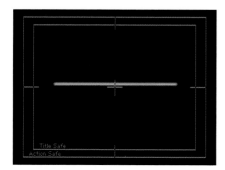

A feathered rectangular mask makes the comet trail.

4   To add a small comet head, use the Elliptical Mask tool (Q) to draw an oval shape near the left end of the new line.

5   Set the oval mask's Mask Feather to 10, 10.

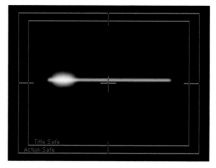

Adding a comet head by using the Elliptical Mask tool

Now you can animate the comet:

1   Turn on the lock next to each mask. Then, go to time to 1;01, where the first flash appears.

2   Line up the oval portion of the white line with the bright spot in the lens flare, and add a Position keyframe to the White Line layer.

3   Back up to time 0;26. To keep the line straight as it moves, hold down Shift while you move the White Line layer off the screen to the right.

4   To complete the cycle, go to time 1;06, and move the line off the screen to the left while pressing the Shift key.

The line should now zip across the screen, and the comet head should line up with the light flash. If you need to refine the size of the line, try changing only the y value of the solid layer's Scale property to thin the line and maintain its proportion relative to the feather.

Tip: You may have noticed that the Position velocity (the speed of the animation for the Position parameter) isn't even from start to finish. If you want to make the line travel at the same speed throughout the animation, expand the Position property in the Timeline, and deselect the box under the middle keyframe to make it a roving keyframe. Doing so makes the middle keyframe interpolate its speed from the previous and next keyframes.

Now that you've created one flying comet, you'll create duplicates of it and align the copies' timing with the other lens flares:

1   Select the Light Flash layer, and press U to reveal its keyframes.

2   Duplicate the White Line layer. Move the In point of the new White Line layer to time 1;16 so that it lines up with the start of the second set of the three Lens Flare keyframes.

3   Repeat step 2 three more times to create the remaining three lines, but align the In point of the new lines with the start of the other sets of Flare Brightness keyframes at times 2;06, 2;26, and 3;16.

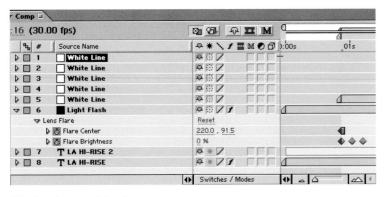

Aligning the remaining lines

Press Home and then the spacebar to preview the animation. A comet should fly across the Comp window from right to left, and a flare should fade in and out to reveal each set of letters in the title.

Stretching the Title

There's just one last animation to complete before this section of the project is finished!

1   Go to time 5;00. Select the LA HI-RISE text layers, press S to display their Scale properties, and add a 100, 100% Scale keyframe to each layer.

2   Go to time 9;29, and change the Scale property for both layers to 130, 100%. This will slowly expand the title horizontally, similar to a tracking effect.

Now Try This

Try some of the following steps to create a suitable background for the animation and to add the remaining elements seen in this chapter's sample movie:

- Create a white solid that's the same size as the composition, and use the Rectangular Mask tool in Subtract mode to make the project's white letterbox.

- Add symbols that represent city life, and scroll them across the bottom of the screen. We used the Webdings font to create these in the project's sample movie, and we applied blending modes to integrate them into the background.

- Add the background movie from the **Chapter 04** folder on the book's DVD, and add Blur and Levels effects to it to enhance its impact. Apply a Drop Shadow effect to the topmost LA HI-RISE text layer to give a sense of depth.

CHAPTER 5

Dancing Type

One fun and powerful text property in After Effects is Source Text, which lets you animate individual characters within a word. You can change a single letter to another character in tandem with any or all of its other properties. For example, you can change the letter *A* to the letter *W* and then to *E* (or set it to random characters) over time.

This chapter shows you how to use the Source Text property to create a dancing figure, with some help from a unique font. In addition, you'll learn how to create a rich ethereal motion background, simply by masking and animating some solids (and blending them, and applying effects to them…OK, it isn't *that* simple!).

It Works Like This

In this chapter, you'll learn a few ways to animate text and a technique for creating motion backgrounds from scratch. Check out the **Ch 5 Final Movie.mov** file to see the animation you'll build. The project's basic steps are as follows:

1. Create an animated background using effects and masked solids.

2. Create a simple logo.

3. Animate the characters in a text layer.

4. Animate a logo in 3D space.

The logo emerges from the background.

As the logo turns to face the viewer, the background colors and tones morph.

The logo's stick figure shakes its groove thang.

Preparing to Work

To prepare for this project, do the following:

1   Quit After Effects, and then install the DANCEMAN TrueType font from this chapter's folder on the DVD onto your computer system.

2   Restart After Effects. You should see the DANCEMAN font listed in the Character palette's Font Family menu.

3   Start with a new project, and save it as Ch 5 Dancing Type.

Setting Up the Composition

The final project contains a master composition and two nested comps. Start by building a comp for the background, which you'll add to the master comp toward the end of the project:

1   Create a new comp named Background using the Preset NTSC DV, with dimensions 720 × 480, Frame Rate 29.97, and Duration 5:00 seconds.

2   Save the project.

Animating the Background

The background layer consists of four solids that are masked, blended, and animated. You have a lot of freedom in this section to create a unique background by defining your own color, shapes, keyframes, and layer blending, but we provide some of our property values in case you want to create something similar to our final results:

1   Create a new solid (Layer > New > Solid), and click the Make Comp Size button. You can use our color (RGB: 252, 208, 0) or any color you'd like.

2   Use the Elliptical Mask, Rectangular Mask, or Pen tool to draw a large shape out of the solid. We used the Elliptical Mask tool and created a mask that surrounds most of the solid but doesn't cover its corners. (Again, it's not important that your mask be exactly like ours. However, if you prefer it to be, draw an oval with the Elliptical Mask tool, and then click the Shape value next to the Mask Shape property in the Timeline and enter -169.72977 for Left, -12.252265 for Top, 889.72913 for Right, and 495.8559 for Bottom. Surely that's not as fun as creating your own mask—but each to their own, eh?)

Tip: If you need to resize and reposition the mask after initially drawing it, be careful that you only change the mask and don't reposition or resize the solid layer. It's a little awkward, but all you need to do is make sure the mask is selected under the solid layer in the Timeline before you drag any of the mask's handles.

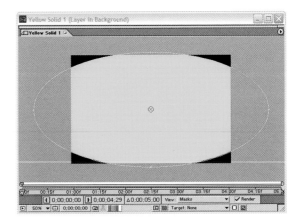

Masking the solid layer

3   Make sure you're at time 0;00. Select the solid layer, press M to display its Mask Shape, and click the stopwatch next to it to create a keyframe for it.

4 Go to time 1;00, and reposition one or more of the mask handles to create the next state of the solid's animation. We dragged the top mask handle to the bottom and vice versa to create a wave effect.

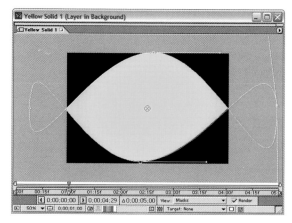

Animating the mask's shape

5 Go to each remaining second in the Timeline, and modify the mask's shape again in the Composition window. When you've completed this step, you should have six Mask Shape keyframes. (Again, you don't have to match our results. Believe us when we tell you it would be too tedious to write out how to get our precise mask shape changes and *way* too tedious for you to replicate the steps. Just drag the handles around to create random shapes.)

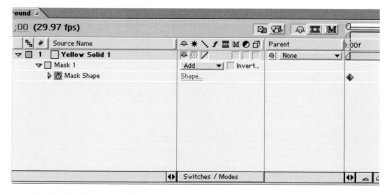

All the Mask Shape keyframes in place

6 To complete the background, duplicate the solid layer three times so that you have four solid layers.

7 Assign each new solid a different color. (We chose RGB: 155, 155, 5 for solid layer 2; RGB: 2, 119, 85 for layer 3; RGB: 195, 152, 21 for layer 4…. Just choose your own colors, and stop making us transcribe this stuff!) Then, modify the mask shape and keyframes so that they don't repeat the same pattern at any time.

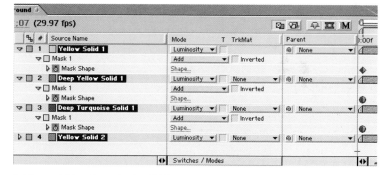

Adding additional masked solid layers

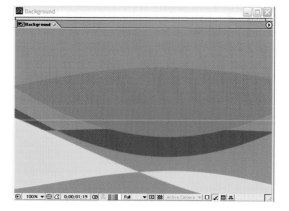

The Background composition at time 1;19

To add some complexity to the shapes, you'll make the layers blend with one another so that their colors change wherever they overlap.

8   Display the Modes column in the Timeline, and then select all the layers. To quickly browse through the blending modes, hold down the Shift key as you press the plus (+) or minus (−) key at the top of your keyboard. We chose the Luminosity blending mode, which uses each layer's level of brightness to determine the results.

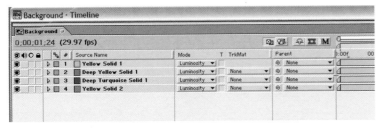

Setting the blending mode for all layers

Press the Home and Spacebar keys to preview your background. The background's look is totally up to you, so tweak it until you're satisfied, save it, and then close it.

Creating the QUICKSTEP Logo

Our QUICKSTEP logo is fairly simple: just lines and text. How would you reproduce it? Lay it out in Adobe Illustrator or some other application and then import it? We created it in After Effects using three text layers and one masked solid—you can't get much simpler than that! Here are the steps:

1   Create a new comp named Logo Comp that uses the preset NTSC DV, dimensions 720 × 480, Frame Rate 29.97, and Duration 5;00 seconds.

2   At time 0;00, create a new comp-size solid layer named Outline that's any color you desire.

3   Use the Rectangular Mask tool in Add mode to draw a filled rectangle on the solid layer; make it a little less than a third the size of the Comp window. This will be the basis for the border that surrounds the QUICKSTEP logo.

Tip: Turn on the Title-Action Safe button at the bottom of the Comp window to help keep the border within the safe zones.

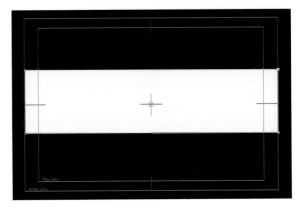

Masking the solid

4   With the Outline layer selected, apply Effect > Render > Stroke. Change the effect's Paint Style to On Transparent, and make sure the effect's Color is set to white.

5   Set the Brush Size to 3.0 to increase the size of the stroke, and turn on the All Masks option so that the masks you subsequently add to this layer also contain this effect.

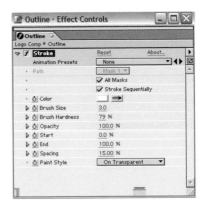

Settings for the Stroke effect

6   Click the Horizontal Type tool, and then set the Font Family to Arial Black, the Text Size to 60, and the paragraph to Center Text.

Setting the Horizontal Type tool properties

7   Type QUICKSTEP in uppercase letters, and then place the layer so that the word ends near the upper-right corner of the white border.

You'll apply a mask to this word in the next step, but we set the text properties and inserted the type beforehand because it's much easier to adjust the mask to the text than to adjust the text to the mask.

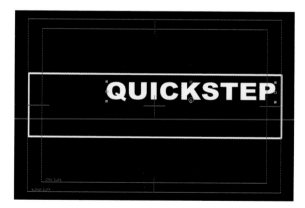

Positioning the text

8   Use the Rectangular Mask or Pen tool to add two lines to the border: One should span the height of the rectangle, and the other should lie perpendicular to the middle of the other line and reach the right side of the rectangle (or just use the illustration as your guide).

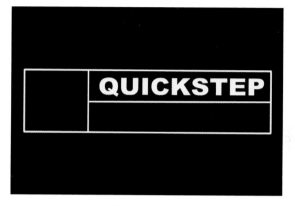

Adding two more masks to the solid

9   Add the subtitle DANCE STUDIO using font Arial Black, Text Size 30, and text Tracking 415. Position the text layer under the word *QUICKSTEP* in the Composition window.

Adding the subtitle

Creating the Dancing Figure

In the next few steps, you'll create the text layer that forms the dancing figure in the logo. Before you begin these steps, make sure you've installed the DANCEMAN font from the Chapter 5 folder on the DVD onto your computer system. Each letter in the DANCEMAN font displays a stick figure in a different dance pose; the lowercase letters put the figure in a mirror image of the corresponding uppercase figure's position.

Once the font is installed, you should see DANCEMAN listed in the Font Family menu in the After Effects Character palette. Now you're ready to go:

1   Click the Horizontal Type tool, and then set the Font Family to DANCEMAN and the Text Size to 150 in the Character palette.

Setting the text properties

2   Click in the box at the left end of the logo, and type the uppercase letter *A*. Instead of the letter *A*, a stick figure appears.

Adding the dancing stick figure

3   Expand the A text layer and its text properties in the Timeline.

4   At time 0;00, click the stopwatch for the Source Text property to create its first keyframe.

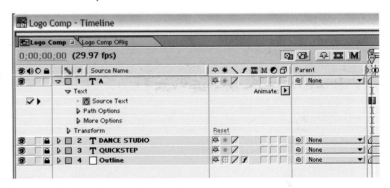

Creating the first Source Text keyframe

5   Go to time 0;05, and change the letter *A* to uppercase *B*. By animating the Source Text, you're making the figure appear to dance.

6   Continue changing the letter every five frames. You can either type new letters until you reach the end of the timeline (using both upper-case and lowercase letters if you prefer) or stop after you've made several keyframes and then copy and paste those to the end. We used only six letters to create the figure's six positions in our final movie and then duplicated those keyframes throughout the remaining Timeline.

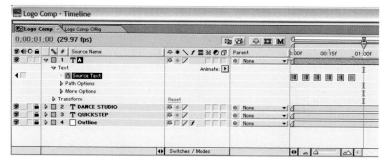

Adding more Source Text keyframes

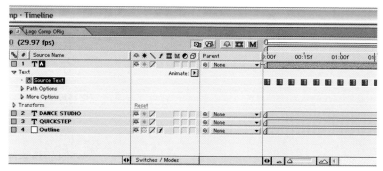

Adding the remaining Source Text keyframes

Click the Ram Preview button in the Time Controls palette to see the stick figure groove.

Pulling It All Together

In this section, you'll create a new parent composition to contain both the Background comp and Logo Comp. You'll add a few effects to soften the background and animate the Logo Comp so that it appears to slice right through the background:

1   Create a new comp named CH5 Master Comp, using the same settings as before (NTSC DV, 720 × 480 preset, Frame Rate 29.97, and Duration 5;00 seconds).

2   Place the Background comp into the Timeline at time 0;00.

3   Place the Logo Comp at time 0;00 and above the Background layer in the Timeline.

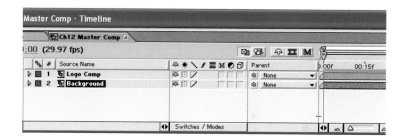

The Master Comp Timeline so far

4   Turn on the 3D switch for both layers so that you can rotate the logo around the Y and Z axes and create some special effects with the background.

5   Add three Position keyframes to the Logo Comp layer:

   • At time 0;00, values 360, 240, 300

   • At time 0;20, values 360, 240, −300

   • At time 02;00, values 360, 240, −10

6   Go back to time 0;20, and add a Y Rotation keyframe to the Logo Comp layer with a value of 0 x –80. This positions the logo at an angle away from the viewer.

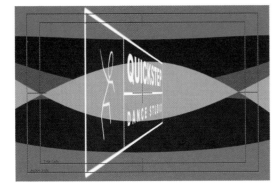

The logo's starting angle

7   Go to time 1;10, and change the Y Rotation to 0 x 0.0 to turn the logo to face the viewer.

8   To adjust the positioning of the logo in the Comp window, set a 100, 100% Scale keyframe at time 1;10, and then go to time 2;00 and change the value to 80, 80%.

9   To soften the background so that the title logo stands out more, apply Effect > Blur & Sharpen > Fast Blur to the Background layer, and set Blurriness to 30.

Click Ram Preview in the Time Controls palette to see the presentation. To add some of the final touches that we used, such as lighting and shadow effects, check out the "Now Try This" section.

Now Try This

This project showed you how to use effects and masks to create your own motion background and animate the text in a word. You can complete the following steps on your own to add the finishing touches that we used to produce the sample movie for this chapter:

• Expand the Logo Comp layer, and turn on the Cast Shadows option in the Material Options.

• Add a Light layer above the other layers in the Ch5 Master Comp, and place it far enough from the background so that the full logo is visible in the light. Adjust the parameters to your taste.

• Fade in the Background layer using Opacity keyframes from 0;00 to 0;10, and fade it out from 3;00 to 3;15 seconds.

• Use the Ramp and Bevel Alpha effects to add a metallic texture to the Logo Comp layer.

| # Auto-Scaling Type

If you're a huge fan of James Bond movies, it's probably not just because of the action but also because of the opening titles. Even if you're not a fan of Bond movies, you have to admit the titles, like 'em or not, make quite an impact and are an integral part of the Bond "dynasty." This chapter may not show you how to design a title as snazzy as those you've seen in Bond movies or elsewhere, but it will demonstrate some really useful techniques for animating type and building a background from scratch.

The new text tools in After Effects 6.0 made animating individual characters in a text layer a piece of cake, and version 6.5 makes it absolutely effortless by providing nearly 300 slick pre-built text animations (see Help > Text Preset Gallery). If the text animation you want appears in the gallery, then lucky you. But eventually you'll want to create your own from scratch (or at least customize an existing text preset), so you really should get to know the text Animator and Range Selectors.

It Works Like This

Check out this project's **Ch_6_Final_Movie.mov** file on the DVD. Most anything you produce in After Effects can be accomplished using a variety of different methods. Show other After Effects users something you've built and ask them how they'd do it, and you're bound to get several different approaches that will all work! But not all methods are equal.

If you were to produce the scaling text effects in this chapter's project on your own, you might choose to create a separate layer for each letter and animate the layers separately, or draw a mask around each letter in a single text layer and animate the masks, or perhaps use some expressions. Instead of those methods, this project will show you that using the text Animator and its Range Selector is probably the most elegant and efficient way to get these results:

1. Animate text by using a layer Animator instead of relying solely on a layer's Transform properties or on a Text Animation Preset.

2. Use effects to give the text a metallic look.

3. Create shadows that react to different implied light sources.

4. Use the Ramp effect to create the back wall and floor of the scene.

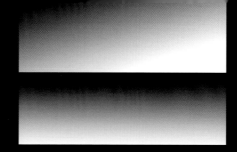

The title's horizon line

The title scales into place, casting shadows both behind and in front of the title.

Scaling Text Comp_1.mov

00:00:05

As the title comes in, background lighting moves from right to left, and foreground lighting moves from left to right.

Preparing to Work

To prepare for this project, do the following:

• Start with a new project, and save it as Ch 6 Scaling Text.

This project doesn't use any source files, so onward to the next section!

Setting Up the Composition

This project uses the NTSC D1 standard for television. Since the project contains text and is destined for broadcast, you'll need to be especially aware of the text's position in the comp:

• Create a new composition named Scaling Text Comp, using the NTSC D1, 720 × 486 Preset with Duration 5;00 seconds.

Creating the Text

When you're designing any composition, you need to consider the destination of your completed project—especially when you're working with titles. If your project will be shown on a television, you should turn on the Title-Action Safe button in the Comp window to show the boundary within which titles won't be cut off by particular displays.

In this section, you'll create the title's text (you'll add texture and animated shadows to the text in later sections):

1 To format the text, click the Horizontal Type tool in the Tools palette, and then set the following properties in the Character and Paragraph palettes:

      Font Family: Arial

      Style: Bold

      Text Size: 55

      Alignment: Center Text

2 To start the Text layer right in the center of the Comp window, choose Layer > New > Text (Ctrl+Alt+Shift+T on Windows or Command+Option+Shift+T on MAC OS), and then type The Omega Future. To get out of text-entry mode, click the Selection tool in the Tools palette or press Enter on your keyboard's numeric keypad.

Save your composition.

Tip: When you use the Text tool in After Effects, the type continuously rasterizes so that it appears clean no matter how much it scales.

Creating the title

Scaling by Letter

You can scale text using the layer's Scale property, but that method gets pretty time-consuming and tedious when you want to build more complex scaling effects. With After Effects 6.0 and 6.5, you have easy and complete creative control of individual text attributes thanks to the Animator and its Range Selector. These features give you greater flexibility while also making it nearly effortless to animate your text.

Every Animator you add to a text layer comes with a default Range Selector, which has a Start value represented by a right-pointing grey arrow and an End value represented by a left-pointing grey arrow. These two arrows and their values define the area of your layer that will be animated. You choose the property to be animated from the Animate menu.

Begin by setting the Text layer's Animator options:

1   Press the Home key to ensure that the Current Time Indicator (CTI) is at time 0;00.

2   Expand the Text layer to reveal the Text property group in the Timeline. Click the Animate menu arrow, and choose Scale from the pop-up menu.

Adding an Animator for scale to the Text layer

3   Set Animator 1's Scale value to 1000, 1000%.

4   Expand Range Selector 1, and click the Start property's stopwatch to create a 0% keyframe for the start of the selection range.

5   Go to time 3;15, and change the Start value to 100%.

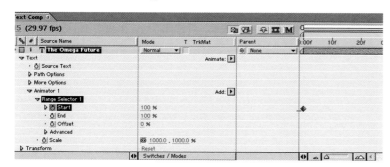

Keyframes for the Range Selector's Start property

Click the Ram Preview button in the Time Controls palette to see the results. The letters should scale from 1000% to 100% one letter at a time from left to right.

By animating only the Start property from 0–100, you move the start of the selection area from the left to the right; at 100%, the Start arrow ends up exactly where the End arrow is, resulting in text being selected and so no more scaling.

The Range Selector's Start property (gray arrow on the left) and End property (gray arrow on the right)

As the Range Selector moves from left to right, it deselects letters, which return to their default scale.

The Animator has scaled the first two words in the title.

Creating the Fade-In Effect

Since you probably don't want the letters to just pop into the screen, you'll create an easy fade-in effect for them. This section guides you through the quick process of fading in the letters one at a time using the same Animator you created in the previous section. Fading in the letters makes the title easier to read as each word develops, and it makes the scaling a little more dramatic:

1 Go to time 0;00. Click the Add menu arrow (just to the right of Animator 1 in the Timeline), and choose Property > Opacity.

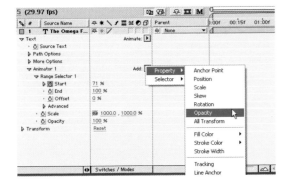

Adding Opacity to the Animator

2 Change the Opacity value to 0%. With that one little step, the Animator also animates each letter's Opacity from 0–100% (in addition to scaling each letter) as the Start of the Range Selector passes over the letter.

Tip: After you apply a text Animator to a text layer, you can rename the Animator to something that will help you identify it in the Timeline, such as `ScaleOpacity` in this project. This is especially helpful when you're working with multiple Animators in a single text layer or you have a deep stack of layers.

---

3 To have the Animator ignore the spaces between the words in *The Omega Future* (because spaces cause pauses in the animation), expand the Advanced property group under the Range Selector and change the Based On property to Characters Excluding Spaces.

Making the animation skip the spaces between words

Click the Ram Preview button in the Time Controls palette to preview the result in real-ish time. After the last letter in a word is animated, the first letter in the next word is animated—there's no pause as the Animator passes over the space between the words.

Building the First Background Layer

Next you'll develop a background that gives the comp more depth by using the Ramp effect. The Ramp effect is like a two-color version of the 4-Color Gradient effect, sharing most of the same properties but with different property names.

Here are the steps:

1 Go to time 0;00, and create a new comp-size Solid layer (Layer > New > Solid) named Bottom Background. The color doesn't matter, because the colors you set for the Ramp effect override the solid's color.

2 Move the Bottom Background layer below the Text layer in the Timeline.

3   Apply Effect > Render > Ramp to the Bottom Background layer.

4   Set the effect's Start of Ramp property to 360, 243 to define the position of the starting color. The Start Color defaults to black, and the End Color defaults to white, creating a color gradient between the two colors.

Settings for the Ramp effect in the Effect Controls window

The result of the Ramp effect with Start of Ramp set to 360, 243

5   Press End on your keyboard so you can see the entire Text layer, and then apply the Ramp effect to the The Omega Future text layer. Set the effect's Start of Ramp to 360, 200 and its End of Ramp to 360, 265.

Tip: After Effects remembers the last effect you applied. You can apply the last effect to a new layer by choosing Effect and the second item in the menu or by using the shortcut that appears next to that menu item.

6   Apply Effect > Perspective > Bevel Alpha to the Text layer. Set the Bevel Alpha effect's Edge Thickness to 2.70, Light Angle to 0 x –60, and Light Intensity to .99.

Save the composition.

The text after the Ramp and Bevel Alpha effects are applied to it

Building the Second Background Layer

At this stage, the background behind the text doesn't quite give you the sense of depth you're looking for. You'll use another layer that contains the Ramp effect to complete the illusion:

1   Duplicate the Bottom Background layer, and press Enter to rename the duplicate layer Top Background.

    You'll use this layer as the floor for the text; it will help give the composition more spatial depth.

2   Select the Top Background layer, press P to reveal its Position property, and set the property to 360, 0.0. (If you chose a different font style or size than we specified for the Text layer, then you may need to adjust the Y value slightly to make the Top Background layer lie right underneath the Text layer's baseline.)

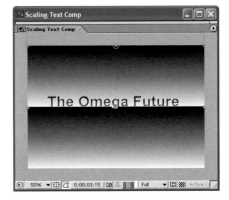

The final position of the background layers

The Ramp effect helps give a sense of space, but the depth is still a little shallow. You can create more depth and dynamism by adding a Drop Shadow effect and then animating the shadow's light source:

1   Select the Text layer, apply Effect > Perspective > Drop Shadow, and set up the effect's properties as follows:

   Opacity: 35%

   Direction: 0 x +67

   Distance: 33

   Softness: 20%

2   Make sure you're at time 0;00, and add a keyframe to the Drop Shadow effect's Direction property.

3   Go to time 4;29, and then change the Direction property to 0 x -59.

By animating the effect's Direction, you make the shadow move behind the Text layer as if the light source is panning in front of the text.

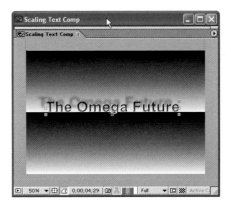

The Drop Shadow effect in the comp's last frame

Animating the Black End of the Ramp

When you added a drop shadow to the text and animated the shadow in the previous section, you created an implied light source that moves over the text. For additional drama, you can animate the gradient behind the Text layer to create a separate moving light source that's hidden behind the text:

1   Expand the Top Background layer's Ramp effect to display its properties.

2   Press the Home key to go to time 0;00, and then create a keyframe for Start of Ramp with values 240, 155.

3   Press the End key to go to time 4;29, and change the value to 440, 155.

The Ramp (color gradient) effect depends on two colors: the Start Color (black, in this project) and the End Color (white, in this project). By animating only the X value for Stamp of Ramp from 240 to 440, you've animated the black end of the gradient from left to right. This technique creates a second implied light source that moves from right to left behind the text.

Creating a Surface Reflection

You're getting close to completing the project. The next task is to create a surface reflection of the text. You'll apply several effects to a single layer to simulate a moving shadow reflected on the floor of the scene:

1 Duplicate the Text layer, and rename the new (top) layer Text Reflection.

2 Expand the Text Reflection layer's Transform group, and change the Scale to 125, –570 to enlarge and invert the image.

You don't need to be concerned about Title Safe in this case because the layer will be a shadow, not the main title.

Starting to build the text reflection

3 To remove the Ramp, Bevel Alpha, and Drop Shadow effects from the Text Reflection layer, select the layer and choose Effect > Remove All.

4 Apply Effect > Blur & Sharpen > Directional Blur to the Text Reflection layer. Set the effect's Direction to 0 x +90 and its Blur Length to 15.

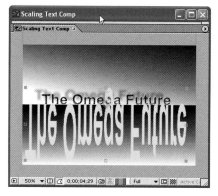

Settings for the Directional Blur effect

Almost finished creating the text reflection

5 To make it easy to reshape and distort the reflection, apply Effect > Distort > Corner Pin to the Text Reflection layer.

6 To align the reflection with the title, set the Corner Pin effect's values to the following:

> Upper Left: 135, 45
>
> Upper Right: 582, 45
>
> Lower Left: 0, 486
>
> Lower Right: 720, 486

Save and preview your work.

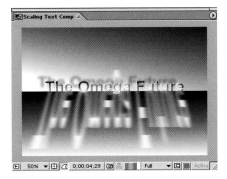

Settings for the Corner Pin effect in the Effect Controls window

The distorted text reflection

Cleaning up the reflection

Currently, the letter *g* in the Text Reflection layer protrudes above the horizon, which is unrealistic and interferes with the text's shadow. So, let's quickly clean that up by masking only the area you want the layer to display:

- Use the Rectangular Mask tool to draw a box around the reflection layer, starting in the bottom right or left corner of the comp and stopping somewhere below the horizon so that the text reflection no longer appears above the horizon.

You may notice that the top edge of the mask doesn't cut off the letters as expected, even if the mask edge is at the horizon. That's because the Text Reflection layer is distorted with the Corner Pin effect.

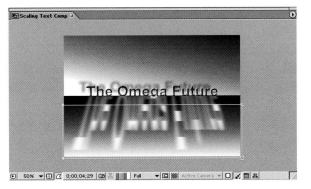

Trimming the Text Reflection layer with a mask

Click the Ram Preview button in the Time Controls palette to review the results.

Select All, Drill Them Up, Lock Them Down, and Save
The keyboard shortcuts for these actions can save you lots of time and protect your project from accidental changes: • Select All Layers: Ctrl+A (Windows) or Command+A (Mac OS) • Drill Them Up: Accent key (layers must be selected) • Lock Them Down: Ctrl+L (Windows) or Command+L (Mac OS) • Save: Ctrl+S (Windows) or Command+S (Mac OS)

Now Try This

Here are a few ways you can continue playing with your project:

- Create an animated accent bar below the title by adding a solid layer that's the same width as the title but only about 5 pixels high. Place the solid under the title in the Timeline, and apply the Ramp effect to it. Finally, animate the X value of the layer's Scale property from 0% at time 0;00 to 72.2% at time 1;28 to 100% at time 3;15.

- To change the text reflection to a shadow, set the Text Reflection layer's Blending Mode to Silhouette Alpha in the Modes column, and then lower the layer's Opacity to about 35%.

- Once you're satisfied with the animation, save and then reuse individual effect properties, animations, or both by saving them as a preset in the Effects & Presets palette. (*Presets* is the term used in After Effects 6.5 to refer to what previous versions called *Favorites*.) To do so, select the items that you want to save in the Timeline and either click Create New Animation Preset in the Effects & Presets palette or choose Animation > Save Animation Preset. After applying an animation preset, you can subsequently modify and enhance the added properties and keyframes in the Timeline.

Adding an animated bar below the title

CHAPTER 7

Animated Columns

Animating columns and filling the columns with video or stills is a technique used in many contemporary television commercials and station IDs. They often start with a main picture that expands to the width of the screen; then columns of images randomly slide back and forth across the screen. It's an effective way to weave together different pieces of footage to create an animated collage-like portrait of a subject.

This chapter shows you some quick techniques for creating this complex and sophisticated look. You'll also discover how to create alternating layers of video that replace each other as the columns float over and under one another.

It Works Like This

Check out this chapter's final movie on this book's DVD to see this project's end result. You'll discover how to create a collage of video that's replaced by other video as the footage moves via columns across the screen. The techniques are as follows:

1. Use a fast and automated method to put together sequences of footage and create transitions.

2. Create multiple animated masks to serve as windows on the footage.

3. Add transparency and richness to the scene by using a blending mode.

4. Use the new Box Blur effect.

The main footage seen through masked windows

As the columns float across the main footage, other footage appears within the columns.

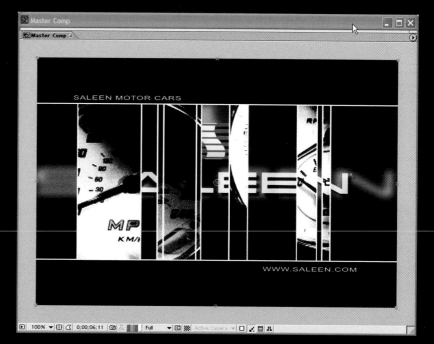

The company logo appears in the background as footage fades in and out inside the floating columns.

Preparing to Work

You'll configure all of this chapter's compositions for digital video by using one of the composition presets. The first comp you'll create contains the sequence of video footage that serves as the focal point of the entire project.

To prepare for this project, do the following:

1   Start with a new project, and save it as Ch7AnimatedColumns.

2   Import the **Footage** folder located in the Chapter 7 folder on the book's DVD.

3   Import the **Saleen_logo_Layers.psd** file from this chapter's folder on the book's DVD as footage with merged layers.

4   Create a new composition named Sequence Comp using the composition Preset NTSC DV, 720 × 480, and set the Duration to 10;00 seconds.

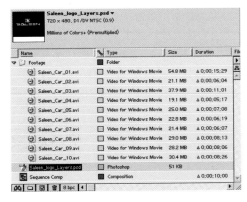

Project window with all your footage

Building the Car Sequence

The subject of this project's movie is a Saleen vehicle, which is featured in the ten pieces of footage you imported. In this section, you'll trim all that footage to the same duration, and then use a really quick method (just one step!) to distribute the footage across the Timeline and create a transition between the pieces:

1   Drag all ten Saleen_Car movies from the Project window into the Sequence Comp Timeline.

2   Go to time 2;00, select all the layers, and then press Alt +] (Windows OS) or Option +] (Mac OS) to trim the layers' Out point to the current time. (If you don't press Alt or Option, you'll move the layers' Duration bars instead of trimming them.)

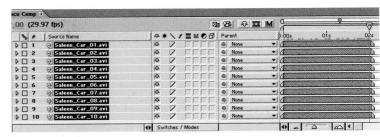

Trimming the layers

You want each layer of footage to fade into the next sequentially, so you'll stagger the layers in time and add a transition between each pair.

3   Make sure all the layers are still selected. From the top of the application, choose Animation > Keyframe Assistant > Sequence Layers.

4   In the Sequence Layers dialog, check the Overlap box, set the Duration to 1;00 second, and set Transition to Dissolve Front Layer.

Settings for the Sequence Layers command

5   With all the layers still selected, press T on your keyboard to reveal their Opacity properties. Notice that Opacity keyframes were created for each layer to fade them out over a 1 second duration.

Click the Ram Preview button in the Time Controls palette to see the results. Each layer should play for a second and then fade away to display the next layer in the sequence.

With one step, all the layers are staggered and dissolve into one another.

Building the Layers

In this section, you'll assemble the master composition to contain all of the project's components (including the composition you made in the previous section). You'll also blend another piece of footage over the entire sequence that makes up the Sequence Comp and fade it in and then out of the composition:

1   Create a new composition named Master Comp using the NTSC DV, 720 × 480 preset, and set the Duration to 10;00 seconds.

2   Drag the Sequence Comp composition from the Project window to the Master Comp Timeline. Make sure the layer starts at time 0;00.

3   Drag the **Saleen_Car_01.avi** file from the Project window into the Timeline, above the Sequence Comp layer.

4   Change the Saleen_Car_01.avi layer's Blending Mode to Difference in the Modes column of the Timeline.

5   Press T to display the Saleen_Car_01.avi layer's Opacity, and add a 0% Opacity keyframe to the layer at time 0;00.

6   Go to time 1;00, and change the layer's Opacity to 100%.

7   Go to time 5;00, and add another 100% Opacity keyframe to the layer.

8   Press End to go to the end of the Timeline, and change the layer's Opacity to 0% to fade out the layer.

First stage of the Master Comp Timeline

Click the Ram Preview button in the Time Controls palette to view the results.

Building the Columns

It's time to create the animated masks that serve as sliding windows over the footage. To make it easier for you to keep track of which mask in the Timeline represents a mask in the composition, you'll turn on a preference that's new in After Effects 6.5:

1   Choose Edit > Preferences > User Interface Colors, and select Cycle Mask Colors.

Now, every time you draw a new mask, one of five colors will be used to identify the mask in the Timeline and in the Composition or Layer window. This will come in handy in the next section when you begin animating the masks.

2   Go to time 0;00, and double-click the Sequence Comp layer in the Master Comp Timeline to open it in a layer window. (Alternatively, you can complete this section in the Composition window; but the Layer window gives you more control.)

3   Click the Rectangular Mask tool in the Tools palette. Draw a vertical column starting below the bottom edge of the composition area and extending above the top edge of the composition.

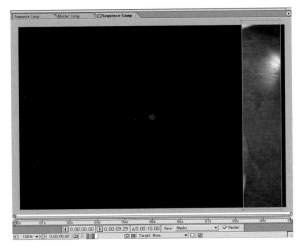

Drawing the first mask in the Sequence Comp's layer window

4   Draw four more columns that also span beyond the top and bottom edge of the comp. Place them in other areas of the composition, and make them varying widths.

Five masks with unique colors in the Sequence Comp layer

Animating the columns

Your next task is to animate the masks horizontally and randomly across the screen. You'll use each mask's Mask Shape property as you would a Position property to animate its location over the Sequence Comp:

1   At time 0;00, expand the Sequence Comp in the Timeline, select all the masks, and then press M to display their Mask Shape properties.

2   With all the masks still selected, click the stopwatch next to any Mask Shape property to add a keyframe to all the masks.

3   Go to time 2;00, and click Mask 1's name in the Timeline to select the mask.

4   Using the Selection tool, drag Mask 1 to the opposite side of the comp.

5   Move the other four masks to new locations on the layer.

Tip: Remember to select the mask's name in the Timeline first in order to select all four vertices before moving the mask. Otherwise, you'll reshape the mask instead of moving it.

---

6   Go to time 4;00, and again move each mask to a new location.

7   Select the Mask Shape keyframes for all five masks, and copy them.

8   Go to time 6;00, and paste the keyframes.

Pasting all the Mask Shape keyframes

9   To add some definition to the boundaries of the masked areas, go to the Master Comp Timeline, select the Sequence Comp layer, and choose Effect > Render > Stroke.

10 Check the All Masks option in the Effect Controls window, and set Color to white (RGB: 255, 255, 255). Now each mask has a white outline.

Settings for the Stroke effect in the Effect Controls window

Branding the Project

You've assembled the footage and animated its masks. Now it's time to add the logo, which is a Photoshop file. You'll set the logo behind the footage so that it teases the viewers by allowing them to see bits of the logo between the masks but never the entire thing:

1 Go to time 0;00 in the Master Comp Timeline, and drag the **Saleen_logo_layers.psd** file from the Project window to the Timeline below the Sequence Comp layer.

2 Duplicate the Saleen_logo_Layers layer, and add a 0% Opacity keyframe to both logo layers.

3 Go to time 3;00, and change both layers' Opacity to 100%.

4 Go to time 7;00, and add another 100% Opacity keyframe to both layers.

5 Go to time 9;00, select only the bottommost logo layer (layer 4), and change the layer's Opacity to 0%.

Now parts of the logo appear as the masks move back and forth over the footage.

Animating and revealing the logo

So far you've set up the logo to only play peek-a-boo with the user, by hiding it behind the footage. Next you'll fade out the footage at the end of the project to reveal the entire logo. You'll also give the logo more life by stretching it over time and adding a halo look to it:

1 Go to time 6;00, and add a 100% Opacity keyframe to the Sequence Comp layer.

2 Go to time 7;00, and change the layer's Opacity to 0%. Now the logo is fully visible.

3 Go to time 0;00, add a Scale keyframe to both logo layers, and set both keyframes to 85, 85%.

4 Press the End key to go to the end of the Timeline (time 9;29). Change layer 3's Scale to 100, 100% and layer 4's Scale to 150, 150%.

5 Select layer 4, and choose Effect > Blur & Sharpen >Box Blur. Set Iterations to 3 and Blur Radius to 10 in the Effect Controls window.

Save the project, and preview your results.

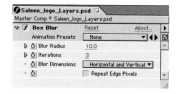

Settings for the Box Blur effect in the Effect Controls window

The logo, fully revealed

Tip: If you often use the same group of settings (or nearly the same) when you use a particular effect, then save that effect with those settings as a preset. To create the preset, set up the effect's settings as you want them, go to the Effect Controls window, and choose Save Selection As Animation Preset from the Animation Presets menu. (Despite the name Animation Preset, animation isn't required.) One way to then use your preset is to apply the effect as you normally would and choose your preset's name from the Animation Presets menu in the Effect Controls window.

Now Try This

Here's a series of steps to bring more attention to the car's logo and add more pizzazz:

1   Create a new comp named Letter Box that uses the same comp preset you've been using, with Duration set to 10;00 seconds.

2   Drag the Master Comp from the Project window into the Letter Box Timeline, starting at time 0;00.

3   Use the Rectangular Mask tool in Add mode to mask over the Master Comp in a format that looks like a 16:9 letterbox.

4   Apply the Stroke effect to the mask.

5   Use the new Text Animation Presets to animate titles in the top and bottom black areas of the screen, above and below the new stroke lines.

6   Use Opacity keyframes to create a 15-frame fade up of the Master Comp layer.

CHAPTER 8

Animating with Illustrator

Making titles that engage the viewer is tough nowadays. Movie and television audiences often treat titles like commercials, during which it's normal for people to talk to others, check cell phone messages…basically do anything but actually read the titles. Sometimes all you need to do to keep people engaged in the titles you create is to add a little mystery that makes the viewer pay attention as they try to figure out what's going on. This chapter's project shows you one technique to accomplish just that.

In this chapter, you'll animate letters so they appear to be drawn onto the screen, sort of like an Etch-a-Sketch drawing. Part of this technique uses a workflow between Adobe After Effects and Adobe Illustrator that helps simplify a seemingly complex task: animating objects along the paths of an intricate font. You can take this technique and apply it to other things besides text, as long as those things contain paths.

It Works Like This

Check out the **Ch8FinalMovie.mov** file in this chapter's folder on the book's DVD to see the final results of this project. You'll use these techniques:

1. Paste Illustrator paths onto solid layers to create masks for the letters in the final project.

2. Use a nonrendering Guide layer as reference when positioning the masks.

3. Use the Stroke effect to create outlines of each letter.

4. Create elaborate and precise animations by pasting the Illustrator paths again.

5. Animate the Stroke effect to create the illusion of live drawing.

6. Use a Keyframe Assistant to instantly create a mirror copy of your animations in time.

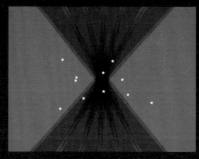

Illustrator files fan out and spin in the background.

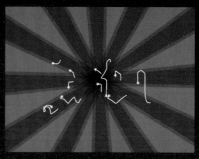

The stars begin drawing white lines.

The lines form a word.

Preparing to Work

You need both Adobe After Effects and Adobe Illustrator to complete this project. If you don't have Illustrator, you can download a free tryout version of the application from the Adobe Web site at **http://www.adobe. com/support/downloads/main.html**. This project uses three Illustrator files, which you'll import from the book's DVD as footage.

To prepare for this project, do the following:

1   Start with a new project, and save it as Ch8AnimateWithIllustrator.

2   Choose File > Import Multiple Files.

3   Select the file **jason.ai** from this chapter's folder on the book's DVD. Set the Import As option to Footage, and click Open. Click the Merged Layers option, and click OK.

4   Press Ctrl (Windows) or Command (Mac OS), and click both the **star.ai** file and the **StarBackground.ai** file from this chapter's folder on the DVD to select them. Set the Import As option to Footage, and click Open.

5   Click Done.

The Project window, containing imported footage

Setting Up the Composition

You'll work within one composition to animate the stars and the letters the stars appear to draw. The stars are provided in a simple Illustrator drawing, and you'll create the letters in the word *jason* by masking solid layers. You'll include the **jason.ai** file for visual reference, but that image doesn't appear in the finished project.

Start with these steps:

1   Create a new composition named Comp 1 using the NTSC D1 Square Pix, 720 × 540 preset. Set the background to blood red (RGB: 170, 0, 0) and Duration to 10;00 seconds.

2   Add **jason.ai** to the Comp 1 Timeline at time 0;00.

3   Since you'll use the jason.ai layer only as a visual reference and don't need to render it, select the layer and choose Layer > Guide Layer. Now the Timeline labels the layer with a blue guide layer icon so you can easily distinguish it from other layers. In addition, you don't need to remember to hide the layer before rendering, since by default a guide layer won't render unless you turn on a particular guide layer option in the Render Queue window.

4   Create five white solid layers at comp size. Name each layer for a unique letter in the word *JASON*.

5   Create a composition marker (Shift+1) at time 0;00, time ;15 (Shift+2), time 2;15 (Shift+3), time 3;00 (Shift+4), time 5;00 (Shift+5), and time 5;15 (Shift+6). You'll use the markers throughout the project to quickly move between those points in time.

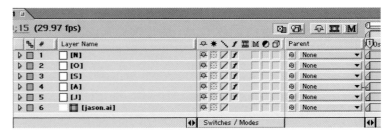

The Comp 1 Timeline

Setting Up Illustrator

You need to have Illustrator and After Effects running simultaneously in this section so you can copy paths in Illustrator and paste them as masks onto the solid layers in After Effects. Each letter in the **jason.ai** file is made of multiple Illustrator paths except the letter *N*, which is made of just one path.

Follow these steps:

1   In After Effects, select the jason.ai layer in the Timeline, and choose Edit > Edit Original. Illustrator should start and display the **jason. ai** file. (Again, if you don't have Illustrator, you can go to the Adobe Web site to download a trial version.)

2   In Illustrator, choose Edit > Preferences > File Handling & Clipboard. In the Clipboard on Quit section, make sure the Copy As option is set to AICB, and select Preserve Paths. Click OK.

3   Choose View > Outline to view only an outline of the **jason.ai** file.

4   Expand all the layers to display all the paths that make up each letter. These paths will enable you to easily animate the act of drawing the letters' outlines.

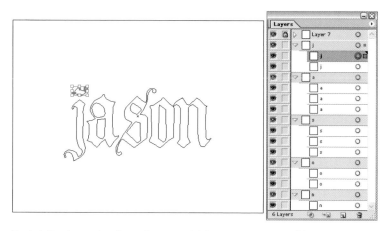

Each letter is made of one layer containing one or more objects.

Creating the Letters' Paths

You can create intricate masks for your solid layers by copying the letters' paths in Illustrator and pasting them onto the solid layers in After Effects. The masks aren't used to display the letters, as you might typically use a mask; instead, you'll apply an effect to the masked layers in the next section to create the letters' outlines.

Create the paths as follows:

1   In Illustrator, click the Selection tool in the Tools palette.

2   To select all paths in the letter *j*, click the target circle next to the layer's name.

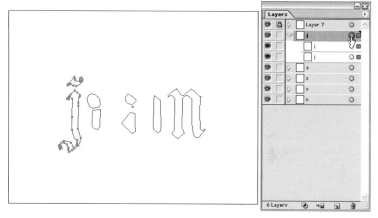

Selecting all paths in the J layer

3   Choose Edit > Copy to copy the paths.

4   Return to After Effects, select the solid layer named J, and then paste.

5 Expand the J layer and the Masks group in the Timeline to display the two masks you just created when you pasted the Illustrator paths.

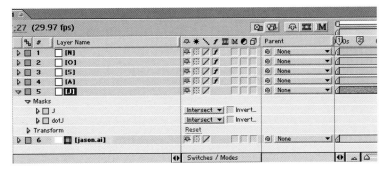

Pasting Illustrator paths creates the masks for the solids.

6 Click a mask's name in the Timeline to select the mask, and then use the arrow keys on your keyboard or the Selection tool to position the mask so that it matches the location of the corresponding letter in the jason.ai guide layer.

7 Repeat steps 1–6 for the other letters, copying the paths of a letter in Illustrator and pasting the paths onto the corresponding solid layer.

8 Hide the jason.ai guide layer, since you no longer need it for visual reference.

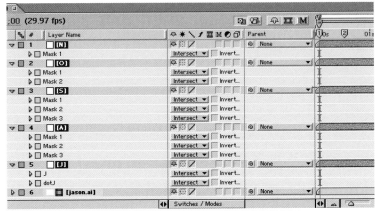

The Comp 1 Timeline after all the Illustrator paths have been pasted

The composition window with the Mask Mode for all masks set to Add

Stroking the paths

Now that you have solid white versions of each letter in the word *jason*, it's time to turn them into outlines by changing their Mask Modes and applying a Stroke effect to each mask's path:

1. Select all the letter layers in the Timeline, press M to display their masks, and then set each mask's Mask Mode to Intersect in the Switches column. (The Mask Mode menu appears at the same level as each mask's name in the Timeline.)

   Now the letters aren't visible, since this mode only displays areas where a mask intersects another mask.

2. Select the J solid layer, and choose Effect > Render > Stroke.

3. Select the Stroke effect in the Effect Controls window, and choose Edit > Duplicate.

4. Set each Stroke effect's Path property to a different mask in the current layer.

5. Set each Stroke effect's Paint Style property to On Original Image.

6. Repeat steps 2–5 for each solid layer, but with the following modifications:

   In step 3, duplicate the effect as many times as you need to in order to have one Stroke effect for every mask in the layer. Layers A and S have three masks, and layer O has two masks; layer N has only one mask, so you can skip step 3 for that layer.

In step 5, set the Paint Style for the O and N layers' effects to On Transparent.

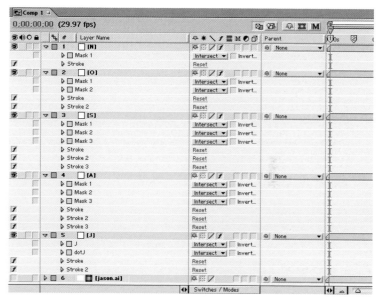

The Comp 1 Timeline with all masks and Stroke effects in place

The Composition window with masked and stroked solids

Adding Stars for Each Letter

Each mask in the final project has a star that travels over it as the stroked path is revealed. So, next you'll add a copy of the **star.ai** file to the composition for every mask in the Timeline:

1 Add the **star.ai** file to the Timeline at time 0;00. Duplicate it 10 times so that you have 11 star.ai layers, one for each mask.

2 Move the star.ai layers in the Timeline stack so that you have one star.ai layer above a solid layer for each mask in the solid layer. For example, since the J solid layer contains two masks, you should move two star.ai layers above the J solid layer in the Timeline.

3 Rename the star.ai layers star_*letter*, where *letter* represents the name of the solid the star.ai layer is above.

4 Press Ctrl (Windows) or Command (Mac OS), and click each of the star layers to select them. Press S to display their Scale properties, and set Scale to 75, 75% for all the star layers.

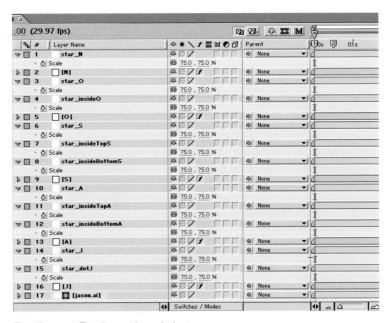

The Comp 1 Timeline with scaled stars

Animating the stars

You were probably worried that animating the 11 tiny stars around the letters' paths would be mind-numbingly tedious, especially since those paths are fairly intricate. And when we tell you that the animation requires several dozen roving keyframes per star, you're probably already turning to the next chapter…but fear not! It's copy and paste all the way, baby!

> **Note:** This time, instead of copying all the paths in a letter, you need to copy one path at a time.

1 Return to Illustrator, and expand the J layer in the Layers palette to display its paths.

2 Click the target circle button to the right of the path that makes up the body of the letter J, and then choose Edit > Copy.

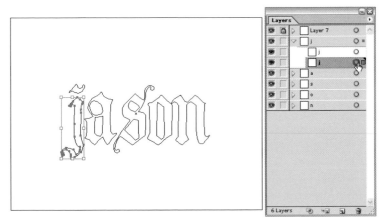

Selecting and copying one path at a time in Illustrator

3   Return to After Effects, select the star_J layer, and press P to display its Position property.

4 Go to time 0;15, select the layer's Position property, and then paste. A slew of Position keyframes appear, for all the points that make up the path of the lower body portion of the letter *j*.

5   With the Position property still selected, use the arrow keys on your keyboard or the Selection tool to position the path in the same location as the letter. (Make sure every keyframe is selected [highlighted]; otherwise, when you press an arrow key, you'll move only one keyframe instead of all of them.)

If you preview your comp, you'll see the little star fly around the letter. That was easy enough, eh?

6   Now repeat steps 1–5 for each star layer by copying a different path in the Illustrator layers and pasting the path onto the Position property of the corresponding star layer in After Effects.

7   When you're done, you can quit Illustrator.

Animating the stars by pasting the Illustrator paths onto the stars' Position properties

"Drawing" the letters

At this point, all the stars travel around the paths of the letters, so the worst is over. Now you need to make it appear as if the stars are drawing the letters onto the screen. You'll accomplish this by animating each letter's Stroke effect simultaneously:

1   Select all the solid layers in the Timeline, press E to display their Stroke effects, and then expand each effect to display their properties.

2   Go to time 0;15, and set each Stroke effect's Start to 0% and End to 0%. Add a keyframe to each effect's Start property.

3   Go to time 2;15, where the stars stop animating, and change each effect's Start to 100%.

Deselect the layers, and then preview your animation. The stars should wander around, appearing to draw the letters in the word *jason* as they go.

Animating the Stroke's Start property creates the drawing illusion.

Fading and rotating the stars

Next, you'll animate the stars' Opacity, Position, and Rotation to make them fade in and fade out while rotating the entire way:

1   Select all the star layers in the Timeline, and press P to display their Position properties. You should see a bunch of round dots (the roving Position keyframes) book-ended by two normal Position keyframes.

2   Press Home to go to time 0;00, and then move the star layers somewhere else in the composition.

3   Press Shift+T to display the layers' Opacity properties alongside their Position properties.

4   Make the stars fade in by adding a 0% Opacity keyframe at time 0;00 and a 100% Opacity keyframe at time 0;15 for each star layer.

5   Go to time 2;15, select all the star layers, press T to display their Opacity properties, and then add a 100% Opacity keyframe to every star.

6   Go to time 3;00, and change every star layer's Opacity to 0%.

7   Move every star layer to a new and unique position in the composition, so the stars appear to fade away from the letters they've just drawn. Consider making each star travel in a direction it's already heading toward.

8   Go to time 0;00, and add a 0 x +0.0 Rotation keyframe to every star layer.

9   Go to time 3;00, and change every star layer's Rotation to 5 x +0.0 to make each star rotate five times from 0 to 3 seconds.

Reversing time

You did a lot of work in the previous section to bring in the stars and add some nuance to their appearance and movement. To get those same results at the end of the Timeline, but in reverse time, might seem like a lot of work; but it isn't, when you outsource the work to a Keyframe Assistant!

1   Select a star layer, and press U to display its keyframes.

2   Click the first property name to select it, and then press Shift while you click each and every property name listed to select all the keyframes for every animated property in the star layer. By selecting a property name, you ensure that you've selected all the property's keyframes.

3   Choose Edit > Copy to copy the keyframes.

4   Go to time 7;00, and paste the keyframes.

5   With the new keyframes still selected, choose Animation > Keyframe Assistant > Time-Reverse Keyframes. This command flips the selected keyframes in time, reversing the animation.

6   Repeat steps 1–5 for every star layer.

7   Repeat steps 1–5 for the letter layers, but go to time 7;15 in step 4 instead of time 7;00.

Save and play back your animation. All the letters are erased toward the end of the composition, with the stars fading and flying out.

Now Try This

Our final movie contains a stylized star spinning in the background. To create this, all you need to do is rotate multiple copies of an Illustrator file we provide. To make rotating the layers as easy as possible, you'll assign a Null Object layer to the background layers and then rotate the null object once to rotate all the background layers:

1   Create a new composition named Background, using the NTSC D1 Square Pix, 720 × 540 preset, with Duration set to 10;00 seconds and the background color set to white (RGB: 255, 255, 255).

2   Add **StarBackground.ai** from the Project window to the Timeline at time 0;00.

3   Choose Layer > New > Null Object, and set the layer's Anchor Point to 50,50.

4   Duplicate the StarBackground layer five times so you have six StarBackground layers.

5   Select all the StarBackground layers, press R to display their Rotation properties, and add a 0 x +0.0 Rotation key frame to each.

6   Go to time 1;00. Change the Rotation of the second StarBackground layer in the stack to 0 x +30, and then set the Rotation of each StarBackground layer below it to 30 degrees more than the last. This sets the position of each layer.

The Background Timeline with rotated backgrounds

7   Shift+click the Rotation property of every StarBackground layer to select all of them, and then choose Edit > Copy to select all their Rotation keyframes.

8   Go to time 9;00, and paste the keyframes.

9   With all the new Rotation keyframes still selected, choose Animation > Keyframe Assistant > Time-Reverse Keyframes.

10 With all the StarBackground layers selected, drag one of the layers' pick whip (curly pigtail button) in the Parent column to the Null 1 layer.

11 At time 0;00, add a 0 x +0.0 Rotation keyframe to the Null layer.

12 Press the End key to go to the end of the Timeline, and then set the Rotation to 8 x +0.0. Close the Background composition.

Animating the background

13 Go to the Comp 1 Timeline, and add the Background composition to the bottom of the stack.

14 Duplicate the Background layer, and set both Background layers' Opacity to 30.

15 Set the bottom Background layer's Scale to 200, 200%.

16 Turn on both layers' Continuously Rasterize switch.

CHAPTER 9

Corporate Open

Adobe After Effects comes with a slew of effects, and the Professional version contains even more; but everyone knows you can never have enough effects to choose from. (So many effects, so little time....) When you can't produce a certain effect using the native tools in After Effects, or you want a different method, you can turn to effects that work in After Effects but that are provided by other companies such as DigiEffects, Profound Effects, and Boris FX. This chapter's project uses effects produced by Boris FX and Zaxwerks.

This project is an open for a corporate video. It features a gold bar that flies in from behind the viewer; the company logo is welded into the bar with sparks flying.

It Works Like This

Check out **Ch9FinishedProject.mov** in this chapter's folder on the book's DVD to see the spot you'll create in this chapter. This project shows you how to build and animate 3D elements using a Boris FX effect and create a unique logo reveal using another effect produced by Boris FX. In addition, you'll use gradients and blending modes to create some atmosphere. The project shows you how to do the following:

1. Design and animate a color gradient for the project's background.

2. Create a scrolling layer of text over the background.

3. Use Boris FX's 3D Invigorator effect with a few Adobe Illustrator files to build a 3D gold bar and the company logo and animate the bar into the scene.

4. Use masking techniques, Boris FX's BCC Sparks effect, and the Lens Flare effect to create the effect of the logo being welded into the gold bar.

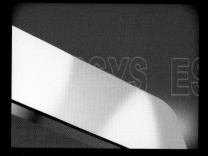

The gold bar flies in from behind the viewer.

Sparks fly as the logo is burned into the gold bar.

The logo is revealed from left to right.

Preparing to Work

This project uses the BCC Sparks effect from the Boris FX Continuum Complete collection. If you don't own this effect, you can install a trial version of it from this book's DVD or download the trial from the Boris FX Web site.

You'll also need the Classic 3.0.9 version of the Zaxwerks 3D Invigorator plug-in, which is provided on its own CD with the Professional versions of either Adobe After Effects 6.5 or the Adobe Video Collection. If you have the Standard version of either product, you can install a trial version from this book's DVD or download a trial version from the Zaxwerks Web site.

To prepare for this project, do the following:

1   Start with a new project, and save it as Ch9CorporateLogo.

2   If you don't already have Zaxwerks' 3D Invigorator effect and Boris FX's BCC Sparks effect installed in After Effects, then install them. Once they're installed, Zaxwerks and BCC submenus appear in the Effect menu in After Effects.

3   Create a new composition named Master Comp using the Medium, 320 × 240 preset; set the background color to black (RGB: 0, 0, 0) and Duration to 5:00.

Creating the Background

You'll build this project's blue and black background by using a solid and animating the Ramp effect. Follow these steps:

1   At time 0:00, create a new comp-size Solid layer named Background using any color. The effect you'll apply in the next step will override the solid's color.

2   Apply Effect > Render > Ramp to the solid.

3   Set the effect's Start Color to a vibrant shade of blue (RGB: 100, 0, 255) and the End Color to black (RGB: 0, 0, 0).

4   To start animating the effect's color gradient, add a keyframe to both the Start of Ramp and End of Ramp properties at time 0:00.

5   Set the effect's Start of Ramp to 160, -50 and its End of Ramp to 160, 0. Now the gradient's starting and ending colors begin offscreen, and the comp is filled with black.

6   Go to time 2:00, and change the Start of Ramp to 160, 120 and the End of Ramp to 160, 240.

At time 0:10, the effect's start and end colors are just coming onscreen.

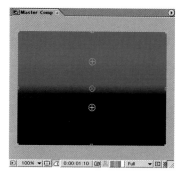

At time 1:10, you can clearly see the icons (circled plus signs) that mark the effect's Start of Ramp and End of Ramp positions.

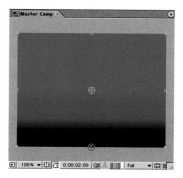

The final position of the solid's Ramp effect

Scrolling Text

In this section, you'll use the Offset effect much as you might use the Position property, to animate text so that it appears to scroll across the screen. In addition, you'll use a blending mode to integrate the text with the background:

1   Press Home to return to time 0:00, and then set the following properties in the Character palette:

>   Font Family: Arial Black
>
>   Font Size: 48 pixels
>
>   Fill Color: None
>
>   Stroke Color: White
>
>   Stroke Width: 1.5
>
>   Tracking: 0

2   To create a text layer in the middle of the comp, choose Layer > New > Text, and then type the company name: ESTORSYS.

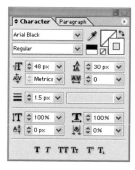

Settings for the company logo

3   In the Timeline's Modes column, set the text layer's Blending Mode to Classic Color Dodge. This gives the letters a pink color, which you'll change in a few steps.

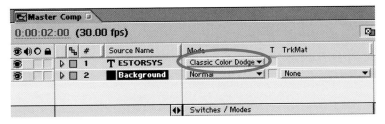

Setting the text layer's Blending Mode

4   Apply Effect > Distort > Offset to the text layer.

5   Still at time 0:00, add a keyframe to the effect's Shift Center To property with a value of 160, 120.

6   Press the End key to go to the end of the Timeline at time 4:29, and then change the Shift Center To value to –160, 120.

7   Select the ESTORSYS layer, choose Layer > Pre-Compose, and click OK.

8   Set the pre-composed layer's Blending Mode to Classic Color Burn. Now the layer's pink color changes to blue hues that complement the background.

Save the composition, and then preview your results. Once the blue gradient is behind the text, you should see the background text scrolling from right to left in a continuous loop.

The company name scrolls from right to left

Building the Gold Bar

You'll create the gold bar by applying the Zaxwerks 3D Invigorator effect to a solid layer and extruding the solid in 3D with the help of a 2D Illustrator file. Once the effect has been set, you can also enhance the image by adjusting the lights to control the reflections:

> **Important:** If you haven't already installed the 3D Invigorator plug-in into After Effects, you'll need to do so before you can complete this section. You can download a demo version of the 3D Invigorator plug-in from Zaxwerks' Web site at **http://www.zaxwerks.com**.

1   Go to time 1:00, and create a comp-size Solid layer named Gold Bar 1. It can be any color, since the effect you apply will determine the solid's color.

2   Apply Effect > Zaxwerks > 3D Invigorator to the solid layer.

3   In the Open dialog that appears, select the **rectangle1.ai** file located in this chapter's folder in the book's DVD, and click Open.

The 3D Invigorator effect prompts you to select a file to work with.

4   Go to time 2:00, and expand the Camera property group in the Effect Controls window.

5   Add a keyframe to every Camera property listed, and set the values to the following:

   Camera Eye X: 300

   Camera Eye Y: 500

   Camera Eye Z: 500

   Camera Target X: 0.00

   Camera Target Y: 0.00

   Camera Target Z: 0.00

   Camera Distance: 330.00

   Camera Tumble Left: 0.00

   Camera Tumble Up: 0.00

   Camera Ortho Size: 500.00

6   Click the camera button next to Update in the Effect Controls window to refresh the Scene preview.

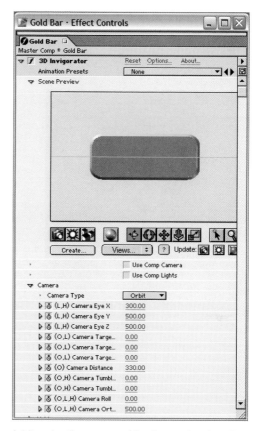

Adding the first group of keyframes for the 3D Invigorator effect

The new steps add texture and animate the solid:

1   Click Options in the upper-right corner of the Effect Controls window to open the 3D Invigorator Set-Up Window dialog. Choose a gold-like style in the Object Styles tab to apply to your solid, and drag the style onto the center portion of the rectangle and then onto the rectangle's edge. Click OK when you're satisfied with its appearance.

Applying texture to the solid

2   Go to time 1:00, and type in the values to move the solid past the viewer :

    Camera Target X: 0.00

    Camera Target Y: 0.00

    Camera Target Z: 30.00

    Camera Distance: 1.00

    Camera Tumble Left: -70.00

    Camera Tumble Up: 70.00

    Camera Ortho Size: 25.00

The object isn't visible in the window because it's been moved offscreen at time 1:00.

Adding the Logo Layer

This is the section of the project where the pyrotechnical fun comes in. You'll hide the logo behind a mask and then reveal it with sparks and a burst of light:

1   Go to time 2:00, and add a new comp-size solid layer named Logo that's any color.

2   Apply Effect > Zaxwerks > 3D Invigorator to the Logo layer, and open the **Rectangle 3.ai** file when prompted.

3   Click Options in the Effect Controls window for the Logo layer, and apply the same Object Style that you applied to the Gold Bar 1 layer.

4   Select the Gold Bar layer in the Timeline, press U to display all its keyframes, and then copy only the keyframes that are at time 2:00.

5   Select the Logo layer, and paste the keyframes at time 2:00. These keyframes align the Logo layer with the Gold Bar layer.

6   Select the Logo layer, and choose Layer > Pre-Compose; name the new composition Logo Comp 1, and click the Move All Attributes Into The New Composition option. By pre-composing the Logo layer, you ensure the mask applies correctly to the layer after its effects are applied.

7   Use the Rectangular Mask tool to draw an outline around the Logo layer, leaving lots of room between the solid and the mask.

Masking the Logo Comp 1 layer

8   Go to time 3:00, and add a keyframe to the effect's Mask Shape.

9   Go to time 2:00, and move the mask to the left just past the left edge of the logo. These two keyframes wipe the logo into view from left to right.

Animating the mask to start offscreen and slide in from the left

10 Change the effect's Mask Feather to 7, 7 to soften the wipe's right edge, which leads the logo's reveal.

Applying the Sparks

The sparks used in this project were created with the BCC Sparks effect from the Boris FX Continuum Complete collection of effects. If you don't own that collection, you can download a demo copy from **http://www. borisfx.com** to use in this section. Or, you might be able to create a similar effect using the Particle Playground effect in After Effects Professional (but you're on your own, in that case). Follow these steps:

1   Go to time 2:00, and add a comp-sized solid layer named Sparks that's colored black (RGB: 0, 0, 0).

2   Apply Effect > BCC3 Generator > BCC Sparks to the new solid.

3   Click the Producer XY stopwatch to create a keyframe for the effect's position. Set the keyframe's value to 65, 120 so the sparks start on the left edge of the Logo Comp 1 layer.

4   Click the Spread stopwatch to add a keyframe for the property, and set its value to 180.

5   Set the effect's Velocity to 220.

6   Expand the effect's Orientation property group, and set Rotate to –90.

7   Go to time 3:00, and change the Producer XY value to 255.0, 120.0 to move the sparks to the right edge of the Logo Comp 1 layer.

8   Change Spread to 360 to expand the direction the sparks fly as the effect moves.

9   Press Alt+] (Windows) or Option+] (Mac OS) to trim the Sparks layer's Out point to time 3:00.

10 Set the Blending Mode of the Sparks layer to Screen in the Timeline's Modes column so layers underneath it are visible.

Save and preview your results. The sparks should move left to right as the logo is unmasked.

Creating a Flickering Light

A flickering light over the flying sparks adds heat to the effect. If you look at this chapter's final movie on the DVD, you'll see that the sparks trail a little behind the flickering light as it travels across the logo, making the light appear to burn away the gold. Here are the steps:

1   Go to time 2:00, and create a new comp-sized solid layer named Light Flicker that's black (RGB: 0, 0, 0).

2   Apply Effect > Render > Lens Flare to the solid, and leave the effect's default settings.

3   Select the Sparks layer in the Timeline, and press U to display its keyframes. Select the effect's Producer XY property to select all three of its keyframes, and then choose Edit > Copy to copy them.

4   Expand the Light Flicker layer's Lens Flare effect in the Timeline, select the Flare Center property, and paste the keyframes you copied in the previous step.

5   Still at time 2:00, add a keyframe to the Lens Flare effect's Flare Brightness property, and set the keyframe to 150%.

6   Go to time 3:00, and change the value to 0%.

7   Press Alt +] (Windows) or Option +] (Mac OS) to trim the Light Flicker layer's Out point to the current time.

8   Set the Blending Mode for the Light Flicker layer to Screen in the Modes column.

Tip: The shortcut key to toggle between display of the Switches and Modes columns is F4. You can display both columns simultaneously by selecting both in the Timeline's fly-out menu, located in its upper-right corner.

9   Select both of the Light Flicker layer's Flare Brightness keyframes at times 2:00 and 3:00, and then choose Window > The Wiggler to display that palette. Change the Noise Type to Jagged, Magnitude to 100, and Frequency to 30, and then click Apply.

The Wiggler makes the light flicker between the two keyframes.

Settings for the Wiggler

Save the composition, and then click the Ram Preview button in the Time Controls palette to see the results.

Now Try This

The following finishing touches will make your project look just like this chapter's final movie (**Ch9FinishedProject.mov**):

- Open Logo Comp 1, and open the Effect Controls window. Animate the logo in the last 15 frames of the project (4:15–4:29) so that the logo moves toward and past the viewer.

- Apply an Animation Preset from the Effects & Presets palette to a text layer that displays the full company name ELECTRONIC STORAGE SYSTEMS, to bring the layer onto the screen from 2:15 to 3:00. Place the text under the Logo Comp 1 layer in the Timeline.

- Apply Effect > Stylize > Glow to the Sparks layer to enhance the flying sparks.

CHAPTER 10 | Unscrambling Type

When you're designing titles and credits, it's a challenge to capture the audience's attention and get them to read the text. I recently created a segment open for a network TV show in which I animated letters that spelled a sitcom character's name, scrambled into nonsense, and then unscrambled to reveal the name of the actor portraying the character. Scrambled words that gradually unscramble can help keep people engaged as they try to figure out what words are forming.

After this project is completed, you'll know how to animate text to unscramble itself. In addition, you'll animate text in 3D space and create a northern lights effect behind the text.

It Works Like This

To see what you'll design with this project, check out the **Ch10FinishedProject.mov** file in this chapter's folder in the book's DVD. In this chapter, you'll create a promo for an electronic exposition at a local convention center. In the process, you'll do the following:

1. Unscramble text using the Character Offset animator to reveal the title.

2. Animate text in 3D space to bring the text in, rotate it, and send it out of the scene.

3. Add a provided background movie and apply a Box Blur effect to it.

4. Create an atmospheric multicolored ghosting effect behind the text.

The first layer of scrambling text comes in from above.

The first word unscrambles while the next word scrambles in.

After all four words unscramble, the layers rotate and separate in space.

Preparing to Work

To prepare for this project, do the following:

1   Start with a new project, and save it as Ch10ScrambledText.

2   Import the **Background.mov** file from this chapter's folder on this book's DVD.

3   Create a new composition named Random Text Basic using the NTSC D1, Square Pix 720 × 540 Preset, with Duration 5;00 seconds.

4   Turn on the Title-Action Safe button at the bottom of the Comp window to display the boundaries outside of which text might be cut off by particular displays.

Creating the Words

You always need to consider the overall look and feel of the elements (font style, background choices, and so on) in any project, to make certain they're appropriate for the project's destination. For example, readability is an important consideration when you're choosing fonts and colors. Some fonts look great and read well when displayed on a computer, television, or printed page but become more difficult to read when they're animated.

Create the title for this project with the following steps:

1   Select the Horizontal Type tool, and set the following properties in the Character and Paragraph palettes:

> Font Family: Century Gothic or a font that looks similar to the title text in the final project's movie
>
> Size: 48 pixels
>
> Fill Color: green (RGB: 0, 255, 0)
>
> Alignment: Center Text

Tip: Double-click a text layer in the Timeline to select the text, and click the font family name in the Character palette (instead of the pop-up menu arrow). Then you can use the up and down arrow keys on your keyboard to go through the fonts one by one while viewing each font's appearance in the Composition window. You can also press a letter to jump to the fonts whose names begin with that letter.

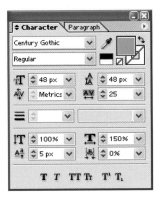

Settings for the Text layers

2   Type the word CYBER in uppercase in the Composition window, and then either press the Enter key on the numeric keypad or click the Selection tool in the Tools palette to get out of text-entry mode.

3 Create three more text layers for the words *WORLD*, *ELECTRONIC*, and *EXPOSITION*. You can put them anywhere in the composition for now; you'll reposition them in the next section.

Four separate text layers in temporary locations

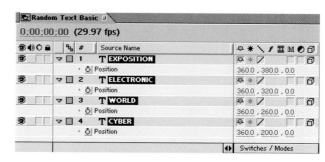

Random Text Basic composition's Timeline

Positioning the Text in 3D

In the next few steps, you'll set up the position each text layer will assume after it flies in through 3D space from behind the user:

1 Select all the text layers in the Timeline, turn on their 3D switches in the Switches column, and then press P on your keyboard to display their Position properties.

2 With all the layers still selected, change their X Position values to 360 and their Z values to 0.0.

3 Deselect the layers. Click the Y Position value for the each layer, and enter the following value listed for that layer. Press Tab (to go forward) and Shift+Tab (to go backward) to navigate through the Position values in a layer and to the next layer's values:

EXPOSITION: 380

ELECTRONIC: 320

WORLD: 260

CYBER: 200

Position values for each text layer

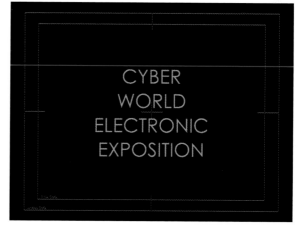

The title's landing position

Randomizing the Text

You'll animate the type using the powerful Animator features, which are only available for text layers—in this case, you'll use the animator to scramble the letters with the Character Offset property:

1   Press Home on your keyboard to go to time 0;00.

2   Select all the layers, and press UU to display the Text and Transform property groups.

3   In the EXPOSITION layer, click the arrow to the right of the word *Animate* to display that menu, and then choose Character Offset.

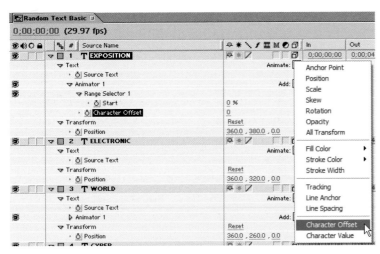

Adding a Character Offset animator to the EXPOSITION text layer

4   Add a keyframe to the Character Offset property, still at time 0;00, and set it to 40.

5   Go to time 0;15, and change the Character Offset value to 0.

6   Click the Animator 1 name to select the entire animator, and then copy it.

7   Press Home to return to time 0;00, select the other three layers, and paste. An Animator 1 and two Character Offset keyframes will appear in each layer's Text property group in the Timeline.

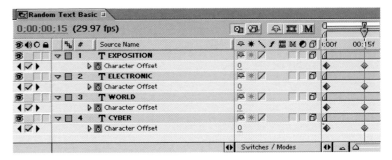

Timeline with Character Offset keyframes in place

How does your text look at time 0;00? It should be an unintelligible mess, thanks to the character-offset settings you applied to the layers. With a Character Offset value of 40, the original letters are each replaced by whatever letter exists 40 letters forward alphabetically. For example, 40 letters forward from the letter C is the letter Q. (Since there are only 26 letters in the alphabet, you must start over at letter A once you hit Z, in order to figure out the letter that will display.) If you go time 14;20, where the Character Offset should already be set to 1, you'll see that every letter is only 1 character away from the letters in the original title.

At time 0;14 seconds, Character Offset is 3, so the letters shown are three letters forward from the original title's letters.

Staggering the Text

Next, you need to stagger the start time of the layers so they arrive in the comp one at a time:

1   Display the In column in the Timeline, and then set the value of each layer's In point as shown here:

>   EXPOSITION: 2;00
>
>   ELECTRONIC: 1;15
>
>   WORLD: 1;00
>
>   CYBER: 0;15

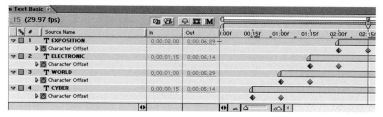

Staggered text layers

2   Close the In column in the Timeline.

Press Home and then the Spacebar to view the results so far. You should see a scrambling word appear; as soon as the word unscrambles itself, the next scrambling word in the title appears.

Making 3D Look Easy

In this section, you'll use a Null Object layer to simplify animating the layers in 3D space. Currently, the project just generates letters that unscramble. The following steps add some depth and dynamism to the effect. You'll parent the text layers to the null object to perfectly synchronize the text by animating one layer (the null object) and maintain the positional relationships.

Follow these steps:

1   With the Random Text Basic composition open, choose View > New View to open a second window for the comp.

2   Set the second Comp window's 3D View pop-up menu to Top so you can see the results of the changes you make in the following steps.

3   Choose Layer > New > Null Object.

4   Turn on the 3D switch for the Null 1 layer in the Switches column. In its default position at 360, 270, 0, you can see the square outline of the entire null object overlapping the words *ELECTRONIC* and *EXPOSITION* in the Comp window.

5   Add a Position keyframe to the Null 1 layer at time 0;00, and set the keyframe to 360, 270, –890. Negative Z values move the Null 1 layer toward the viewer, so now you can only see the null object's upper-left corner.

6   Go to time 2;15, and change the Position to 360, 270, 0. Now the Null 1 layer moves away from the viewer from time 0;00 to 2;15 and lands in the same point along the Z axis as the text layers.

7   Still at time 2;15, add a keyframe to the null layer's Orientation, and set it to 0.0, 300, 0.0. Notice how the null object is now angled away from the viewer in both comp views.

8   Go to time 4;00, and add another Position keyframe with the same value (360, 270, 0) as the keyframe at time 2;15.

9   At time 4;00, change the orientation to 0.0, 0.0, 0.0.

10 Go to time 4;29, and change the Position to 360, 270, –1020. This negative value for Z puts the null object out of view behind the viewer.

11 Go to time 2:15, and lock the null layer.

12 Select all the layers except the Null 1 layer, and display the Parent column in the Timeline.

13 Choose Null 1 from the Parent menu adjacent to any selected layer in the Timeline to set the value for all the selected layers.

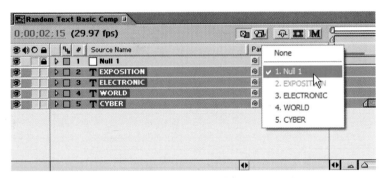

Assigning the null object as the parent of the other layers

14 With all the text layers still selected at time 2;15, add a Position keyframe to each of them.

15 Deselect the layers, go to time 4;00, and change the layers' Position values as follows:

EXPOSITION: 0, 110, –200

ELECTRONIC: 0, 50, –100

WORLD: 0, 0, 0

CYBER: 0, –70, 100

Before you changed the layers' Positions, the layers all resided at the same point on the X and Z axes and differed only in the Y value. The changes in the Position values at time 4;00 create depth between the layers by separating them along the Z axis. Meanwhile, the layers rotate as they imitate the null object's orientation.

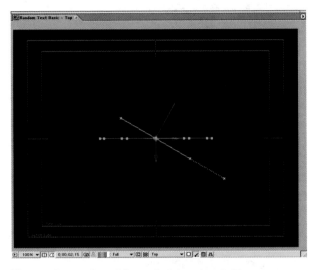

The text layers viewed from above at time 2;15

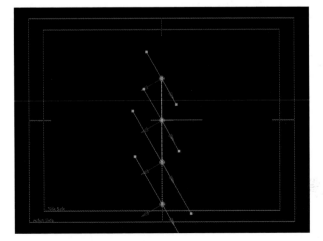

The layers viewed from above at time 4;00

Select all your layers, drill them up, lock them down, and save the project. If you preview your work, the letters should unscramble as they fly into the scene, face the viewer unscrambled, turn counterclockwise by 30 degrees, and then fly at and beyond the viewer.

Adding an Atmospheric Background

Adding a background to this project gives the viewer a frame of reference for the text, which currently floats unanchored in 3D space. Lucky for you, we've provided the foundation for the background by giving you the **Background.mov** file, and you just need to add some finish to it:

1   Create a new composition with the same measurements as the other— NTSC D1 Square Pix, 720 × 540, with Duration 5;00—and name it Random Master Comp.

2   Drag the Random Text Basic composition from the Project window into the Random Master Comp Timeline at time 0;00.

3   To give the text a cloudy fill, apply Effect > Noise & Grain > Fractal Noise to the Random Text Basic layer. The effect's default settings are fine.

4   Drag the **Background.mov** file from the Project window to the Timeline at time 0;00, under the Random Text Basic layer.

5   Change the Background movie's Scale to 115, 115% to compensate for its dimensions, which are smaller than the composition. Because the background is a nonsquare pixel movie and the composition uses square pixels, there will be some distortion; but in this case, it will work to your advantage as a motion background.

6   Apply Effect > Adjust > Brightness & Contrast to the Background movie. Set the effect's Brightness to −70 and Contrast to 45.

7   Add a Box Blur effect with Blur Radius set to 15 and Blur Dimensions set to Vertical.

Creating the Text Lights

In this section, you'll add to the background by duplicating the existing text layer, animating the new layer, and changing it to a supplemental shadow. You can easily do this using a only a few additional effects:

1   Duplicate the Random Text Basic layer, and rename layer 2 Fill Text.

2   Change the Fill Text layer's Scale to 150, 150%.

3   Apply Effect > Blur & Sharpen > Box Blur, and set the Blur Dimensions to Vertical and Iterations to 3.

4   Set a keyframe for a Blur Radius of 0 at time 0;00.

5   Go to time 2;15, and change Blur Radius to 55.

6   Expand the Fill Text layer's Fractal Noise effect, and change the effect's Blending Mode to Hue.

Now Try This

To add the remaining finishing touches that complete the look of this chapter's **Ch10FinishedProject.mov** movie file, do the following:

- Apply Effect > Perspective > Drop Shadow to the top text layer (Random Text Basic), and set the effect's Opacity to 85%, Direction to 282 degrees, Distance to 80, and Softness to 20.

- Create a letterbox, some supporting content, and a basic light zoom in just a few steps:

  1 At time 0:00, create a black, comp-size solid (720 × 540), and place it between the Random Text Basic layer and the Fill Text layer.

  2 Use the Rectangular Mask tool to draw over the center of the solid, and then change the mask's Mask Mode to Subtract.

  3 To outline the letterbox, apply a Stroke effect to it using the default effect values.

CHAPTER 11

Raining Slogans

Designing elaborate text animations in After Effects became breathtakingly easy and pretty fun when text Animators were added to the application. Actually, let's qualify that statement—animating text in After Effects became breathtakingly easy and pretty fun *if* you managed to figure out how to *use* the text Animators. The text Animator and its group of sidekicks, the Selectors, aren't *that* difficult to master, but they do take some getting used to when you're accustomed to animating text the old (painfully slow) way.

If you haven't mastered the text Animator and its Selectors yet, then you'll especially welcome the nearly 300 prebuilt text-animation presets provided in version 6.5 of After Effects. Not only can you use the text-animation presets to instantly produce sophisticated text animations, you can also use the results of a preset in the Timeline to explore how the text Animator and Selectors work. That's because the presets all rely upon some combination of text Animators, expressions, and effects.

In this chapter's project, you'll start with several text-animation presets and then work with the results to customize the presets.

It Works Like This

Check out the **Ch11FinishedProject.mov** file in this chapter's folder on the book's DVD. The sexy aspects of the movie were created instantly with text-animation presets; the rest is just good ol' fashioned hard work (not that hard, actually) done in the Timeline.

You'll perform the following techniques:

1. Animate the scale of the first slogan.

2. Bring slogans into and out of the scene by using the Raining Characters In and Out presets.

3. Animate text in 3D space, and create a camera fly-through effect to transition to the next message.

4. Add depth to a scene by using an Adjustment layer.

5. Create a vertical Venetian blind effect for the closing title sequence.

6. Fly the company's phone number onto the screen by using the Smooth Move In text-animation preset.

Text-animation presets animate the letters so they scramble and fall.

Falling letters eventually unscramble to reveal the original text.

The text flies behind the viewer to create a camera fly-through effect.

Preparing to Work

This project consists entirely of content created in After Effects 6.5. The majority of the text layers are contained within two nested compositions. You'll create folders in your project window to help organize the project's elements.

To prepare for this project, do the following:

1   Start with a new project, and save it as Ch11TextPresets.

2   Create a folder named **Comps**.

3   Create a new composition named Base Text Comp using the NTSC D1 Square Pix, 720 × 540 preset, with Duration 8;00 seconds.

4   Turns on the Composition window's Title-Action Safe button, and set the Magnification Ratio pop-up menu to 100% so you can see your text better in the next section.

Creating the First Slogan

First, you'll set up the text layers that are the foundation for the wall of text that rains into the scene. You'll work backward by laying out the landing position for the layers in this section and then animating them from their starting positions in the next section. Follow these steps:

1   Click the Horizontal Type tool in the Tools palette, and set the following properties in the Character and Paragraph palettes:

Text Size: 12 pixels

Font Family: Arial Black

Fill Color: white (RGB: 255, 255, 255)

Leading: Auto

Horizontal Scale: 125%

Alignment: Center Text

Character settings for the first text layer

2 In the Base Text Comp window, type the text From Dreams to Ideas to Business Solutions as a single line of text at time 0;00, and then press Enter on your keyboard's numeric keypad or click the Selection tool to get out of text-entry mode.

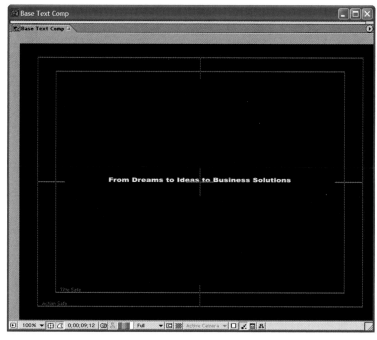

The first slogan

3 Duplicate the text layer eight times so you have nine layers total.

4 Select all the layers, press P to display their Position properties, and change the X value of any one of the selected layers to 360 to set the value for all of them.

5 Deselect all the layers, and then click the Y Position value of the first layer and set it to 110. Press Tab twice to go to the next layer's Y Position value, and change the remaining layers' Y Positions as follows:

Layer 2: 360, 150

Layer 3: 360, 190

Layer 4: 360, 230

Layer 5: 360, 270

Layer 6: 360, 310

Layer 7: 360, 350

Layer 8: 360, 390

Layer 9: 360, 430

Position values for the nine text layers

The layers should be evenly distributed between the first and last layers, forming a vertical stack.

The text layers in formation

Raining Letters into Place

It's time to instantly create a falling letters effect with the text layers you just created. You can certainly build the animation yourself, but why bother when a motion graphics designer (a great one!) has already done the work for you?

To preview the text-animation presets you have at your disposal, choose Help > Text Preset Gallery. Now, in addition to muttering, "So many cool effects, so little time…" as you work in After Effects, you'll also mutter, "So many clever text-animation presets, so little time…."

Proceed as follows:

1   At time 0;00, select all the layers in the Base Text Comp.

2   In the Effects & Presets palette, expand the **★Animation Presets**, **Text**, and **Animate In** folders, and then double-click the Raining Characters In preset to apply it to all selected layers.

Applying the Raining Characters In text-animation preset

Press U on your keyboard to display only the properties that have key-frames; the Timeline then shows a Range Selector with Offset keyframes. The Range Selectors are evidence that the Raining Characters In preset added a text Animator to every layer. You'll also notice that the animation starts 1 second into the Timeline, which you could change to customize the animation (but do that on your own time, after you've first completed this project, Grasshopper).

Keyframes created by the Raining Characters In preset

Press UU to display all properties that were modified by the preset, not just those with keyframes. You'll notice the preset did quite a lot of work for you.

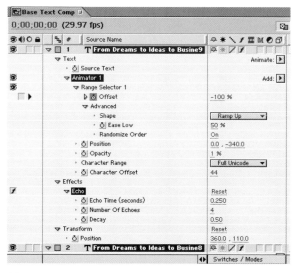

All properties affected by the Raining Characters In preset

Click the Ram Preview button in the Time Controls palette to preview the animation. Just as the preset's name suggests, the letters in all nine text layers fall in from the top side of the composition like random drops of rain from time 1;00 to 3;15. In addition, this preset animates the source text of the letters so that as they fall, different letters display until the letters land and display the characters you originally typed. Unlike in previous chapters, when you animated the source text by adding Character Offset and Source Text keyframes, this preset uses Offset keyframes that work in tandem with the current Character Offset value.

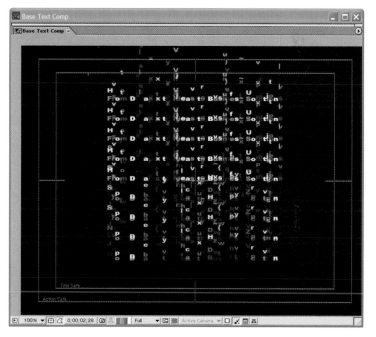

The animation at time 2;28

Flying through Text in 3D Space

Next you'll animate the wall of text through 3D space to create a camera fly-through effect. There is more than one way to create a fly-through effect, but you'll use one of the easier methods: animating a Null Object layer and parenting it to the other layers. Here are the steps:

1   Create a new comp named Text Stack Comp, using the same composition preset as the Base Text Comp: NTSC D1 Square Pix, 720 × 540, with Duration 8;00 seconds.

2   Place the Base Text Comp into the Text Stack Comp's Timeline at time 0;00. These layers will be used to stagger the effect into 3D space and give the project the depth needed for the fly-through.

3   Choose Layer > New > Null Object to create the layer you'll use to animate the Base Text Comp layer.

4   Drag the text layer's pick whip in the Parent column to the Null 1 layer.

5   Turn on the 3D switch for both layers in the Switches column.

Assigning the Null Object layer as parent to the text layer

6   Duplicate the Base Text Comp layer seven times so you have eight copies of that layer.

7   Select all the Base Text Comp layers, and press P to display their Position properties. Deselect the layers, and then set the first Base Text Comp layer's Z Position value to 100. Change the Z value of each of the remaining Base Text Comp layers, each time increasing the value by 100 more than in the previous layer.

New Z positions for the text layers

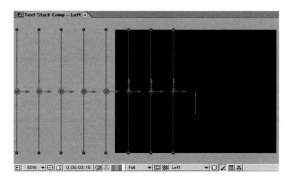

The text layers viewed from the Left 3D view

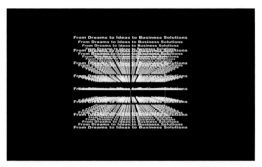

The text layers viewed from the Active Camera view

Tip: If you notice that your system slows down now that you've turned on the 3D switch for every layer, you can improve performance by setting the Composition window's Resolution to Half, its Fast Previews option to Adaptive, and the text layers' Quality switches to Draft.

8   To make the text layers fly toward and behind the viewer, add a Position keyframe to the Null 1 layer with the values 360, 275, –450.

9   Press End on your keyboard to go to time 7;29, and then change the Null 1 layer's Z Position value to –1800.

Clarifying the Text

If you preview the animation at this point, you'll notice that the text is much too difficult to read because the letters appear to merge into one another. You'll make the viewer focus on the topmost text layer and increase its readability by fading in all the text layers behind it and changing their color. This technique will also add more impact when the topmost text layer lands in place:

1   Select the Base Text Comp layers 3 through 9 (leaving Base Text Comp layer 2 unselected), press T, and then add a 0% Opacity keyframe at time 0;00.

2   With layers 3–9 still selected, go to time 5;00 and change their Opacity values to 30%. Then, go to time 6;00, and change the values to 70%.

3   Create an Adjustment layer (Layer > New > Adjustment Layer), and place it below the topmost Base Text Comp layer in the Timeline at time 0;00.

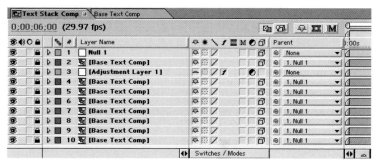

Completed Text Stack Comp Timeline

4   Apply Effect > Image Control > Tint to the Adjustment layer, and set the effect's Map White To color to RGB: 130, 230, 254 and the Amount of Tint to 100%.

Settings for the Tint effect in the Effect Controls window

The Adjustment layer works just like a Photoshop Adjustment layer, so all layers below the Adjustment layer in the Timeline are affected by its settings. In your project, all the Base Text Layers except the top one should display the blue color that you set in the Adjustment layer.

Composition at time 3;00

Adding the Slogans

Now you'll pull the project elements together in a master composition. You'll animate a new slogan with the Raining Characters Out preset and use the resulting animation as a faint background:

1   Create a comp named Master Comp, using the NTSC D1 Square Pix, 720 × 540 preset, with Duration 15;00 seconds.

2   Select the Horizontal Type tool, and set the following in the Character and Paragraph palettes:

Font Family: Arial Black

Font Size: 24px

Alignment: Center Text

3   At time 0;00, create a new layer in the middle of the Composition window by choosing Layer > New > Text. Type MANAGE THE FUTURE on one line, press Enter or Return on your keyboard, and type OF YOUR BUSINESS on the next line.

The new text slogan

4   Still at time 0;00, apply Animation > Apply Animation Preset >Text > Animate Out > Raining Characters Out to the text layer.

Note: When you choose Animation > Apply Animation Preset, After Effects should open the **Presets** folder. If it doesn't, you can locate that folder by navigating to the **After Effects application folder > Support Files > Presets > Text**.

---

5   Go to time 0;00, and add a Scale keyframe of 1000, 1000% and a 0% Opacity keyframe to the text layer.

6   Go to time 1;00, and change Scale to 100, 100% and Opacity to 100%.

These keyframes are timed to fade in the slogan just as the Text Stack Comp animation starts to rain in the letters in the text *From Dreams to Ideas to Business Solutions.*

7   At time 4;00, press Alt +] (Windows) or Option +] (Mac OS) to trim the layer's Out point.

8   Go to time 0;00, and add the Text Stack Comp from the Project window to the Timeline.

9   Go to time 7;00, and add the Text Stack Comp to the Master Comp Timeline again—but below the MANAGE THE FUTURE text layer. Now the Timeline has a Text Stack Comp starting at time 0;00 and another copy starting at time 7;00.

10   Set the Opacity of the bottom Text Stack Comp (located at time 7;00) to 30%, and don't add a keyframe.

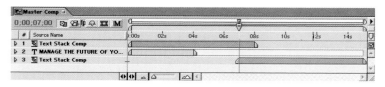

The Master Comp Timeline

At time 0;07, the slogan *MANAGE THE FUTURE* fades in.

At time 1;14, the *MANAGE...* text rains out of the scene as the other text rains in.

Raining in the next slogan

You'll add another slogan to the project and animate it by using the Raining Characters In preset again. (Presets don't do all the necessary work for you, but they're mighty handy, aren't they?) Even though you used the same preset for the wall of text that you created in an earlier section, the results will look unique after you scale the text and assemble the sequences:

1   Select the Horizontal Type tool, and make sure the properties in the Character and Paragraph palettes are still set as follows:

> Text Size: 24px
>
> Font Family: Arial Black
>
> Alignment: Center Text

2   Go to time 6;00, and choose Layer > New > Text to create a text layer in the middle of the Composition window. Type TURNING IDEAS on one line and INTO SUCCESS on the next.

The TURNING... text layer at time 6;00

3   With the new text layer selected, choose Animation > Recent Animation Presets > Raining Characters In.

4   Add a Scale keyframe of 40, 40% at time 6;00, and change the Scale to 100, 100% at time 8;00.

5   With the TURNING... text layer selected, press U on your keyboard to reveal the layer's keyframes. Move the layer's Offset keyframe at time 7;00 to time 6;00 and its Offset keyframe at time 9;15 to time 8;00.

Tip: Press Shift as you drag a keyframe to snap it to a particular point in time.

---

6   Move the TURNING... layer in the Timeline's layer stack so it's layer 2. Now the TURNING... layer comes in beneath the text in the topmost Text Stack Comp as the composition's text fades out.

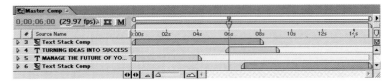

The Master Comp Timeline

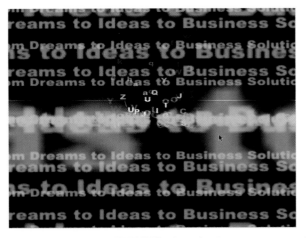

The white text of the TURNING... layer begins to appear at time 7;00 behind the blue text.

Flipping Venetian Blinds

You'll animate the TURNING… text by building a false vertical Venetian blinds effect that flips the text to reveal the company name. To accomplish this fake flip, you'll actually squeeze and expand the text and modify the text's existing text Animators:

1   Expand the TURNING… text layer in the Timeline, and expand its Text group.

2   Choose Scale from the Animate menu next to the Text group in the Switches column to add a second Animator to the layer.

3   To help you keep track of what's what in the Timeline, click the Animator 1 name in the Timeline, press Enter or Return on your keyboard, and then type `Raining In` (since that Animator was created by the Raining Characters In preset). Click the Animator 2 name, press Enter or Return, and type `Scale Animator`.

4   Go to time 8;15, and add a 100, 100% Scale keyframe to the Scale Animator. At time 9;00, change the Scale to 0, 100%. Now the TURNING… text squeezes itself into oblivion from time 8;15 to 9;00.

5   Go to time 9;00, and press Alt +] (Windows) or Option +] (Mac OS) to trim the layer's Out point to the current time.

6   Still at time 9;00, make sure the Horizontal Type tool's properties are set as follows:

> Text Size: 24px
>
> Font Family: Arial Black
>
> Alignment: Center Text

Then, choose Layer > New > Text to create a text layer in the middle of the Composition window.

7   Type `TIME HONORED` on one line and `CONSULTING, INC.` on the next line.

Adding the company name

8   Reveal the Text group for this layer by pressing UU, and then choose Animate > Scale in the Timeline.

9   Add an Animator Scale keyframe at time 9;00 with a value of 0, 100%, and then go to time 9;15 and change the Scale value to 100, 100%. Now the text expands itself into view just after the TURNING… text layer squeezes itself out of view.

10   Choose Property > Tracking from the Add menu next to Animator 1, and add a Tracking Amount keyframe of 0 at time 9;15.

11   Go to time 14;29, and change the Tracking value to 3. This results in the letters moving away from one another very subtly between the two keyframes.

If you preview the animation between time 8;15 and 9;15, you should see the letters in the TURNING… layer squeeze out of view and the letters in the TIME… layer expand into view. When you play the animation in real time, this technique creates the illusion of turning vertical Venetian blinds.

Sliding In the Phone Number

Only a few more elements remain. Your next task is to bring the company's phone number onto the screen with—you guessed it—another text animation preset. Are you feeling spoiled yet?

1   At time 10;00, make sure the Horizontal Type tool's properties are still set as follows:

>   Text Size: 24px
>
>   Font Family: Arial Black
>
>   Alignment: Center Text

Then, type 800.555.1234.

2   Set the layer's Position to 360,335. (No keyframe is needed.)

3   In the Effects & Presets palette, expand ★ Animation Presets > Text > Animate In, and double-click Smooth Move In to apply it to the 800… text layer.

4   With the text layer selected, press U to display the layer's keyframes, and then move all the starting keyframes to time 10;00 and all the ending keyframes to time 11;00.

Realigning the keyframes

If you preview the animation between time 10;00 and 11;00, the telephone number falls into place from left to right.

Now Try This

You can do the following to add the remaining elements that appear in this chapter's finished project movie:

- Add a white horizontal line between the CONSULTING, INC. text and the phone number, and animate its Scale from 0, 0% to 100, 100% to bring it into the scene.

- Add a clock to the background to reiterate the company name, Time Honored Consulting. You can create the entire clock from scratch in only a few minutes by using solid layers. The one shown in the finished movie uses a white, comp-size solid with an elliptical mask set to –10 Mask Expansion. The lines are created with five 600 × 10 solid layers angled in increments of 30 degrees for each layer. The clock hands are solids, with rotation keyframes set at time 9:29 of 1 × 0 for the minute hand and 12 × 0 for the hour hand.

| # Sonic Promo

When you first import layered files into an After Effects project, you have to make an important decision: Do you want to retain the layers, or should you flatten them? Until Adobe released version 6.5 of After Effects, this choice was a permanent one; if you subsequently changed your mind about the file's layered status, you had to reimport the file and use the Replace Footage feature.

Now you still have to decide whether to retain a file's layers when you first import it, but the decision is no longer permanent. If you subsequently decide that you want access to the file's layers, you can make the change in one step; then you must decide whether to replace all instances of that file throughout the entire project or just a single instance. To replace all instances, you select the file in the Project window and choose File > Replace Footage > With Layered Comp; to convert a single instance, you select the layer in a Timeline window and choose Layer > Convert To Layered Comp. Easy!

In this chapter, you'll design a spot with Illustrator layers that you'll make bounce to the beat of some audio. The project includes a background of translucent speakers that vibrate according to the audio and another virtual speaker that replaces a letter in the title you build.

It Works Like This

Check out the **Ch12FinishedProject.mov** movie file in this chapter's folder on the book's DVD to see the results of this chapter's project. This chapter shows you how to make a composition come alive with rhythm, first by animating an Illustrator file to sound and then by animating other elements that synchronize with the beat. The project you'll build uses the following techniques:

1. Create keyframes from an audio file, and then use expressions to animate layers based on those keyframes.

2. Use the Sequence Layers command to loop a layer in time.

3. Create an animated background of pulsing circles.

4. Use Time Remapping to manipulate layers in time.

A background of circles pulsing to the beat

The title scales in and then rotates in space.

The logo is brought in as if by audio waves.

Preparing to Work

This project requires three Adobe Illustrator files and an audio file, all of which are provided for you on this book's DVD. When you import the Illustrator files, the project should contain three new compositions (one for each file) and a folder of footage for each composition.

Tip: Check out the sidebar "Import As Options: Do You Really Understand Them?" in Chapter 1 ("Spinning Squares") for a thorough explanation of the three options for importing footage.

To prepare for this project, do the following:

1   Start with a new project, and save it as Ch12SonicPromo.

2   Choose File > Import Multiple Files, and open the three Illustrator files (**sonic.ai**, **recordingBox.ai**, and **sOnic Radar.ai**) from this chapter's folder on this book's DVD. Set the Import As option to Composition – Cropped Layers for each file, and then open the audio file **Sonic_track.aif** with Import As set to Footage. Click Done.

3   Create a new composition named Sonic Promo, using the NTSC D1 Square Pix, 720 × 540 composition preset, with Duration 15;00 seconds.

4   Set the composition's Background Color to HSB: 198, 100, 65.

5   Add the **Sonic_track.aif** file to the Sonic Promo Timeline at time 0;00.

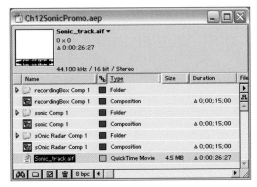

The Project window with imported items and the Sonic Promo composition

Creating the First Speaker

The sOnic Radar composition was created when you imported the **sOnic Radar.ai** file as a Composition with cropped layers. It contains eight layers that create what appears to be a solid white circle, which is actually a stack of stroked and unfilled circles. You'll position these circles in 3D space to add depth and create a virtual speaker.

The original Illustrator file's dimensions are only 111 × 113, so your first task is to enlarge the composition:

1   Open the sOnic Radar Comp 1 composition, and change its settings (Composition > Composition Settings) to use the NTSC D1 Square Pix, 720 × 540 preset, with Duration 1;16.

2   Select all the circle layers, and turn on their 3D switches in the Timeline.

3   With all the circle layers still selected, press the P key to display their Position properties. Deselect the layers.

4   Starting with the circle 2 layer, set each layer's Z value -5 degrees away from the previous layer. As a result, the Z-axis value of circle 1 is 0, the value for circle 2 is -5, the value for circle 3 is -10, and so on.

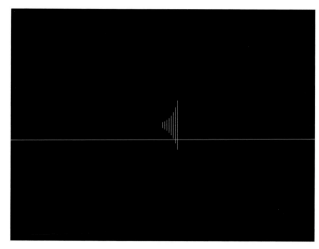

The circle layers with new Position values

The circle layers viewed from the left

5   Save the composition. Duplicate the sOnic Radar Comp in the Project window, and rename one Still Radar and the other Radar Pulse.

Animating with Audio

Now you'll animate your virtual audio speaker so that it seems to reverberate to the beat of an audio track. The speaker fades into the scene to replace the letter *O* in the word *SONIC* in the final project. You'll also edit expressions to intensify the results; if you're not comfortable working with expressions yet, this example shows you how easy they can be.

Follow these steps:

1   Open the Radar Pulse composition. Drag **Sonic_track.aif** from the Project window into the Timeline at time 0;00, and place it below all the circle layers.

2   Choose Animation > Keyframe Assistant > Convert Audio to Keyframes. A new layer named Audio Amplitude is automatically added at the top of the Timeline. Select the layer, and press U on your keyboard to see the resulting keyframes.

The keyframes reflect the amplitude of all audio in the composition at each frame. Using expressions, you can make the properties of other layers animate according to the audio amplitude in this layer.

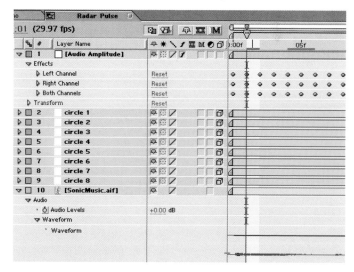

Creating keyframes based on the audio amplitude at each frame

3 Return to the sOnic Radar Comp 1 Timeline, select all the circle layers, and then press T to display their Opacity properties.

4 Select the Opacity property of all circle 1 layers, and then choose Animation > Add Expression. Expand each circle layer's Opacity property to display the new property named Expression: Opacity. Also expand the Audio Amplitude layer, its Effects group, and its Left Channel, Right Channel, and Both Channels. (You don't need to expand the Sliders.)

5 Drag the pick whip next to each circle layer's Expression: Opacity property, and choose the Audio Amplitude layer's Slider option for the Left Channel, Right Channel, or Both Channels. Cycle through the channel you link to so that each layer is linked to a different channel than its adjacent layers.

The circle 1, 4, and 7 layers should be linked to the Left Channel; the circle 2, 5, and 8 layers should be linked to the Right Channel; and the circle 3 and 6 layers should be linked to Both Cannels. A bunch of code is added to each circle layer's Expression Opacity property.

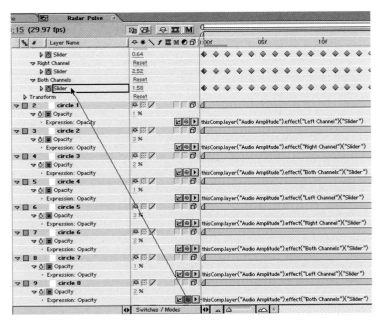

Using the pick whip to link each circle's Opacity to an audio channel

Currently, the audio amplitude is so low that the circles aren't visible in the composition. You'll fix this in the next step by increasing the effect of the expressions.

6 Click at the end of the code next to circle 1, and type *20 to multiply the effect by 20.

7 At the end of the next layer's expression line, increase the *20 by 10 until you reach 50; repeat, starting at 20.

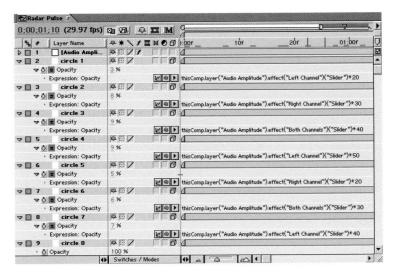

The Radar Pulse Timeline after editing the expressions

8 Delete the **Sonic_track.aif** audio file in the Timeline, and close the sOnic Radar composition.

Now you can see the circles in the composition and their varying levels of transparency. If you preview the animation, you'll see the circles pulsing to the beat.

Looping the pulse

Next you'll create a parent composition for the Radar Pulse composition and make it loop in time:

1   Create a new composition named Sonic Loop, using the NTSC D1 Square Pix, 720 × 540 composition, with Duration 15;00 seconds.

2   Drag the Radar Pulse composition to the Sonic Loop Timeline at time 0;00 to automatically center it in the Comp window.

3   Duplicate the Radar Pulse layer nine times, so you have ten layers.

4   Select all the layers, and choose Animation > Keyframe Assistant > Sequence Layers. Deselect Overlap, and click OK. This automatically places each layer in succession in time.

5   Save the project, and close the composition.

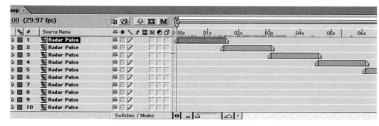

The Sequence Layers command lets you quickly distribute layers across time.

Making a Pulsing Background

To create the foundation for this project's animated background, you'll start with the Sonic Loop composition, which also serves as the pulsing letter O in the finished movie:

1   Create a new composition named Radar_background, using the NTSC D1 Square Pix, 720 × 540 preset, with Duration 15;00 seconds.

2   Drag the Sonic Loop composition to the Radar_background Timeline at time 0;00, and change the layer's Scale to 200.0, 200.0.

3   Duplicate the layer four times so you have five layers total.

4   Go to time 0;10, select all the layers, and press P. Set the layers' X Position values to 0, 180, 360, 540, 720, to distribute the layers evenly across the entire width of the composition.

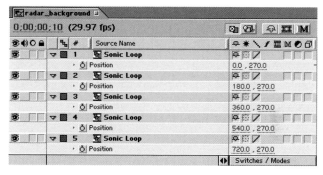

Distributing the layers along the X axis

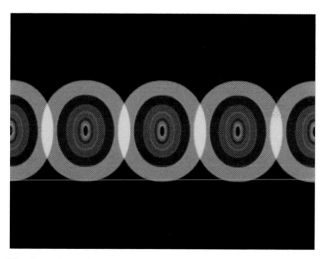

The Sonic Loop layers in formation

5   Stagger the layers' In points by five frames from time 0;00 to time 0;20 so they first appear at different times. For example, we set the In Point of layer 1 to 0, of layer 2 to 0;10, of layer 3 to 0;05, of layer 4 to 0;20, and of layer 5 to 15.

6 Select all the layers, and pre-comp (Layer > Pre-Compose) them. Name the composition radar_5across.

7 Duplicate the radar_5across layer four times for a total of five layers.

8 Select all the layers, and press P. Set the layers' Y Position values to 0, 135, 270, 405, 540, to distribute the layers evenly across the entire height of the composition.

9 Stagger the layers' In points by five frames from time 0;00 to time 0;20 so they first appear at different times. For example, we set the In Point of layer 1 to 0, of layer 2 to 0;10, of layer 3 to 0;05, of layer 4 to 0;20, and of layer 5 to 15.

If you preview the animation, you should see pulsing circles appear at different points in time. They fill the entire composition and continue pulsing in and out.

10 Close the Radar_background composition, and open the Sonic Promo composition.

11 Drag the Radar_background composition to the Timeline at time 0;00, and set the layer's Opacity to 25%.

Animating Illustrator Layers

When you imported the **sonic.ai** file into your project at the start of this chapter, a new composition was automatically created with a layer for each layer in the original Illustrator file. The composition contains the word *sonic*, with two layers for each letter: a stroked version of the letter and a filled version of the letter.

The composition's default settings are based on the dimensions of the original file, so your first task will be to change those to fit the current project. Then you'll animate the text onto the screen:

1 Open sonic Comp 1, change its composition settings to use the NTSC D1 Square Pix, 720 × 540 preset, and set its Duration to 4;26. The composition contains ten layers.

2 Select all the layers, and then turn on each layer's 3D switch in the Timeline.

3 Deselect only the c4 and c1 layers by pressing Ctrl (Windows) or Command (Mac OS) as you click them. Turn on the Shy switch next to all the other selected layers, and then turn on the Shy button at the top of the Timeline to display only the c4 and c1 layers.

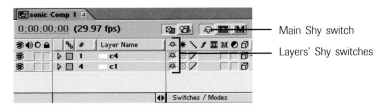

Hiding all layers but two by using the Shy switch

4 Create a Position keyframe for layer c4 at time 0;00 seconds with the values 415, 274, -700. The negative Z value moves the layer closer to the viewer so it appears much larger than the other letters.

5 Go to time 0;10, and change the position to 542, 282, 0.

6 At time 1;00, change the layer's Position to 669, 282, 700. If you scrub the Timeline from time 0;00 to 1;00, you'll see an outline of the letter C start at a really large size and then scale to a smaller size.

7 At time 0;15, add a 100% Opacity keyframe to the c4 layer, and then go to time 1;00 and change the layer's Opacity to 0%.

8 Go to time 0;14, and add a 0% Opacity keyframe to the c1 layer. Go one frame forward to time 0;15, and change layer c1's Opacity to 100%.

9 Turn off the Timeline's Shy button to display all the layers.

10 At time 0;00, add a Position keyframe to each of the following layers with the values listed:

     i4: 392, 263, -700

     n4: 369, 282, -700

o4: 336, 273.2, -700

s4: 304, 274, -700

Now the letter outlines appear very large in the composition, with the filled letters behind them at their original size.

11 To animate the scale of the letter outlines, go to time 0;10 and change the Position value for each of the following layers:

i4: 468, 263, 0

n4: 392, 282, 0

o4: 281, 282, 0

s4: 175, 282, 0

12 To scale the letter outlines even smaller, go to time 1;00, and change the layers' Positions as follows:

i4: 544, 263, 700

n4: 409, 282, 700

o4: 226, 291.2, 700

s4: 44, 282, 700

13 Select the c4 layer's Opacity property name, and then choose Edit > Copy to copy all of the property's keyframes.

14 Go to time 0;15, select the i4, n4, o4, and s4 layers, and then paste the keyframes you copied in the previous step.

15 Select the c1 layer's Opacity property, and copy the property's keyframes.

16 Go to time 0;14, select the i1, n1, o1, and s1 layers, and paste the keyframes.

17 Pre-comp (Layer > Pre-Compose) each pair of layers that share the same letter in their name, and name them *letter*_precomp (c_precomp, i_precomp, and so on).

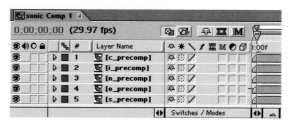

The sonic Comp 1 layers after pre-comping them

18 To fade the letters into the scene, select all five layers and press T to display their Opacity. To each layer, add a 0% Opacity keyframe at time 0;00 and a 100% Opacity keyframe at time 0;07.

19 To fade out the letters *s*, *n*, *i*, and *c*, go to time 4;10 and add a 100% Opacity keyframe to all the layers except o_precomp. Then go to time 4;25 and add a 0% Opacity keyframe to all the layers except o_precomp.

20 To fade out the o_precomp layer, go to time 1;15 and add a 100% Opacity keyframe; then go to time 1;20, and change the layer's Opacity to 0. You've faded out the letter *o* sooner than the others because it will be replaced by the pulsing speaker you'll add in later steps.

The sonic Comp 1 Timeline with all fades added

If you preview sonic Comp 1, you should see the letter outlines scaling from large to small and the filled letters appearing midway through the sequence.

Putting the Beats Together

Now it's time to assemble all the pieces you've built so far into the master Sonic Promo composition:

1   Open the Sonic Promo composition, go to time 2;00, and add sonic Comp 1 and Sonic Loop to Sonic Promo's Timeline.

2   Turn on the 3D switch for the sonic Comp 1 and Sonic Loop layers in the Timeline.

3   Set the Sonic Loop layer's Position to -30, 63, 0 and its Scale to 90, 90, 90%.

4   Go to time 3;15, and add a 0% Opacity keyframe to the Sonic Loop layer. Go to time 3;20, and change the layer's Opacity to 100%.

5   Go to time 6;10, and add another 100% Opacity keyframe. Go to time 6;15, and change Opacity to 0.

6   Create a new composition named Still Radar Long, using the NTSC D1 Square Pix, 720 × 540 preset, with Duration 15;00.

7   Add the Still Radar composition to the Still Radar Long Timeline at time 0;00.

8   Select the layer, and choose Layer > Enable Time Remapping.

9   Go to time 14;29, press Alt (Windows) or Option (Mac OS), and press the] key to stretch the layer out to the composition's entire duration.

10   Right-click the second Time Remap keyframe at time 1;16, and choose Edit Value. Enter 1;15, and click OK.

11   Go to time 14;29, and add a Time Remap keyframe. Right-click that keyframe, choose Edit Value, and then enter 1;15.

12   Open the Still Radar composition, and add a 0% Opacity keyframe to the circle 1 layer. Go to time 0;05, and change the layer's Opacity to 100%.

13   Copy both of circle 1's Opacity keyframes, and paste them on the next circle layer at time 0;05. Repeat this step for each successive layer, moving forward in time by five frames before pasting.

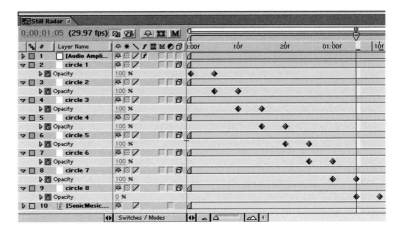

Fading in the circles in succession

If you preview the Still Radar animation at this point, the circle outlines should fade in from the smallest circle to the largest.

14   Close the Still Radar comp, save your project, and then open the Sonic Promo composition.

15   Go to time 6;10, and add the Still Radar Long comp to the Timeline above Sonic Loop.

16   Turn on Still Radar Long's 3D switch, and set its Position to 50, 50, 0.

17   Go to time 2;00, and add a Null Object layer. Turn on the layer's 3D switch in the Timeline, and set the layer's Anchor Point to 50, 50, 0.

18   Select the sonic Comp 1, Sonic Loop, and Still Radar Long layers, and choose Null 1 in the Parent column. Now you can rotate the Null 1 layer to rotate the parented layers and use Null 1 to keep everything aligned.

19 Go to time 2;15, and create an Orientation keyframe of 0, 0, 0 for the Null 1 layer.

20 Go to time 6;10, and change the Y-axis for Orientation to 296.

21 Go to time 6;25, and set the Orientation to 0, 280, 0. As a result, the Null 1 layer and the parented layers rotate around the Y-axis and away from the viewer between the two keyframes.

If you preview the animation at this point, the circles in the Radar_background layer should fade in. Then the letters in the sonic Comp 1 layer scale in and turn away from the viewer. Next, the pulsing circles in the Sonic Loop layer fade in as the letter O fades out from the sonic Comp 1 layer.

That's it; you're finished! Render out the animation, and nod your head to the groovy beat.

Now Try This

You can use the following techniques to add the titles and exercise your new skills in syncing audio:

- To add color to the background, create a solid with a color of your choosing, and then use the Convert Audio to Keyframes command and expressions to animate the solid's color in sync with the music.

- Use the new After Effects text-animation presets to animate the phone number and Web site address into the scene. If you haven't already explored Chapter 11, "Raining Slogans," check it out; it shows you how to work with several different text-animation presets.

- Open recordingBox Comp 1 (created when you imported the **recordingBox.ai** file), and set the BOX layer's Track Matte to Alpha Inverted Matte "RECORDING" to make the text cut out the box so the viewer sees the background in the letters. Create a Track Matte for the recordingBox comp by creating a new composition that contains multiple copies of the Sonic Promo composition laid out horizontally. Animate the Opacity of the layers sequentially from the rightmost layer to the left.

CHAPTER 13 | Sci-Fi Storm

Brick, Cloth, Fire, Granite, Rain, Reptilian, Rock, Snow, Sparks, Veined Marble, Weave, Wood Grain, and Wooden Planks. What do these things have in common? They're all realistic and very malleable surfaces you can instantly create and animate with just a solid layer in After Effects. Yes, only a solid layer in After Effects—oh, and you'll also need a group of effects provided by Boris FX in its Continuum Complete collection

Effects that generate imagery and textures, like the Boris FX effects listed here and some of the Render effects in After Effects, are fun to work with because they enable you to create virtually an entire world with very little effort. This chapter shows you how to create a storm-riddled planet and a steel box with a combination of effects that are native to After Effects and effects provided by Boris FX.

It Works Like This

To see what you'll create with this project, check out the **Ch13FinishedProject.mov** movie file in this chapter's folder on the book's DVD. The project consists of several layers that are integrated in 3D space. The shapes form a sphere of clouds inside of a 3D box.

You'll use these techniques:

1. Create a stormy sky from a solid layer by using the Fractal Noise and Advanced Lighting effects.

2. Convert the stormy sky to a stormy globe by using the BCC Sphere effect from Boris FX, and then animate the globe so it spins.

3. Create a title that orbits the stormy globe by using the BCC Sphere effect.

4. Create a steel box to contain the spinning globe by applying the BCC Steel Plate effect to solid layers.

5. Animate the steel box and its text label by using a Null Object layer in 3D space.

A steel box flies through space.   The box's lid slides open.

A stormy globe spins as the title orbits around it.

Preparing to Work

Amazingly, this industrial-looking project doesn't require any footage; everything is created with After Effects and the Continuum Complete collection of effects from Boris FX, which you must purchase and install into After Effects. But of course you already own that collection, right? No? Then install the trial version provided on this book's DVD or the Boris FX Web site (**www.borisfx.com**), and then make sure you finish this chapter within the next 14 days, before your trial period expires! (Actually, once the trial period ends, you can still follow along with the chapter; but any layer that uses a trial version effect will appear with a black X through it.)

Once the Boris FX effects are installed in After Effects, all you need to do is create a new project and the master composition before you're on to the real work.

To prepare for this project, do the following:

1   If you don't already have the Boris FX Continuum Complete collection of effects installed with After Effects, you can install a trial version from the book's DVD or from the Boris FX Web site at **www.borisfx.com**. Once it's installed, you should see numerous submenus labeled BCC in the Effect menu in After Effects.

2   Start with a new project, and save it as Ch13Sci-FiClub.

3   Create a new composition named Ch 13 Sci-Fi Club Logo, using the Medium, 320 × 240 comp preset, with Duration 10:00 seconds.

Creating Clouds

Your first task is to generate some clouds for the stormy sky that will cover your spinning globe. The Fractal Noise effect in the Professional version of After Effects is great for generating and animating clouds or other fluid things (such as flowing water) from scratch, and it doesn't require any footage.

Note: The Fractal Noise effect is available only with the Professional version of Adobe After Effects or the Adobe Video Collection. If you have the Standard version of either product, you can install a demo version of the Professional version of After Effects from this book's DVD.

Follow these steps:

1   Go to time 3:00 in the Ch 13 Sci-Fi Club Logo Timeline, and create a comp-sized solid layer named Sphere (320 × 240) using any color. (The solid's color doesn't matter, because the effect that you'll apply overrides it.)

2   To create clouds from the solid, apply the Effect > Noise & Grain > Fractal Noise effect to the layer, and set the effect's Contrast to 150.

3   Still at time 3:00, add an Evolution keyframe to the effect with a value of 0 × 0.0.

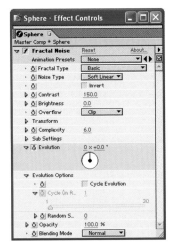

Settings for the Fractal Noise effect

4   Press End to go to time 9:29, and change Evolution to 3 × 0.0.

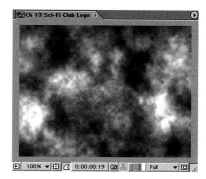

The Sphere layer using the Fractal Noise effect

5   To add color to your clouds, apply Effect > Adjust > Hue/Saturation to the Sphere layer. Turn on the Colorize option (below Master Lightness), and then set Colorize Hue to 0 × +220, Colorize Saturation to 45, and Colorize Lightness to –30. This creates a moody, dark-blue sky.

Settings for the Hue/Saturation effect In the Effect Controls window

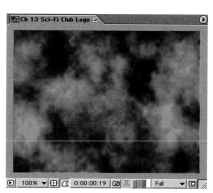

The Sphere layer using the Fractal Noise and Hue/Saturation effects

Creating a Lightning Storm

You've made a cloudy sky; now you need to add a lightning storm to it. Fortunately, there's an effect devoted to just that. This is one of those effects that you can tweak for hours and still get new and interesting results:

1   Apply Effect > Render > Advanced Lightning to the Sphere layer, and use the following settings for the effect:

Origin: 0.0, 120

Direction 320, 120

Glow Radius: 35

Glow Opacity: 50%

Glow Color: #FFD200

Decay Main Core: checked

Composite on Original: checked

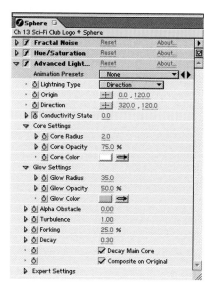

Settings for the Advanced Lightning effect at time 0:00

2 Still at time 9:29, add a Conductivity State keyframe to the effect with a value of 15.

3 Go to time 3:00, and change the Conductivity State value to 0.

The Sphere layer using the Advanced Lightning, Hue/Saturation, and Fractal Noise effects

Currently your so-called Sphere layer looks nothing like a sphere and just fills the comp window in 2D. You'll make the layer live up to its name in the next section.

Creating a Planet

The starring element of this project is a stormy planet revolving in space. There are a number of ways to create a convincing sphere in After Effects without any plug-ins, but those methods are pretty laborious. Instead, you'll use a Boris FX effect devoted to making spheres; it gives you more control over your sphere's attributes than you'll ever need, including multiple ways to apply texture and animate the globe.

> **Note:** This section requires the BCC Sphere effect from the Boris FX Continuum Complete collection of effects. If you don't have this collection installed, you can install a trial version of it from this book's DVD.

Follow these steps:

1 Select the Sphere layer, choose Layer > Pre-Compose, select the Move All Attributes option, and click OK. You pre-compose your Sphere layer so that the Sphere effect maps the solid's image after the three other effects have been applied to the solid.

2 Select the Sphere Comp 1 layer, and choose Effect > BBC3 Distortion & Perspective > BCC Sphere. The default values for this effect work very well to start.

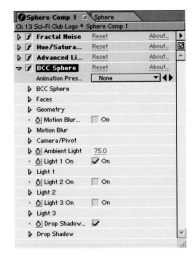

Settings for the BCC Sphere effect in the Effect Controls window

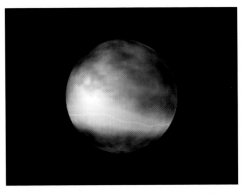

The Sphere Comp 1 layer using the BCC Sphere effect

3   Go to time 3:00, add a Spin keyframe in the effect's Geometry group, and set it to 0 × 0.0.

4   Press End to go to time 9:29, and change the Spin value to 1 × 0.0. These keyframes make the sphere turn one full revolution.

At time 7:00, you can see the rear of the sphere where the left and right edges of the solid layer meet, creating an undesirable seam in the sphere's skin. You'll fix this in the next step.

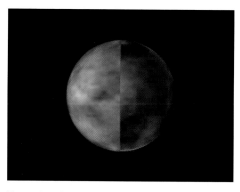

The sphere's seam destroys the illusion.

5   Expand the effect's Faces group, and change the Wrap property's value to Back And Forth Repeat.

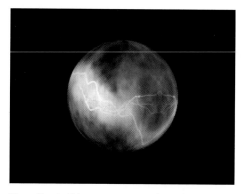

The effect's Wrap property makes the sphere seamless.

Creating an Orbiting Title

Making text orbit your stormy planet is fairly straightforward; you'll use the same effect you used to make the solid layer a sphere, and then tweak the effect's settings to make the text appear to hover or orbit over the planet. Here are the steps:

1   Select the Horizontal Type tool, and set the following properties in the Character and Paragraph palettes:

> Font Family: Arial Black
>
> Text Size: 36 pixels
>
> Alignment: Center Text

The text's fill color is irrelevant, because effects you'll apply to the layer will override the layer's original color.

2   Type SCI-FI CLUB in uppercase, and set the text layer's Position to 160, 135.

Creating the title

3   Apply Effect > BCC3 Distortion & Perspective > BCC Sphere to the SCI-FI CLUB layer.

4   Turn on the effect's Drop Shadow On property, and set the Shadow Distance to 10. Expand the effect's Faces group, and set the value of Faces to Front.

5   At time 3:00, add a Spin keyframe in the effect's Geometry group with a value of 0 × –180. This positions the first letters in the text layer along the right side of the sphere so the title can be read from left to right as the globe spins.

6   Press End to go to time 9:29, and change the Spin value to 0 × 135.0.

7   Set the Scale property in the Geometry group to 130. This makes the text-wrapped sphere larger than the solid-wrapped sphere, so the type appears to float above the stormy orb. The distance gives the overall scene a greater sense of depth.

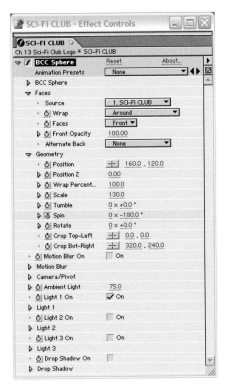

Settings for the BCC3 Sphere effect

Adding style to the orbiting title

Now you'll use the Ramp and Bevel Alpha effects to add a color gradient and substance to the type:

1   Apply Effect > Render > Ramp to the SCI-FI CLUB layer.

2   To equally divide the effect's color gradient between the top and bottom halves of the letters, apply these settings:

> Start of Ramp: 160, 116
>
> End of Ramp: 160, 137
>
> Start Color: Royal blue (#1301FF)
>
> End Color: Bright yellow (# ECFB02)
>
> Ramp Shape: Linear Ramp
>
> Set the effect's remaining two properties to 0.

3   To add some depth to the letters, apply Effect > Perspective > Bevel Alpha to the SCI-FI CLUB layer with these settings:

> Edge Thickness: 3.3
>
> Light Intensity: 1.0
>
> Light Angle: 0 x –60
>
> Light Color: #FFFFFF

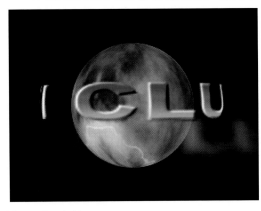

The stylized title

Assembling a Steel Box

You'll make solid layers appear metallic by applying a steel texture with the Boris FX effect appropriately named Steel Plate. Then you'll form a box from your steel plates in 3D space to surround your stormy globe.

Do the following:

1   Go to time 0:00, and create a solid named Floor with dimensions 300 × 300 using any color. The effect you'll apply to the solid will override the solid's color.

2   Apply Effect > BCC3 Generators > BCC Steel Plate to the Floor layer.

3   To brighten the effect's highlight, change the effect's Specular Intensity value to 45 in the Lighting group. You'll enhance these highlights in later steps with other effects.

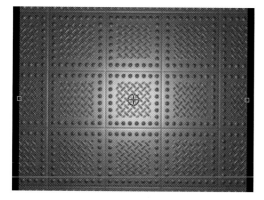

Adding texture to the Floor layer

4   Turn on the 3-D switch in the Timeline for all layers.

5   Duplicate the Floor layer five times so you have six layers total. Rename the new Floor layers Front, Back, Right, Left, and Top.

6   Select the six solid layers, and press P to display their Position properties. Set the values as specified here:

> Front: 160, 120, –150
>
> Back: 160, 120, 150
>
> Right: 310.0, 120, 0.0
>
> Left: 10.0, 120, 0
>
> Top: 160, –30, 0.0
>
> Floor: 160, 270, 0.0

7   Press R to display the layers' Rotation properties, and set their Orientation values as specified here:

> Front: 0.0, 0.0, 0.0
>
> Back: 0.0, 0.0, 0.0
>
> Right: 0.0, 90.0, 0.0
>
> Left: 0.0, 90.0, 0.0
>
> Top: 90.0, 0.0, 0.0
>
> Floor: 90.0, 0.0, 0.0

8   Select the Horizontal Type tool, and apply these settings:

> Font Family: Arial Black
>
> Text Size: 48px
>
> Fill Color: Black (#000000)
>
> Alignment: Center Text

Then, type OPEN THIS SIDE in uppercase with one word per line.

9   Turn on the 3D switch for the new text layer, and set the layer's Position to 160, 80, –150 so that the text appears above the Front layer.

10 In the Timeline's Parent column, choose the Front layer for the OPEN THIS SIDE layer. This way, whenever the Front layer moves, the text appears to be attached to the Front layer.

Creating the box's label

Animating the Steel Box

To simplify animating the steel box and its text label, you'll animate a Null Object layer instead and parent the other layers to it. You can think of a Null Object layer as basically an invisible solid; when it serves as a parent to other layers, the other layers imitate its every move. As a result, your box will fly in from space, and the side labeled *OPEN THIS SIDE* will slide open to reveal the spinning globe:

1   Choose Layer > New > Null Object.

2   Assign the Null 1 layer as the parent to all the layers except the OPEN THIS SIDE text layer.

Parenting the layers

3   Turn on the Null 1 layer's 3D switch, and set the layer's Position to 160, 120, 120.

4   Go to time 3:00, and add a Position keyframe to the Null Object and to the Front layer.

5   Still at time 3:00, add an Orientation keyframe to the Null 1 layer with a value of 0.0, 0.0, 0.0.

6   Go to time 4:00, and change the Front layer's Position to 0.0, 270, –150 to open the door.

7   Go to time 0:00, and change the Null 1 layer's Position to 0.0, 120, 2000 and Orientation to 50.0, 220, 300.

Click the Ram Preview button to see the results.

Now Try This

The project's remaining elements include a starry sky and a galaxy from which the steel box emerges. You can quickly generate these items with aptly named effects provided by Boris FX. Other finishing touches include intensifying the colors and giving various elements a more monochrome appearance:

- Create a new solid layer, and use effects from the Boris FX BCC3 Generators group to generate stars and galaxies for the background.

- Create an Adjustment layer, and apply the Hue & Saturation effect to colorize the entire animation and give it a uniform color and intensity.

- Add additional information such as show times and air dates.

- Create another comp-size solid layer that uses the BCC Steel Plate effect, and make a letter box from it by masking out the central area.

CHAPTER 14

Station ID

If someone asked you how to add more depth to a scene in After Effects, you might first rattle off the names of several effects, such as any of the Perspective or Distort effects, or the various Emboss effects. Those work well to give depth to individual elements in a scene. But to give the entire scene more depth, you can add elements to the foreground or frame the scene to create the illusion.

This chapter's project uses a combination of both those methods to create a "deep" scene. To give you a running head start, the book's DVD provides you with some video footage of a city landscape on top of which you can build your project. You'll create an animated iris or aperture to frame the scene and use effects to give the aperture its style and some substance. Finally, you'll use Zaxwerks' 3D Invigorator effect to extrude and animate a 2D drawing.

It Works Like This

Check out the **Ch14 Finished Project.mov** file in this chapter's folder on the book's DVD to see the final results of this chapter's project. This project is created using only one composition and a few layers, yet the results contain a lot of depth and visual interest.

You'll use the following techniques:

1. Give footage of a cityscape a stylized night look with some effects.

2. Add a layer of scrolling text to the background.

3. Create an animated aperture that frames the city view.

4. Create a 3D object with the 3D Invigorator effect, a solid, and an Adobe Illustrator file.

The TV channel slowly spins in the center of the scene.

As the channels rotates, text scrolls upward.

The text scrolls off the screen after the channel lands in position.

Preparing to Work

You'll need to import a file and make sure a third-party effect is installed into After Effects in order to complete this chapter's project. The project uses some video footage, provided on the book's DVD, to create the background. To create the 3D channel number 2, you'll use an Illustrator file and the Zaxwerks 3D Invigorator effect. You won't need to import the Illustrator file into your project, since the 3D Invigorator effect prompts you to open the Illustrator file from its actual location on your computer.

To prepare for this project, do the following:

1   Start with a new project, and save it as Ch14StationID.

2   Import the **City_Background.mov** file as footage from this chapter's folder on the book's DVD.

3   Create a new composition named Master using the NTSC DV, 720 × 480 composition preset, with Duration 5;00 seconds.

Creating the Background

You'll create the background in three easy steps by importing your movie file and applying two effects to it. The Hue/Saturation effect helps give the footage a uniform appearance, and the Glow effect further stylizes the imagery:

1   Add the **City_Background.mov** file to the Master Timeline at time 0;00.

2   To give the City_Background.mov layer a blue hue, apply Effect > Adjust > Hue/Saturation to the layer. Use these effect settings:

> Colorize (under Master Lightness): On
>
> Colorize Hue: 0 × 220
>
> Colorize Saturation: 45

Settings for the Hue/Saturation effect

3   To add some radiance to the city background, apply Effect > Stylize > Glow to the layer. Use these effect settings:

> Glow Threshold: 27%
>
> Glow Radius: 18
>
> Glow Intensity: .3

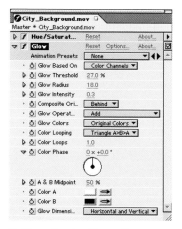

Settings for the Glow effect

The City_Background.mov layer with Hue/Saturation and Glow effects

Adding the Scrolling Text

A text layer that displays the names of 11 cities (presumably the news station's broadcasting area) scrolls upward on top of the city. To create this effect, you'll animate your text layer's Position property. Once you're done with this project, you can try using any of the Multi-Line text animation presets (in the Effects & Presets palette) to animate the layer instead.

Follow these steps:

1   Use these Settings for the Horizontal Type tool:

> Alignment: Center Text
>
> Font Family: Arial
>
> Text Size: 34px
>
> Leading: 72
>
> Tracking: 300
>
> Fill Color: White (RGB: 255, 255, 255)
>
> Stroke Color: None

Settings for the text layer

2   Type the names of 11 cities, with one city name per line, in a single text layer.

3   To set the starting position of the text layer, add a Position keyframe of 360, 505 at time 0;00. This keyframe starts the first line of text just outside the bottom edge of the composition and centered in the composition's width.

4   Press your keyboard's End key to go to time 4;29. Change the text layer's Position to 360, -725 to position the layer above the top edge of the Composition window.

The text's motion path starts below the composition and ends far above.

Save your project, and then preview your results. The text layer should now start offscreen at the bottom of the composition and scroll upward until every line of text is out of view.

Creating an Aperture

The city background is viewed through an aperture you'll create by masking two solid layers. You have a lot of freedom to make your aperture unique when you draw and position your masks; use our illustrations and masking instructions as a general guide. The solids' appearance is created with the Ramp and Bevel Alpha effects:

1   At time 0;00, create a comp-size Solid layer named Border 2 that's any color. Make sure the Solid layer is above the other layers in the Timeline.

2   Use the Elliptical Mask tool on the Solid layer to draw an oval shape that encompasses about two thirds of the composition. The right side of the mask in this chapter's final movie is within the composition, and the left side is out of view to the left of the composition. Use the illustration of the first iris as a guide.

3   Set the Mask's Mode to Subtract so you see the city through the oval shape.

Tip: Choose Layer > Mask > Free Transform Points after you select your mask in the Timeline to more easily move, rotate, and reshape your mask.

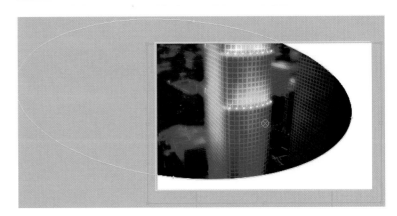

Making the first aperture

4 Still at time 0;00, add a Mask Shape keyframe to the Border 2 layer's mask.

5 Press End on your keyboard to go to time 4;29. Rotate and move the mask's shape up or down to a new location near the mask's current location, to create a slow and subtle movement.

Note: Make sure you move only the mask and not the Solid layer.

---

6 To create the second half of the iris, duplicate the Border 2 layer and rename the new layer Border 1.

7 At time 0;00, move the Border 1 mask so it encompasses the area opposite the Border 2 layer's mask. In this chapter's final movie, the left edge of the mask is within the composition, and the right edge is out of view on the right side.

8 At time 4:29, rotate and move the Border 1 mask up or down in the opposite direction of Border 2's mask.

The masked solids create a basic frame over the city scene.

Adding style to the aperture

Currently, your solids appear very flat, and their shapes appear to merge into one another (if you used the same fill color with each). You'll use the Ramp effect with unique settings for each solid so their colors are distinct from one another, and then you'll use the Bevel Alpha effect to give the solids some volume:

1 Select both Border layers, and apply Effect > Render > Ramp to both.

2 To complement the blue hue in the city background, set the effect's Start Color to a yellow color and the End color to a blue color for one Border layer. Reverse the colors in the other Border layer's effect.

3 Select both Border layers, and apply Effect > Perspective > Bevel Alpha. Set the effect's properties as follows:

> Edge Thickness: 15
>
> Light Color: White (RGB: 255, 255, 255)
>
> Light Intensity: 0.70

4 Set the Bevel Alpha effect's Light Angle to 90 for the effect in Border 1 and to 0 in Border 2.

The Border layers using the Ramp and Bevel Alpha effects

Adding the News Channel

In this section, you'll create a 3D TV channel number by extruding an Illustrator file's shape from a Solid layer. You'll assign prebuilt surface textures and lighting to the object to quickly create the number's look. To make the number rotate in space, you'll animate a virtual camera instead of the number itself.

> **Note:** If you don't already have the 3D Invigorator effect installed into After Effects, quit After Effects, and then install a trial version of the effect from the book's DVD.

Follow these steps:

1   At time 0;00, create a new comp-size Solid layer named 2, using any color.

2   Apply Effect > Zaxwerks > 3D Invigorator to the new solid, checkmark Move Objects to Center in the dialog prompt, and then open the **2.ai** file from this chapter's folder on the book's DVD.

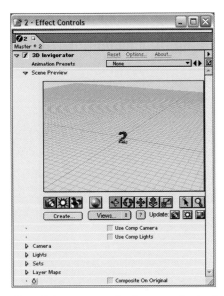

The 3D Invigorator effect's properties in the Effect Controls window

3   To assign a texture to the number, click Options in the upper-right corner of the Effect Controls window. Drag an object style onto the object in the Scene Preview area of the dialog, and click OK.

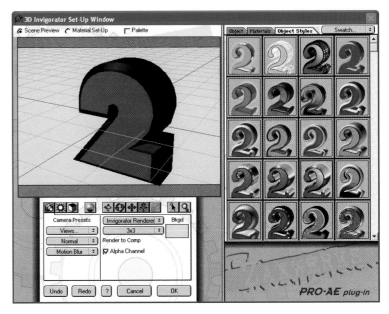

Applying the object style to the number

4   Expand the triangle next to the effect's Camera group in the Effect Controls window, add a keyframe to every property in the group, and set the camera properties as follows:

Eye X: 300

Eye Y: 500

Eye Z: 500

Target X: 0

Target Y: 0

Target Z: -15

Distance: 907

Tumble Left: 116.29

Tumble Up: 22.21

Roll: 0

Ortho Size: 500

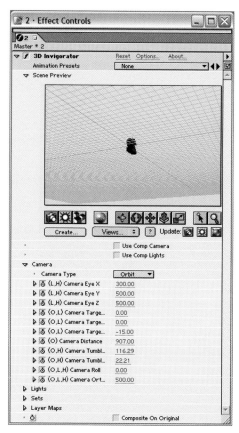

The camera's view with the 2 layer's first set of keyframes

5   Go to time 3;00, and change the effect's camera properties as follows:

Target Z: –10

Distance: 143.73

Tumble Left: –31.54

Tumble Up: 33.27

Ortho Size: 97.67

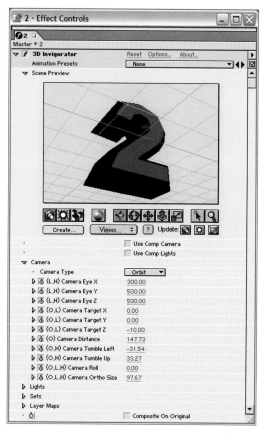

Animating the camera instead of the object

6   To assign a lighting style to the number, click Options in the upper-right corner of the Effect Controls window. Click the Light button (next to the Camera button), and then click the Lighting Styles tab in the right panel of the dialog. Drag a lighting style from the list onto the number in the scene preview area of the dialog, and click OK.

7   Apply Effect > Perspective > Drop Shadow to the layer named 2. Set the effect's Distance to 70 and Softness to 50.

Settings for the drop shadow

Save your project, and then preview your results. The number 2 should initially appear small and with its back to the viewer and then slowly rotate counter-clockwise as it moves closer to the viewer.

Adding Text to the Channel

The remaining finishing touch is to add the phrase *ON TUESDAY* in front of the channel number when the number comes to a stop at time 3;00:

1   Go to time 3;00, and create a text layer that displays *ON TUESDAY* above the 2 layer in the Timeline. Use these settings for the new text layer:

> Font Family: Arial Black
>
> Text Size: 18px
>
> Tracking: 300
>
> Fill Color: White (RGB: 255, 255, 255)
>
> Stroke Color: Red (RGB: 255, 0, 0)
>
> Stroke Width: 2px
>
> Stroke Style: Fill Over Stroke

2   Turn on the new text layer's 3D switch, and adjust the Position and Orientation values until the text lies on the front of the bottom stroke of the character and appears aligned with the front of the number.

Adding a phrase to the channel number

If you preview your animation, the words *ON TUESDAY* should appear at time 3;00.

Now Try This

At this point, your animation should look very similar to the finished movie in this chapter's folder on the book's DVD, although your animation may have different colors and styles and the aperture may look different. Here are a number of suggestions that you can perform to refine this project even further:

- Select the individual Border layers, and animate the Light Angles of the Bevel Alpha effect to give the edges of the animated aperture more visual interest.

- Change the background text so that the names of the cities animate in alternating directions across the screen—some from right to left, and others from left to right.

- To really jazz up the scrolling text, remove the Position keyframes from the layer, and then apply a text animation preset from the Multi-Line category in the Effects & Presets palette to the layer. You can refine the resulting animation by tweaking the preset's settings in your Timeline. Press UU to reveal all the properties that were modified by the preset.

| # Fog of Text

This chapter was actually inspired by the accident of duplicating a text layer more times than necessary. Instead of removing the extra layers, I began playing around with them and animated them in from various locations on the screen. It's an effect that you can use many ways: as the main feature of a project, as a background to fill space, and so on.

In this chapter, you'll create a virtual fog made of words that scale and move through 3D space until they settle into uniform rows. A woman's figure walks through the fog of words, revealed only by the words that fall upon her form.

It Works Like This

Check out the **Ch15 Finished Project.mov** file in this chapter's folder on the book's DVD to see the final results. With the exception of the movie footage of a walking figure, the entire project is created in After Effects using only text layers and an effect. These are the main steps:

1. Create several layers of text, and animate the layers' Scale and Positions in 3D space.

2. Randomize the layers' Scale and Positions in space.

3. Use the Displacement Map effect to make an animated figure appear to be walking invisibly through the layers of text. Key out the background around the figure, and invert the track matte.

4. Animate the Tint effect to change the background text's color.

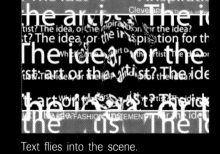

Text flies into the scene.

Text that overlaps the walking figure appears distorted.

The multilayered text appears stenciled by a word and the figure.

Preparing to Work

This project works fine in any composition preset, but you'll use a relatively small preset that requires fewer system resources and less time to render or preview your work.

To prepare for this project, do the following:

1   Start with a new project, and save it as Ch15FogofText.

2   Import the **Woman_Walking.mov** file as footage from this chapter's folder on the book's DVD.

3   Create a new composition named Text Tracks 1 with dimensions 320 × 240, a Pixel Aspect Ratio of Square Pixels, Frame Rate 30, and Duration 10:00 seconds. Make the composition's background color black (RGB: 0, 0, 0).

Creating Layers of Text

Your first task is to create and position the layers of text that you'll animate into the scene in the next section. Your main objective is to create a line of text that spans the width of the composition; so, you can type any words you like, or you can type the text we specify in step 2.

Follow these steps:

1   Select the Horizontal Type tool, and set its properties in the Character and Paragraph palettes:

Font Family: Arial

Text Size: 18

Fill Color: white (RGB: 255, 255, 255)

Alignment: Center Text

Settings for the Horizontal Type tool

2   Type Which came first: art or the artist? The idea, or the inspiration for the idea? or other text that covers the entire width of the composition once it's positioned in the next step.

3   Set the text layer's Position to 5, 20 so the line of text starts in the upper-left corner of the Composition window.

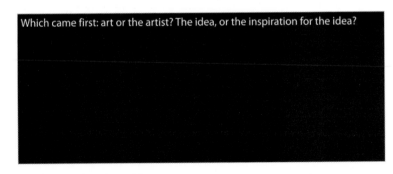

The first text layer's position

4   Duplicate the text layer seven times, so you have a total of eight layers. Set their Position properties as listed here:

> Layer 1: 5, 20
>
> Layer 2: 5, 50
>
> Layer 3: 5, 80
>
> Layer 4: 5, 110
>
> Layer 5: 5, 140
>
> Layer 6: 5, 170
>
> Layer 7: 5, 200
>
> Layer 8: 5, 230

Which came first: art or the artist? The idea, or the inspiration for the idea?
Which came first: art or the artist? The idea, or the inspiration for the idea?
Which came first: art or the artist? The idea, or the inspiration for the idea?
Which came first: art or the artist? The idea, or the inspiration for the idea?
Which came first: art or the artist? The idea, or the inspiration for the idea?
Which came first: art or the artist? The idea, or the inspiration for the idea?
Which came first: art or the artist? The idea, or the inspiration for the idea?
Which came first: art or the artist? The idea, or the inspiration for the idea?

The text layers' landing positions

Animating the Text

You'll randomly animate your text layers' Scale and Position along the Z axis in this section so the layers appear scattered throughout space. There's no science to this part; you'll come up with your own settings by randomly scrubbing the values:

1   Turn on the 3D switch for each text layer in the Timeline's Switches column.

2   Go to time 4:00, and add a Position keyframe and a Scale keyframe to each layer.

3   Go to time 0:00, and change each layer's Z Position value (only the Z value!) and Scale value so that no layer has the same Z Position or Scale value as another layer. Make half the Z Position values negative and half positive so that some layers are closer to the viewer (negative Z value) and others appear in the distance (positive Z value).

You don't want to skew the text when you modify a layer's Scale, so leave on the Constrain Proportions button to the left of each set of Scale values.

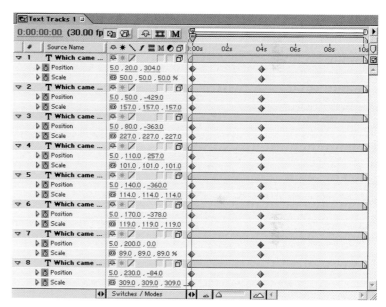

The Timeline after adding the Position and Scale keyframes

The Composition after adding the Position and Scale keyframes

Animating more text

So far, you've created only half the text layers you need for this project. Your next task is to create more lines of animated text by duplicating the composition you've already created and modifying the keyframes. The text layers in the new composition will appear in between the lines of text in the original composition. Here are the steps:

1   Close the Text Track composition, and duplicate it in the Project window.

2   Open the Text Tracks 2 composition, and go to time 4:00.

3   Increase each layer's Y Position value by 15 pixels. This moves each layer vertically so that when you combine the two Text Tracks compositions into one, the layers of text won't overlap. The top layer's Y Position value will be 35, the second layer's 65, and so on.

4   Go to time 0:00, randomly animate each layer's Scale (with proportions constrained), and change each layer's Z Position value to its opposite negative or positive value. (For example, change a Z Position value of −304 to 304.) Be certain to only change the Z value for each layer's Position.

Completing the text wall

Your next task is to combine the two text comps into a new composition and modify one layer's Position so the lines of text appear staggered:

1   Create a new composition named Master, using the Medium, 320 × 240 composition preset, with Duration 10:00 seconds.

2   Add the Text Tracks and Text Tracks 2 compositions to the Timeline at time 0:00.

3   Still at time 0:00, add a Position keyframe to each layer, and set each layer's Position to 300, 120.

4   Press End to go to time 9:29, and then change each layer's Position to 20, 120.

5   Click the Position property name of the Text Tracks 2 layer to select all of its keyframes. Choose Animation > Keyframe Assistant > Time-Reverse Keyframes to switch the layer's Position keyframes in time.

The text layers in their final positions

Making a Woman Invisible

The text wall is complete, so it's finally time to add a mysterious figure: the **Woman_Walking.mov** file you imported at the start of this project. The walking woman animation is an animated 3D model of a blond woman in a t-shirt and slacks, but viewers never really see her. Instead, they see her outline as it walks through the layers of text in space and pushes the words out of place. What's her secret? The Displacement Map effect that you'll apply to the text layers.

The Displacement Map effect moves the Text Tracks layer's pixels by an amount determined by the color values of the Woman_Walking layer and the Maximum Displacement amounts you specify for the effect. Because the animated woman is surrounded by black, which has no color value, the Text Tracks Master layer is only affected by her figure and its colors.

Note: The Displacement Map effect is available only with the Professional version of After Effects. You can install a trial version of After Effects Professional from this book's DVD or from Adobe's Web site at **www.adobe.com**.

Follow these steps:

1   Select the Text Tracks layers in the Master composition's Timeline, and choose Layer > Pre-Compose to combine the layers into a new composition. Name the pre-comp Text Tracks Master.

2   Drag the **Woman_Walking.mov** file from the Project window to the Master Timeline at time 0:00, above the other layer.

3   Turn off the visibility switch for the Woman_Walking layer in the A/V Features column.

4   Apply Effect > Distort > Displacement Map to the Text Tracks Master layer. Use these settings for the effect:

>   Max Horizontal Displacement: 10
>
>   Max Vertical Displacement: 10
>
>   Displacement Layer: Woman_Walking layer

If you preview the animation, you should see the outline of a walking woman created by text that appears to flow over her figure as she moves.

The Displacement Map effect at time 0:00

Inverting the invisible woman

Your final task is to make the walking woman appear to separate from the background of text and animate the background text's color. Since the Woman_Walking animation contains a black background, you can easily key out the background to isolate the woman's figure. Follow these steps:

1   Turn on the Visibility switch next to the Woman_Walking layer so you can select a color in the layer in the next step.

2   Apply Effect > Keying > Color Key to the Woman_Walking layer. Click the effect's Key Color eyedropper button, and then click anywhere in the black area that surrounds the woman's figure in the Composition window. Make sure you turn off the Woman_Walking layer's Visibility switch once you've set the effect's Key Color.

3   Since the black color that surrounds the woman contains different black colors, set the effect's Color Tolerance to 7. Set the effect's Edge Thin to 1 and Edge Feather to 3.

4   Select the Woman_Walking and Text Tracks layers, choose Layer > Pre-Compose, and name the composition Walking Woman Matte 1.

The Walking Woman Matte 1 comp at time 0:00

5   Select the Walking Woman Matte 1 layer, and duplicate it.

6   Rename the bottommost Walking Woman Matte layer Walking Woman Matte 2.

7   Open the Walking Woman Matte 2 composition Timeline, and then change the Text Track Master's Track Matte to Alpha Inverted "Woman_Walking.mov".

9   Add an Amount To Tint keyframe to the effect at time 2:00 with a value of 0%, and then change the property's value to 100 at time 3:00.

The Master composition at time 3:00

Walking Woman Matte 2 composition at the end of the Timeline

8   Return to the Master composition, and apply Effect > Image > Tint to the Walking Woman Matte 2 layer. Set the effect's Map Black To property to black (RGB: 0, 0, 0) and the Map White To property to blue (RGB: 45, 45, 254).

Now Try This

To give your project its promotional context and to add some visual structure to the scene, add the remaining elements you see in this chapter's final movie:

- Create a letterbox by adding a grey-colored solid layer and masking out the central area. Apply the Stroke effect to the solid to outline the masked area.

- Add the titles *Los Angeles* and *Dream of Fashion* within the letterbox, and animate them to slide horizontally into place.

- Add a text layer at time 3:00 above the Walking Woman Matte 2 layer that displays the word *inspiration* with Text Size set to 150 pixels. Set the layer's Blending Mode to Stencil Alpha, and animate the layer's X Position value so that the word slowly scrolls in the background.

CHAPTER 16 | Fast and Easy Lighting

One of the most interesting aspects of light is how it interacts with objects, causing them to cast shadows and creating a sense of space. The most effective lighting programs are generally higher-end 3D modeling applications, but this chapter will show you how to obtain dramatic results using After Effects and a few third-party effects.

In this chapter, you'll develop a movie promo for an independent film named *Alvarez & Cruz*. You'll use a clip from the movie as a background both to serve as a background texture and to give the viewer a glimpse of the film. You'll accent the screen with light and shadows as the 3D title flies in from behind the viewer.

It Works Like This

Check out the **Ch16 Finished Project.mov** file in this chapter's folder on the book's DVD to see the results of the completed project. In this project, you'll see how to leverage the power of After Effects' Light layers and effects to create dramatic lighting. The main steps are as follows:

1. Use a movie clip and several effects to create an atmospheric moving background.

2. Create 3D text extruded from a 2D file for the main title by using the Zaxwerks 3D Invigorator effect.

3. Animate the title into the scene.

4. Create a smooth motion path nearly instantly for your light layer by using a mask.

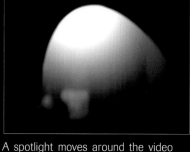

A spotlight moves around the video footage.

The 3D title flies into the scene.

Animated shadows accentuate the 3D title's shape.

Preparing to Work

This project requires one composition, some video footage (provided), an Adobe Illustrator file (provided), and a few solid layers. You'll create a 3D title by extruding the Illustrator file with the Zaxwerks 3D Invigorator effect. The primary lighting effect will be created using native After Effects features; you can further enhance the lighting results with effects provided by the company Trapcode.

To prepare for this project, do the following:

1   If you don't already have the Zaxwerks 3D Invigorator effect (Classic 3.0.9 version) installed into After Effects, you can install it with the CD provided with the Professional versions of After Effects or the Adobe Video Collection. If you have the Standard version of either product, you can install a trial version of 3D Invigorator from this book's DVD or from the company's Web site at **www.zaxwerks. com**. Once the effect is installed, a Zaxwerks submenu appears in the Effect menu in After Effects.

2   Start with a new project, and save it as Ch16Lighting.

3   Import the **Alvarez&Cruz.mov** file as footage from this chapter's folder on the book's DVD.

4   Create a new composition named A&C Master using the Medium, 320 × 240 comp preset, with Duration 10:00 seconds.

Creating the Motion Background

You'll use the footage that you imported from the book's DVD to lay the foundation for your spot's background:

1   At time 0:00, create a comp-size white (RGB: 255, 255, 255) solid named Background, with Pixel Aspect Ratio set to Square Pixels.

2   Place the **Alvarez&Cruz.mov** file in the Timeline starting at time 0:00, above the Background layer.

3   To fit the footage to the composition's size, set the Alvarez&Cruz layer's Scale to 50, 50%.

4   To make the footage fade in to the scene, add a 0% Opacity keyframe at time 1:00; then, go to time 2:00 and change the Opacity to 100%.

5   To make the footage fade out of the scene, add a 100% Opacity keyframe at time 5:00 and a 0% Opacity keyframe at time 7:00.

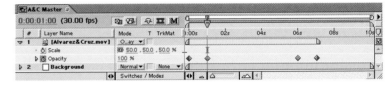

The A&C Master composition at time 1:00

Adjusting the video

The movie clip needs to be adjusted to help push the clip into the background so the focus of the spot will be on the foreground elements. To do this, you'll colorize, blur, and modify the layer's levels:

1   To give the video footage a blue hue, apply Effect > Adjust > Hue/Saturation to the Alvarez&Cruz layer. Use these effect settings:

   Colorize (below the Master Lightness option): On

   Colorize Hue: 0 × –120

   Colorize Saturation: 50

   Colorize Lightness: 0

2   To blur the video footage so it's less of a focal point in each frame, apply Effect > Blur & Sharpen > Fast Blur to the Alvarez&Cruz layer. Use these settings for the effect:

> Blurriness: 20
>
> Blur Dimensions: Horizontal and Vertical
>
> Repeat Edge Pixels: On

3   Apply Effect > Adjust > Levels to the Alvarez&Cruz layer. Use these settings:

> Input Black: 20
>
> Input White: 90

Settings for the movie clip in the Effect Controls window

Extruding the Main Title

To create the main title, you'll use the Zaxwerks 3D Invigorator effect, which generates three-dimensional objects from two-dimensional Adobe Illustrator files. Once you generate the 3D object, you can animate it in 3D space and view it from any angle. Follow these steps:

1   Go to time 1:00, and create a new comp-size Solid layer named A&C Title that's any color. Make sure the solid is above the other layers in the Timeline.

2   Apply Effect > Zaxwerks > 3D Invigorator to the A&C Title layer, and open the **A&C.ai** file from this chapter's folder on the book's DVD.

Options for the 3D Invigorator effect in the Effect Controls window

3   To assign a style to the title, click Options next to the 3D Invigorator name in the Effect Controls window to open the 3D Invigorator Set-Up Window dialog. In the Object Styles tab, select a style that will make the title complement the video footage; drag the style to the text in the Scene Preview area of the dialog, and click OK.

Assigning a style to the title

4   In the Effect Controls window, expand the 3D Invigorator effect's Camera group, and add a keyframe at time 1:00 to each property in the group.

5   To set the title to start nearly offscreen, set the effect's properties as listed here:

Camera Eye X: 300

Camera Eye Y: 500

Camera Eye Z: 500

Camera Target X: 0.62

Camera Target Y: 3.51

Camera Target Z: 8.51

Camera Distance: 9.37

Camera Tumble Left: 1.24

Camera Tumble Up: 81.51

Camera Roll: 0.00

Camera Ortho Size: 5.16

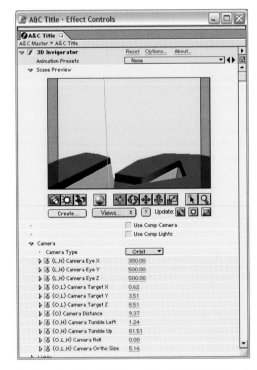

Settings for the 3D Invigorator effect's first keyframe

6   Go to time 3:00, and change the 3D Invigorator effect's properties to the following:

> Camera Distance: 554.29
>
> Camera Tumble Left: -2.78
>
> Camera Tumble Up: 17.19
>
> Camera Ortho Size: 305.56

7   Expand the A&C Title's Material Options group in the Timeline, and turn on the Casts Shadows option. This enables the layer to cast shadows caused by the lights you'll add in the next section.

If you preview the animation now, you should see the title fly into the scene as if from behind the viewer and land in position facing the viewer.

Creating a Spotlight

It's finally time to begin the lighting section. There are several ways to animate After Effects Light layers, which are 3D by default. One technique is to manually create the light's motion path by animating the light's Position property: You add a Position keyframe at one point in time and then reposition the light at other points in time. This usually requires working with your composition in multiple views and subsequently refining the path by using the Pen tool. This method gives you great control over the light's animation but can require a lot of manipulation and time.

Instead of that approach, you'll create your light's motion path by drawing the path with the Elliptical Mask tool and then copying and pasting its keyframes. If you wanted to subsequently refine the path, you could do so with this method by using the Pen tool. Fast and easy.

Here are the steps:

1   Turn on every layer's 3D switch in the Timeline's Switches column.

2   To create a spotlight, go to time 0:00, choose Layer > New > Light, and use the following values in the Light Settings dialog:

> Light Type: Spot
>
> Intensity: 130
>
> Cone Angle: 55
>
> Cone Feather: 15
>
> Color: white (RGB: 255, 255, 255)
>
> Casts Shadows: checked
>
> Shadow Darkness: 55
>
> Shadow Diffusion: 20

3   Make sure the light layer is above the other layers in the Timeline.

4   Use the Elliptical Mask tool to create a circular mask in the Alvarez&Cruz layer and surrounding the composition area. It doesn't matter what point of time you're at in the Timeline.

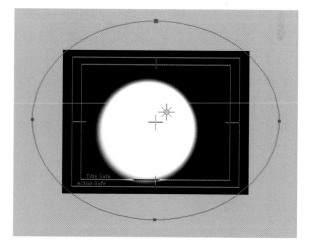

Creating a motion path with a mask tool

5 Select the Alvarez&Cruz layer, and press M to display the mask's Mask Shape property. Click the Mask Shape property's name to select it, and then choose Edit > Copy to copy it.

6 Select the Light layer's Position property in the Timeline, and choose Edit > Paste to paste the mask. You've just created a smooth, perfect oval motion path for your light.

Well, almost perfect. You need to make a few adjustments. Currently, the light has no real distance from your Z axis, so it doesn't appear to point at anything. However, this is easy to fix in the next steps.

7 Since you don't need the mask in the Alvarez&Cruz layer anymore, expand the layer in the Timeline and delete the layer's mask.

8 At time 0:00, set the Z value of the Light layer's Position keyframe to −100.

9 For each of the Light layer's remaining Position keyframes, set the Z value to −300. Press the K key to go to the next keyframe or J to go to the previous keyframe in the layer.

This technique creates an effect in which the light circle is close to the title at the beginning of the animation and then moves away from the title as the title animates into view. As a result, the lighting is softened.

10 To spread the keyframes over the composition's entire duration, click the Light layer's Position property to select all of the property's keyframes, hold down the Alt key (Windows) or Option key (Mac), and drag the last keyframe to time 9:29.

If you preview your animation at this point, you should see the spotlight on an empty scene; then, the title flies in at center stage.

Now Try This

To add the remaining design elements for this project, do the following two tasks:

- Create a fake 16:9 letterbox with a comp-size, black (RGB: 0, 0, 0) solid by cutting out the solid's center with the Rectangular Mask tool in Subtract mode. Apply a Stroke effect to the solid to outline the letterbox.

- Add the text line *An Urban Drama* to the top left and *tonight at 11pm* to the bottom right of the Letterbox layer. Be sure to consider the Title and Action Safe boundaries in the composition when creating your letterbox.

To continue experimenting with After Effects lights, explore the Lux effect provided by Trapcode:

- Visualize your light's source by applying the Trapcode company's Lux effect to a solid layer. If you don't have this effect, you can download a demo version from the company's Web site at **www.trapcode.com**. The Lux effect works seamlessly with the properties of existing lights in your composition. Based on these settings, the Lux effect creates a visual representation of the light. If your light is positioned offscreen, then you won't see the effect (obviously).

- To add the light rays that appear to project around the title layer from a light behind the title, apply the Trapcode company's Shine effect to a duplicate copy of the A&C Title layer. Set the effect's Colorize option to One Color, colored black (RGB: 0, 0, 0). Select the Shine effect's Source Point property in the Timeline, and choose Animation > Add Expression. Drag the Expression's Pick Whip to the Position parameter of the Light 1 layer.

| # Heartbeat Car Commercial

The original idea for the heartbeat you'll visualize with this chapter's project was inspired by a project in which I set an oscilloscope waveform inside a logo. I really liked the idea and began to experiment with it as a means of expressing the excitement someone may feel the first time they drive a Saleen S7 car.

In this project, you'll learn how to use a variety of effects and a mask to create and animate the heartbeat. You'll also use effects to build a heart monitor to contain the heartbeat and to frame some video footage. The lessons you'll learn as you animate the heartbeat's path can be applied to other projects in which you want to animate lines and outlines.

It Works Like This

Check out the **Ch17 Saleen Heartbeat.mov** file in this chapter's folder on the book's DVD to view the final results of this chapter's project. Video footage featuring a Saleen automobile serves as the background for the real star of this spot: an animated heartbeat. You'll learn to use combinations of effects and blending modes to create the layered look of the final project.

You'll use the following techniques:

1. Draw the path of a heartbeat with the Pen tool, and stroke the path with color.

2. Animate the heartbeat's path by animating the Stroke and Lens Flare effects.

3. Fade out the heartbeat's path by animating the Ramp effect and assigning a Track Matte to the heartbeat's layer.

4. Build a monitor for the heartbeat's path by using the Grid effect and an Adjustment layer.

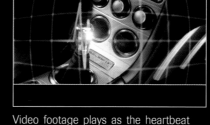

Video footage plays as the heartbeat goes across the screen.

A ball of light leads the heartbeat's path across the screen.

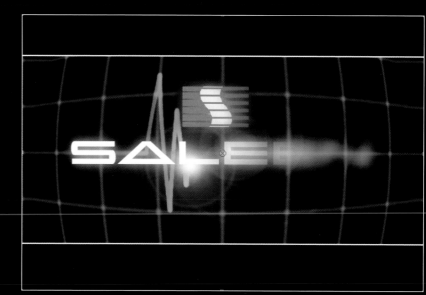

The logo blurs into the scene.

Preparing to Work

This project requires three movie files, an audio file, and a graphic still, all of which are provided on the book's DVD. You need to import these items into your project and create your first composition before the real work begins.

To prepare for this project, do the following:

1   Start with a new project, and save it as Ch17HeartbeatCar.

2   Import the folders named **Audio**, **Footage**, and **Stills** from this chapter's folder on the book's DVD. The **Footage** folder contains two AVI files and a MOV file, the **Stills** folder contains one PSD file, and the **Audio** folder contains one WAV file.

3   Create a new composition named Heartbeat using the NTSC DV, 720 × 480 comp preset, with Duration 1;00 second.

4   To keep your Project window organized, create a new folder named **Comps** and add the Heartbeat composition and all subsequent comps in this chapter to it.

The Project window

Creating the Heartbeat

You'll draw the heartbeat's path with the Pen tool by using the eyeball technique—that is, you'll draw the path by hand using an audio layer's waveform as your visual guide. As a result, your heartbeat path may not look exactly like the path in the illustrations or this chapter's finished movie; that's okay.

Follow these steps:

1   Add the **heartbeat.wav** file to the Timeline, and press your keyboard's L key twice to display the layer's audio track in the Timeline. You'll use the sound as a visual guide when drawing the path for the line in the heart monitor.

2   Create a new comp-size (720 × 480) Solid layer named Heartbeat, colored black (RGB: 0, 0, 0).

3   Use the Pen tool to draw a shape on the Heartbeat layer that resembles the waveform in the audio layer.

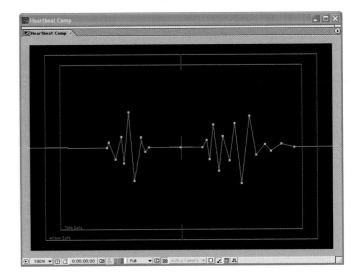

Drawing a heartbeat's path

4 Apply Effect > Render > Stroke to the Heartbeat layer to outline the path. Set the effect's Color to bright green (RGB: 0, 255, 0) and the Brush Size to 3.0.

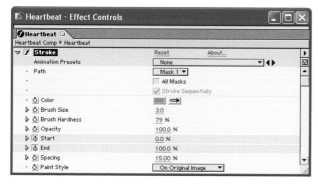

Stroking the heartbeat path

Animating the heartbeat

The Stroke effect has Start and End properties, which let you control the areas of a mask or path that are affected. If Start is set to 0% and End is set to 100% (or vice versa), then the entire path appears stroked. If both properties are set to the same value, then nothing is stroked. To animate the heartbeat's stroke so it moves from left to right, you'll animate the Stroke effect's End property in the following steps; you could just as easily animate the Start property with End set to 0%, instead, to get the same results. You'll use the eyeball technique again to get the right values for each keyframe:

1 Go to time 0;00, add a keyframe to the effect's End property, and change the property's value to 0%.

2 Go to the point in time that's just before the first spike in the audio layer's Waveform path, and scrub the Stroke effect's End value upward until the green stroke lies before the spikes in your mask's path.

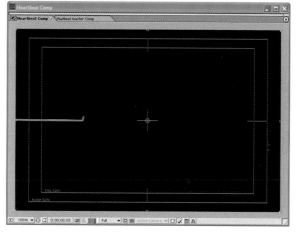

After adding the Stroke effect's second End keyframe

3 Go to the point in time that's at the end of the first group of spikes in the audio layer's Waveform path, and then increase the End property's value until the stroke is at the end of the group of spikes in the mask.

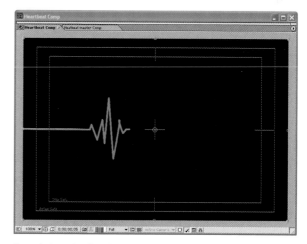

Completing the first heartbeat

4   Repeat steps 2 and 3 for the remaining spikes in the paths of the audio layer's Waveform and your mask.

5   Go the end of the Timeline, and set the End property to 100%.

6   To give the path some radiance, apply Effect > Stylize > Glow to the Heartbeat layer. Use these effect settings:

> Glow Threshold: 40%
>
> Glow Intensity: 2.0
>
> Color A (the inside color): Bright yellow (RGB: 255, 255, 0)
>
> Color B (the outside color): Bright green (RGB: 0, 255, 0)

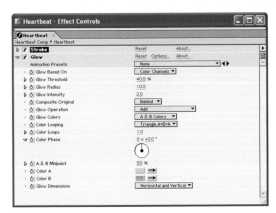

The Glow effect's settings in the Effect Controls window

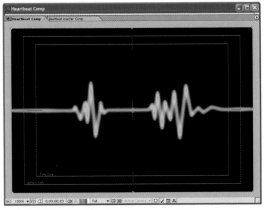

The glowing heartbeat

Fading out the heartbeat

In this section, you'll use an easy technique to fade out the tail end of the heartbeat's stroked path as it moves from left to right, so it's more realistic. You'll animate a color gradient that's created with the Ramp effect and then use the layer as a Track Matte for the heartbeat's layer:

1   At time 0;00, create a new comp-sized Solid layer named Ramp that's any color. Place the layer above the other layers in the Heartbeat Timeline. (The solid's color will be overridden by the Ramp effect.)

2   Apply Effect > Render > Ramp to the Ramp layer to create the gradients you'll need. Set the effect's Start of Ramp to 0, 240 and End of Ramp to 185, 240. These values fill most of the comp with white color that graduates to black on the left edge.

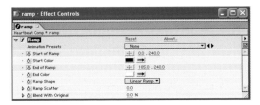

The Ramp effect's settings

The results of the Ramp effect and its settings at time 0;00

3 Set the Heartbeat layer's Track Matte to Luma Matte "Ramp", and press U on your keyboard to display the layer's keyframes

4 Go to the point in time where the Heartbeat layer's second keyframe lies, and add Start of Ramp and End of Ramp keyframes to the Ramp effect in the Ramp layer. Adjust the X value of the End of Ramp property until the End of Ramp marker (a circled plus sign) lies to the left of the rightmost point of the visible green stroke.

End of Ramp marker

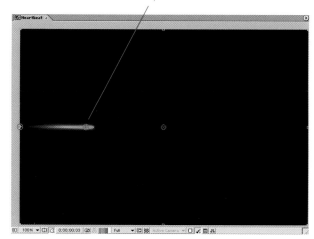

The End of Ramp marker should be to the left of the stroke's leading point.

5 Go to the point in time where the Stroke effect's next keyframe lies, and increase the X value of the Ramp effect's End of Ramp property until it lies to the left of the stroke's leading point, so the rightmost point is fully revealed and the rest of it is fading out.

6 At the same point in time as the Stroke effect's fourth keyframe, repeat the previous step; but this time also increase the Start of Ramp property's X value so that you can't see most of the first heartbeat.

7 At the same point in time as the Stroke effect's fifth keyframe, increase the X value of the Ramp effect's End of Ramp property until it lies to the left of the stroke's leading point. Also increase the Start of Ramp property until you see only the last half of the second heartbeat.

Fading out the first heartbeat's stroke

8 Press End to go to the end of the composition, and then increase the X values of the Start of Ramp and End of Ramp properties until you can't see the heartbeat's stroke.

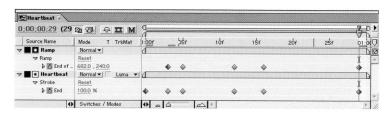

The Heartbeat Timeline

Adding a ball of light

Next, you'll use the Lens Flare effect to create and animate a ball of white light that leads the stroked path across the screen. Follow these steps:

1   At time 0;00, add a new comp-size Solid layer named White Dot that's colored black (RGB: 0, 0, 0).

2   Apply Effect > Render > Lens Flare to the White Dot layer, and set the effect's Flare Brightness to 70%.

3   Add a Flare Center keyframe to the effect, and set it to -50, 240. This starts the light offscreen.

Settings for the Lens Flare effect at time 0;00

4   Set the White Dot layer's Blending Mode to Screen in the Timeline's Modes column. This lets the viewer see both the stroke and the lens flare.

5   Go to the point in time where the Heartbeat layer's second keyframe lies, and increase the Flare Center property's X value until the light ball is at the tip of the line stroke.

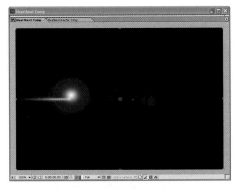

Aligning the Lens Flare to the stroke's leading point

6   Continue to move along the Timeline one frame at a time, and adjust the Flare Center property's position so that it always appear at the leading tip of the stroked path.

To position the Flare Center property, click the button that appears to the immediate left of the property's values in the Effect Controls window and then click in the Composition window where you want the Flare Center. Two white lines follow your mouse pointer to show you where the new point will be: where the lines intersect. Alternatively, you can drag the Flare Center icon in the Composition window to each new position. You can use the Page Up and Page Down keys to navigate along in time as you make the adjustments.

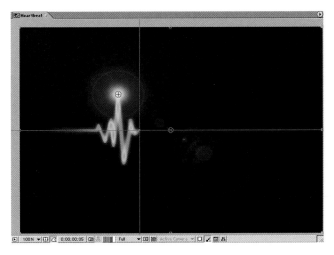

The place where the two white lines intersect defines the new position for the light flare.

Building the Heart Monitor

The style of the monitor enclosure you'll build to contain the heartbeat's path is like a relic from the earliest days of such devices. Before you build the monitor, you'll create a sequence of your heartbeat animation so that it loops continuously in the background. Here are the steps:

1 Create a new composition named Heart Monitor in your Project window's **Comps** folder, using the NTSC DV, 720 × 480 comp preset, with Duration 10;00 seconds.

2 Add the Heartbeat composition to the Heart Monitor Timeline at time 0;00.

3 Duplicate the Heartbeat layer nine times so you have a total of ten layers.

4 Select all the Heartbeat layers, and choose Animation > Keyframe Assistant > Sequence Layers. Make sure the Overlap option is unchecked and Transition is set to Dissolve Front Layer.

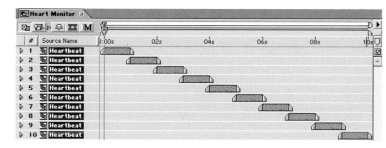

The Heartbeat Timeline after sequencing the layers

5 Create a new comp-size Solid layer named Grid that's any color. Make sure the layer is above all the other layers in the Timeline.

6 Apply Effect > Render > Grid to the Grid layer, and set the effect's Border (grid line size) property to 2.5. Change the color to green.

7 To smooth out the grid lines, apply Effect > Blur & Sharpen > Fast Blur effect to the Grid layer, and set the effect's Blurriness property to 2.

Settings for the Grid layer's effects

8 To create a bulge in the virtual glass of your monitor, choose Layer > New > Adjustment Layer, and name the layer Bulge. Since an Adjustment layer only works on layers that are below it, make sure the layer is at the top of the Timeline.

9 Apply Effect > Distort > Bulge to the Bulge layer. Use these effect settings:

   Horizontal Radius: 320

   Vertical Radius: 320

   Bulge Height: 0.7

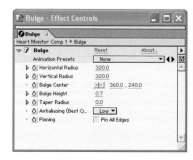

Settings for the adjustment layer's   The Heart Monitor composition
Bulge effect

Building the Movie Sequence

It's finally time to use the movie footage that you imported at the beginning of this project. All you need to do is put the movies in sequence, one after the other, and add transitions to them. You'll use the Sequence Layers command again, but with different options. Follow these steps:

1   Create a new composition named Car Movie in the **Comps** folder using the NTSC DV, 720 × 480 comp preset, with Duration 6;00 seconds.

2   Add the **Saleen_Car_02.avi**, **Saleen_Car_01.avi**, and **SaleenCar_ 04.mov** files to the Timeline at time 0;00. Saleen_Car_02 should be layer 1, Saleen_Car_01 should be layer 2, and Saleen_Car_04 should be layer 3.

3   Go to time 3;00, select all three layers, and press Alt-] (Windows) or Option-] (Mac OS) to trim the layers' Out points to the current time.

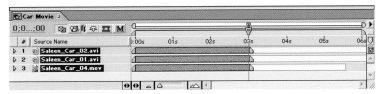

Trimming the Out points of the Saleen_Car layers

4   With the three layers still selected, choose Animation > Keyframe Assistant > Sequence Layers. Use these effect settings:

   Overlap: On

   Duration: 1;15

   Transition: Dissolve Front Layer

Press U on your keyboard to view the Opacity keyframes created by this command.

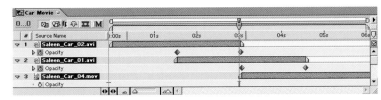

Viewing the sequenced layers

Putting It All Together

Now that all the major components are finished, you can assemble them into a master composition:

1   Create a new composition named Heartbeat Master in your **Comps** folder using the NTSC DV, 720 × 480 comp preset, with Duration 10;00 seconds.

2   Add the Heart Monitor composition to the Heartbeat Master Timeline at time 0;00.

3   To fade in the Heart Monitor layer, add a 0% Opacity keyframe at time 0;00 and a 100% Opacity keyframe at time 0;15.

4   To fade out the Heart Monitor layer, add a 100% Opacity keyframe at time 8;15 and a 0% Opacity keyframe at time 9;29.

5   Add the Car Movie composition to the Heartbeat Master Timeline at time 0;00, above the Heart Monitor layer.

6   To fade the Car Movie layer in and out, copy the Heart Monitor layer's Opacity keyframes, paste them onto the Car Movie layer at time 0;00, and then move the third Opacity keyframe to time 5;00 and the fourth keyframe to time 6;00.

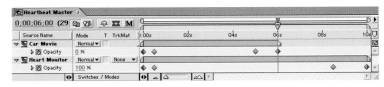

Adding Opacity keyframes to fade the layers in and out

7   Set the Car Movie layer's Blending Mode to Add in the Timeline's Modes column. This mode combines the color in the layer with those below it.

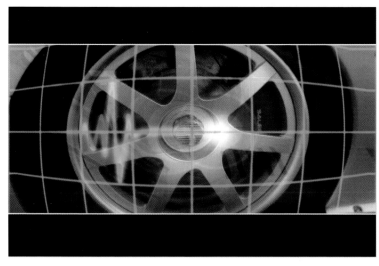

The grid and heartbeat appear within the Car Movie layer.

Now Try This

To add this project's finishing touches, create the following remaining elements:

- To blur the Saleen logo into the scene, drag the **Saleen_logo_Layers** file to the Heartbeat Master Timeline at time 6;00, and duplicate the layer. Move one of the Saleen_logo layers to start at time 7;00. Apply the Fast Blur effect to the Saleen_logo layer that starts at time 6;00.

- Add a letterbox to the scene by adding a new comp-size Solid layer at time 0;00, colored black (RGB: 0, 0, 0). Use the Rectangular Mask tool to outline the letterbox's middle area, and set the Mask Mode to Subtract. Apply Effect > Render > Stroke to the Solid layer to outline the subtracted area with color, and set the effect's Color to white (RGB: 255, 255, 255).

- Add a text layer that displays *THE DRIVE OF YOUR LIFE*, and position it so it appears below the SALEEN logo in the composition window. Fade in this text layer so it appears after the text layer *THE DRIVE...* is totally in focus.

| # Exotic Sketch-a-Car

I'm a huge sports car fan, so I was easily inspired when I finally got my hands on a Saleen S7. Taking that car for a spin was an experience right out of the many commercials you've probably seen, where driving appears tantamount to an out-of-body experience as the driver speeds through the countryside. I started thinking about how much fun it must be to design a car like this—not the hard parts, such as aerodynamics, electromechanicals, and such, but drawing the car and watching it come to life. That's when Chapter 18 was born.

In this chapter, you'll use a third-party effect from Boris FX that makes tracing an image of a car like the Saleen S7 quite simple. Not only does the effect create a drawing of the car, but it also automatically animates the drawing as the footage of the rotating car plays. In addition, you'll learn how to make the drawing appear to be drawn onto the screen by using a different effect provided in After Effects.

It Works Like This

Check out the **Ch18FinishedProject.mov** file in this chapter's folder on the book's DVD. To achieve those results, you'll do the following:

1. Use the Cartooner effect to create animated sketches from video footage.

2. Create a still image from a frame of your footage.

3. Use the Vector Paint effect to matte the car sketch, and animate the matte so the sketch appears to be drawn onscreen.

4. Quickly create some masks that will frame videos with color strokes.

5. Create a gridded background.

6. Use a quick method to isolate the car from its black background.

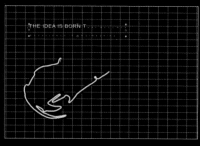

A sketch of the car draws itself onto the screen as the first slogan scales in.

The car reveals itself as other footage plays.

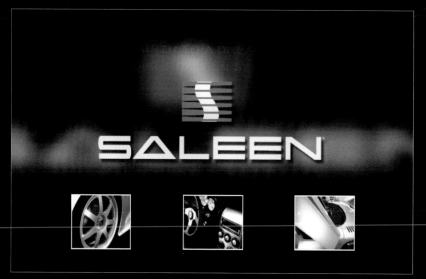

The car footage moves into place as the logo reveals itself.

Preparing to Work

This chapter's project requires four movie clips and a still, all of which are provided on the book's DVD. The car sketch you'll design requires the Cartooner effect from Boris FX. To animate the sketch, you'll need the Vector Paint effect, which is only available with the Professional version of After Effects. You'll start by importing the project files and creating a new composition.

To prepare for this project, do the following:

1   This project requires the Vector Paint effect, which is only available with the Professional version of After Effects. If you don't have the Professional version of After Effects installed, you can install a demo version of the software from this book's DVD.

2   If you don't have the Continuum Complete collection of effects from Boris FX installed into After Effects, you can install a trial version of the effects from this book's DVD. Once you've done so, a slew of submenus named BCC will appear in the Effect menu in After Effects.

3   Start with a new project, and save it as Ch18CarSketch.

4   Import the **Footage** and **Stills** folders from this chapter's folder on the book's DVD. The **Footage** folder contains four AVI files: **Saleen_Car_01**, **Saleen_Car_02**, **Saleen_Car_4**, and **Saleen_Car_07**; the **Stills** folder contains a PSD file named **Saleen_logo_Layers**.

5   Create a new composition named Car, using the NTSC DV, 720 × 480 composition preset, with Duration 10;00 seconds.

Sketching the Car

There are a number of ways to create a sketch of the Saleen car that is featured in all the movie clips you imported. To make the sketch appear to be drawn onto the screen, you'll animate the Vector Paint effect, so it really doesn't matter how you create the underlying sketch for the initial sequence. You could use one of the filters from the Artistic category in Photoshop to transform the car's appearance into a sketch, or simply draw a stroked path in After Effects. In this project, though, we'll show you how to quickly generate a more malleable sketch by using the Cartooner effect from Boris FX. The primary advantage of using this effect is that the lines the effect generates automatically move as the footage the effect is affecting moves; so, as the Saleen car rotates, the effect's sketch rotates too.

Follow these steps:

1   Place the **Saleen_Car_07.avi** file in the Car Timeline at time 3;00.

2   Apply Effect > BCC3 Effects > BCC Cartooner, and set the effect's property values as listed here:

Edge Source: None

Edges From: Luma

Threshold: 127

Pre Blur: 2

Width: Constant

Stroke Width: 2.5

Stroke Distance: 0

Post Blur: 1

Post Blur Quality: Gaussian Low

Intensity: 50

Color: RGB: 235, 235, 235

Ambient Light, Ambient Follow: 0

Alpha: Source Alpha

Reduce Flicker: Off

Apply Mode: Normal

Apply Mix: 100

Mix with Original: 0

Pixel Chooser: Off

In addition to outlining the highlights on the car, the Cartooner effect outlined the shape of the object on the left side of the composition. You don't want that object sketched into the scene, so you'll mask it out next:

1   To exclude the shape on the left, use the Pen tool to draw a mask around the Saleen car.

2   The car rotates in the footage, so go to time 6;00 and adjust the shape of the mask if the mask cuts off the car's shape.

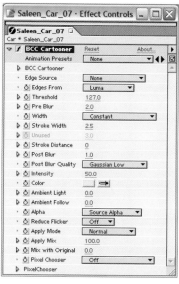

Settings for the BCC Cartooner effect in the Effect Controls window

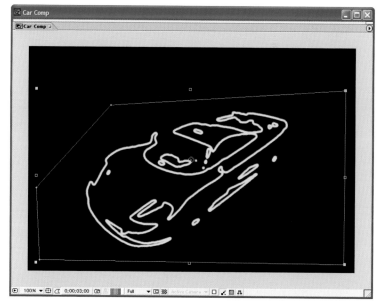

Masking the car to restrict the layer's visible area

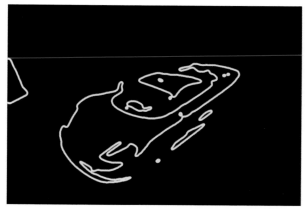

The Cartooner effect applied to the Saleen_Car_07 layer

Capturing a Still

You need the car to stay still as it's sketched onto the screen, but the car in the Saleen_Car_07 layer begins rotating as soon as the footage is played. To get around this behavior, you'll capture the first frame of the footage and add the resulting file to the Car Timeline. The captured Photoshop file will play first, followed by the car's footage. You'll animate the Cartooner effect to create a transition between the two sequences:

1 To capture a frame of the composition, go to time 3;00, choose Composition > Save Frame As > File, and save the file as **Car (0;00;03;00).psd** to the same location as the main project file. (Notice that the default filename helpfully reflects the name of the comp and the current time.)

   The Render Queue window opens for you to render the frame to a file in the next step.

2 Expand the Output Module option in the Render Queue window, set the Post-Render Action option to Import, and then click Render.

   When the rendering is complete, the rendered frame appears in the Project window using the name that you assigned it.

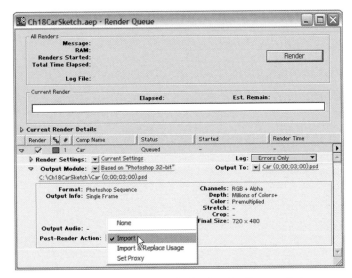

Rendering the captured frame with the Render Queue window

3 Place the **Car (0;00;03;00).psd** file in the Car Timeline so it starts at time 0;00 and is above the Saleen_Car_07 layer.

4 Go to time 3;00, and press Alt (Windows) or Option (Mac OS) and the] key to trim the Car (0;00;03;00) layer's Out point to the current time.

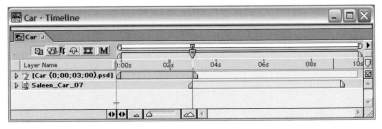

Trimming the Photoshop layer's duration

5 Still at time 3;00, add a Mix With Original keyframe with a value of 0.0 to the Saleen_Car_07 layer's BCC Cartooner effect.

6 Go to time 5;00, and change the Mix With Original value to 100%.

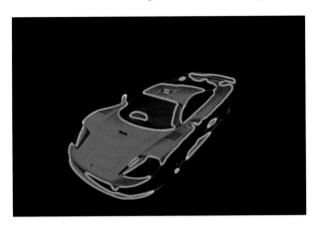

The Cartooner effect fades away to reveal the Saleen car.

Click the Ram Preview button in the Time Controls palette to view the current results. The still of the sketched car plays (actually, it sits still—heh, heh) for the first three seconds, and then the outlines of the car fade away to reveal the car footage.

Animating the Sketch

It's time to animate the car sketch so it appears to be drawn onscreen. Instead of animating the lines in the frame that you captured from the Saleen_Car_07 footage, you'll animate a continuous paint stroke that you'll draw with the Vector Paint effect. The paint stroke will serve as a matte, which you'll animate to reveal the car's sketch over time:

1   Rename the Car (0;00;03;00) layer to AniSketch in the Car composition.

2   Apply Effect > Paint > Vector Paint to the AniSketch layer. Expand the effect's Brush Settings group, and then set the effect's Radius to 7.0. This brush size will make it easy to cover the entire width of the lines you created with the Cartooner effect.

Set the effect's color to something other than white or black so you can make sure you paint over all the white lines in the car sketch and can see your paint strokes over the black background.

Note: Now that you've applied the Vector Paint effect, notice that Vector Paint tools appear in the upper-left corner of the Composition window. The tools appear only when you have the Vector Paint effect selected in either the Timeline or Effect Controls window.

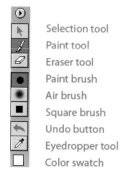

Selection tool
Paint tool
Eraser tool
Paint brush
Air brush
Square brush
Undo button
Eyedropper tool
Color swatch

The Vector Paint effect's tools and properties

3   Using the effect's Paint tool and Paint brush, trace the car line in the AniSketch layer at time 0;00. Don't release your mouse button until you've traced over every line; trace the car body first and then the accents. The resulting car outline will look pretty messy.

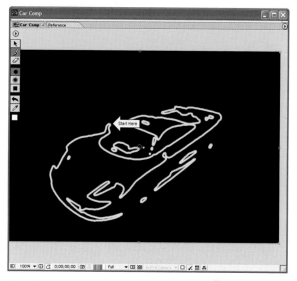

Start the paint stroke where the arrow is pointing in this illustration.

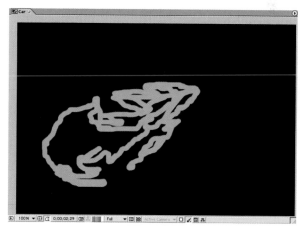

The result of painting over the car lines with the Vector Paint tools

4   Go to time 3;00, and set the Vector Paint effect's Playback Mode to Animate Strokes. When you change the Playback Mode, a new Playback Speed effect property appears, and a short fat stroke appears over only a small part of the car outline.

5   Still at time 3;00, scrub the Playback Speed value until the fat paint stroke completely covers the car outline. You want to find the minimum value that covers the outline completely so there is no delay in the animation when it transitions to the movie layer.

6   Set the Composite Paint option to As Matte. Now you should see the car sketch instead of the Vector Paint stroke.

Click the Ram Preview button in the Time Controls palette to view your animation. The car's sketch should appear to be drawn onscreen by an invisible hand, followed by the footage of the car. If you need to adjust the paint stroke, you must retrace the entire car outline—you can't adjust the stroke as you can other paths in After Effects.

Adding the Three Movies

You've placed, sketched, and animated the primary element of this project: the footage of the Saleen car's exterior. Now you'll stack three smaller videos to the right of the car. After you position and scale the movies, you'll mask them without ever touching the Composition and Timeline windows or the menu commands (intrigued?), and then you'll outline the movies in white to give them more definition.

Here are the steps:

1   To semi-automatically put the remaining footage into the Timeline in the right layer order, click the **Saleen_Car_04.avi** file in the Project window to select it. Then hold down Ctrl (Windows) or Command (Mac OS), and click the **Saleen_Car_02.avi** file followed by the **Saleen_Car_01.avi** file.

2   Go to time 3;00, and drag the selected footage items to the Car Timeline above the other two layers. The new layers should be stacked with the first item you selected in the Project window at the top of the layer stack, followed by the other items you selected, in the order you selected them.

3   Select the top three layers, press the S key on your keyboard, and set the layers' Scale values to 20, 20%.

4   Reduce the Scale for the AniSketch and Saleen_Car_07 layers to 90, 90%.

5   Set the Position for each layer as follows:

Layer 1: 570, 370

Layer 2: 570, 240

Layer 3: 570, 110

Layer 4: 280, 240

Layer 5: 280, 240

Positioning the layers

The layout

6 Select the first layer in the Car Timeline, and then double-click the Rectangular Mask tool in the Tools palette to automatically make a mask that surrounds the layer.

Repeat this step for layers 2 and 3.

7 Select all three top layers, and choose Effect > Render > Stroke. Set the effect's Brush Size property to 15. The effect uses the mask's path by default, so a white line surrounds each video.

Stroking the three footage items

Sketching the three videos

One of the most useful aspects of the Cartooner effect is that the resulting sketch is automatically animated if the footage you applied the effect to contains motion. For example, if you watch the Saleen_Car_07 layer, you'll see that the lines in the Cartooner effect rotate along with the car the effect sketches. In this section, you'll use the same effect to sketch the three small videos and then fade out the effect to reveal the videos:

1 To keep the three small videos from popping on the screen in unison, move layer 2 to start at time 3;10 and layer 1 to start at time 3;20.

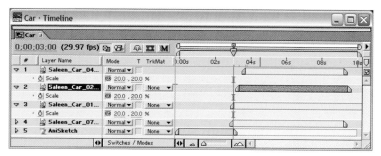

Staggering the In points

2 Go to time 8;00, select the top four layers (not the AniSketch layer), and then press Alt+Shift+T (Windows) or Option+Shift+T (Mac OS) to add a 100% Opacity keyframe to each selected layer.

3 Go to time 9;00, and change the selected layers' Opacity values to 0%.

4 Select only the top three layers in the Car Timeline, and then apply Effect > BCC3 Effects > BCC Cartooner to them.

5 Go to time 4;00, and add a Mix With Original keyframe with a value of 0 to the BCC Cartooner effect for each of the top three layers.

Notice that you must add each keyframe separately; you can't create the keyframe for all three layers simultaneously as you can with native effects.

6 Go to time 5;00, and change the top three layers' Mix With Original values to 100% in the BCC Cartooner effect. This setting fades in the full color of the original movies in unison with the main movie.

Animating the videos

To make room for the logo reveal that closes the animation, you need to animate the three video boxes to slide downward and to the left below the Saleen car:

1   In the Car Timeline, select the top three layers, and press P to display the layers' Position properties.

2   Go to time 6;15, and add Position keyframes to the top three layers.

3   Go to time 7;00, and change the Position values as follows:

> Layer 1: 170, 370
>
> Layer 2: 570, 370
>
> Layer 3: 570, 240

4   Go to time 7;15, and change the Position values as follows:

> Layer 2: 370, 370
>
> Layer 3: 570, 370

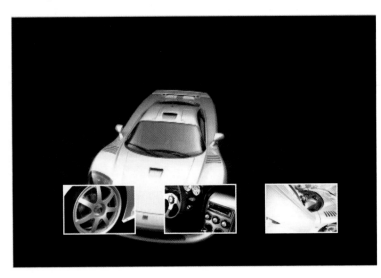

The final layout of the three video boxes

Adjusting the levels

Now that the base project is complete, you may notice a few things that could use a little adjusting. For starters, the top video box is brighter than the others, and it's a different color. Instead of correcting the top video, though, you'll brighten the other two layers since their tones are a little flat. You'll adjust the color in the next section after you've nested the Car composition into a new parent composition; then you can adjust the color of all the layers by applying an effect to the nested composition.

Follow these steps:

1   Select the Saleen_Car_02 and Saleen_Car_04 layers in the Car Timeline, and apply Effect > Adjust > Levels to the layers.

2   With both layers still selected in the Timeline, set the Levels effect's Input White property to 150 in the Effect Controls window. (Setting this value for one of the layer's Levels effect sets the value for both selected layers.)

Creating a Grid

Now you'll give the project some added pizzazz by creating a gridded background. Creating the grid is easy, thanks to the Grid effect, but making the black area around the Saleen car transparent is tricky. You'll start by creating a new composition to contain the work you've done so far, the grid, and the remaining elements of this project, including the company logo and slogans:

1   Create a new composition named Master, using the NTSC DV, 720 × 480 composition preset, with Duration 10;00 seconds.

2   Drag the Car composition into the Master Timeline starting at time 0;00.

3   Select the Car layer and apply Effect > Adjust > Hue/Saturation. Turn on the effect's Colorize option (under the Master Lightness property), and set the effect's Colorize Hue property to 0 x +140.0

4 Go to time 0;00, and create a new comp-size Solid layer named Grid that's any color. (The Grid effect that you'll apply to this layer will override the layer's original color.)

5 Move the Grid layer to the bottom of the layer stack in the Master Timeline.

6 Apply Effect > Render > Grid to the Grid layer, and set the effect's properties as follows:

> Size From: Width & Height Sliders
>
> Border: 3.0
>
> Opacity: 50.0%
>
> Color: Green (RGB: 0, 255, 0)

7 To fade in the Grid layer, add a 0% Opacity keyframe at time 0;00 and then change the layer's Opacity to 100% at time 0;15.

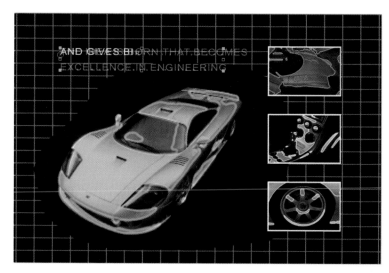

The underlying grid reveals a black-colored miasma around the car.

Removing the car's black background

The black area that surrounds the car currently covers the underlying areas of the grid and needs to be removed. The first solution that might come to your mind is to use the Color Key effect, which hides all pixels that contain a range of colors that you specify. Unfortunately, the black background contains a wide range of dark hues that also appear within the car; as a result, portions of the car would become transparent, and the grid would appear through the car's frame.

You could use the Inner/Outer Key effect and a new mask drawn around the car to restrict the layer's visibility to the car, but that would require you to animate the mask. That effect provides the best results but requires the most time and patience.

Instead, you'll create a duplicate layer and use blending modes to quickly hide the car's black background:

1 Open the Car composition, and duplicate the Saleen_Car_07 layer.

2 Set the Track Matte of the bottommost Saleen_Car_07 layer to Luma Matte "Saleen_Car_07.avi 2".

3 Add a 100% Opacity keyframe to each Saleen_Car_07 layer at time 6;16, and then change each layer's Opacity to 0% at time 7;15.

***

Tip: If you return to the Master composition, you'll see that the black area isn't visible around the car; however, the grid bleeds through the car in different areas as a result of the Luma Matte. To fix this, you can add solid layers and mask them to fill in the headlights and windshield; these shapes are simple enough that you can then animate the position of each solid layer as needed.

Adding the Background Car

The background is almost done, now that you've created the grid and fixed up the foreground car. To finish it, you'll add another version of the Saleen_Car_07 footage that you'll make play at a slightly different rate than the original. Do the following:

1   Go to time 3;00 in the Master composition's Timeline, and add **Saleen_Car_07.avi** from the Project window to the Timeline at the bottom of the layer stack.

2   Select the new layer, and choose Layer > Time Stretch. Set the Stretch Factor New Duration to 7;00 in the resulting dialog, and click OK.

As a result, the layer plays at a slower rate than the same footage that appears in the Car composition.

3   Set the layer's Scale to 200, 200%.

4   Apply Effect > Blur & Sharpen > Fast Blur to the Saleen_Car_07 layer, and set the effect's Blurriness to 10.

5   To fade in the layer, add a 0% Opacity keyframe at time 3;00 and a 100% Opacity keyframe at time 5;00.

6   To fade out the layer, change its Opacity to 50% at time 8;00 and 0% at time 9;00.

Now Try This

To finish your project, you need to add a company slogan that reveals itself as the car is sketched onto the screen and another slogan that replaces the first when the car reveals itself. Both slogans scale themselves into place one character at a time. You can quickly create that effect by using a Text Animator rather than animating the Scale property in the Transform group. In addition, you can animate the Saleen logo for the final closing sequence.

To complete these remaining elements, follow these steps:

1   In the Master composition at time 1;00, add a text layer that displays *THE IDEA IS BORN THAT BECOMES* on one line followed by *EXCELLENCE IN ENGINEERING.*

2   Choose Scale from the layer's Animate menu in the Timeline. Add a Start keyframe and a Scale keyframe to the Animator with a value of 0 for each keyframe, and then change each property's value to 100% at time 3;00.

3   Animate the layer's Opacity from 100% at time 4;00 to 0% at time 5;00.

4   Add the second slogan by duplicating the THE IDEA IS… text layer, and move the top text layer so it starts at time 4;00.

5   Double-click the top text layer in the Timeline to select the characters, and then type AND GIVES BIRTH TO A DREAM on one line and THE INCREDIBLE SALEEN S7 on the next line.

Because of the Scale and Opacity animation in the text layer, you won't see all the text you type unless you go to time 6;00.

6   Add the **Saleen_logo_Layers.psd** file to the top of the Master Timeline, and then duplicate the layer.

7   Animate the Scale of the bottom logo layer to simulate a text-tracking effect.

8   Apply a Blur effect to the bottom logo layer, and then animate the blur.

9   Animate the Opacity of both logo layers from 0% at time 6;00 to 100% at time 7;00 to fade the layers into the scene.

10   Apply the Drop Shadow effect to the top logo layer.

Tip: To save the text animation (Opacity and Scale) for reuse later in another project, select the text layer in the Timeline, and choose Animation > Save Animation Preset. To save only the Scale animation, expand the text layer's Text group in the Timeline, click the Animator 1 name to select it, and then choose Animation > Save Animation Preset.

CHAPTER 19

Tracking Reflections

Reflections are often used in advertising to communicate things subtly—and sometimes not so subtly. For example, some liquor advertisers have included subliminal images in the ice in shots of their product. I was inspired by such usage when I was trying to find a way to enhance some footage of the dashboard in a Saleen S7 car. By adding content in virtual reflections in the dashboard gauges, I was able to make the dashboard footage show off additional angles of the car and a woman. In this case, the effect isn't intended to be subliminal; instead, the reflections are meant to excite the viewer's curiosity.

This chapter's project shows you how to use the Motion Trackers in After Effects to track the motion in video footage, and how to deal with motion that runs offscreen. In addition to tracking the position of a region, you'll track Scale (new in version 6.5) by tracking the distance between two regions.

It Works Like This

Check out the **Ch19FinishedProject.mov** file in this chapter's folder on the book's DVD to see the final results of this project. The primary steps will show you how to create the first sequence of the finished movie. The project's remaining sequences are fairly straightforward to create and are listed in the "Now Try This" section at the end of the chapter.

You'll do the following:

1. Scale and mask footage to fit within the dashboard's three gauges to create virtual reflections.

2. Create motion paths for two of the virtual reflections by tracking the Position and Scale of the car gauges.

3. Use a layer's Anchor Point to animate it offscreen.

4. Use parenting to create the motion for a third virtual reflection.

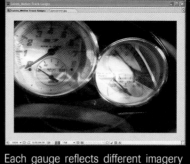

Each gauge reflects different imagery on the car's dashboard.

The dashboard footage fades into footage of the car's exterior.

The logo and slogan animate into the scene

Preparing to Work

The primary element in the first sequence of the final project is moving footage of a Saleen car's dashboard. The dashboard contains three circular gauges on which you'll create virtual reflections of two additional movies and a still image. You'll import that footage and the Saleen logo in this section and create the composition for the first sequence.

To prepare for this project, do the following:

1   Start with a new project, and name it Ch19TrackingReflections.

2   Import the **Footage** and **Stills** folders as footage from this chapter's folder on the book's DVD. (The **Footage** folder contains three AVI files, and the **Stills** folder contains one JPEG file and a PSD file.)

3   Create a new composition named Reflections, using the NTSC DV, 720 × 80 composition preset, with Duration 10;00 seconds.

Creating the First Reflection

The dashboard in this project's first sequence contains three gauges: a speedometer, an RPM gauge, and a fuel gauge. In this section, you'll create a reflection over the speedometer. To create the reflection in the dashboard, your first tasks are to position and scale the reflection's source imagery and to mask the face of the gauge. You'll animate the reflection in the next section.

Follow these steps:

1   Add the **Saleen_Car_06.avi** and **Saleen_Car_02.avi** files to the Reflections Timeline at time 0;00. **Saleen_Car_06.avi** is the dashboard footage, and **Saleen_Car_02.avi** will be the source for your first reflection, so make sure the **Saleen_Car_02.avi** file is the top layer.

2   Rename the Saleen_Car_02 layer Speedometer and the Saleen_Car_06 layer Car Gauges.

3   Change the Speedometer layer's Opacity to 50% and Scale to 73, 73%.

4   Line up the Speedometer layer so that the base of the gearshift is at the center of the first gauge (the speedometer).

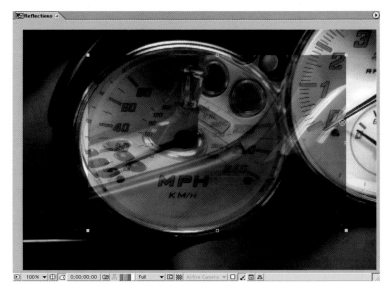

Positioning the Speedometer layer

5   Use the Elliptical Mask tool in the Speedometer layer to create a circular mask that surrounds the white face of the speedometer.

Tip: Press Shift as you drag with the Elliptical Mask tool to create a circular shape instead of an ellipse. Press Shift-Ctrl (Windows) or Shift-Command (Mac OS) as you drag to draw a circle that's centered around the spot where you first click.

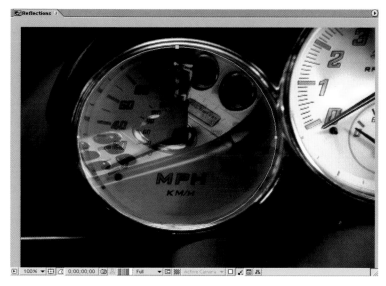

Masking the speedometer's face

6   To soften the edges of the mask so the resulting reflection is more realistic, set the mask's Mask Feather to 50, 50.

7   To give the Speedometer layer more punch, apply Effect > Adjust > Brightness & Contrast to the layer. Set the effect's Brightness to –7 and Contrast to 39.

Animating the first reflection

You've shaped the speedometer's first reflection (the Speedometer layer). Now you need to animate it so it mimics the position of the speedometer in the Car Gauges layer. To animate the reflection, you'll track the Position and Scale (new in After Effects 6.5) in the speedometer gauge in the Car Gauges layer and apply the motion path to the reflection:

1   Select the Car Gauges layer in the Reflections composition, and choose Animation > Track Motion. The Layer window opens for the Car Gauges layer, and a Track Point is added in the middle of the window.

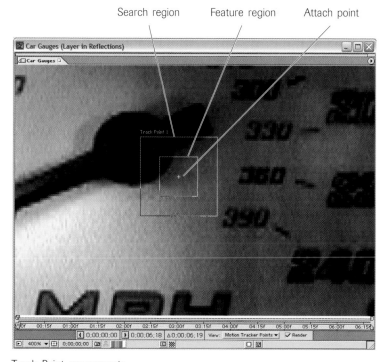

Track Point components

2 Drag the entire Track Point to the number 0 on the RPM gauge on the right side of layer window.

To drag the entire Track Point, hold your mouse pointer anywhere within the Track Point except on a line or the attach point (the crosshairs in the center); when your mouse pointer is in position to move the entire Track Point, the pointer displays the Move Track Point icon .

Dragging with this mouse pointer moves the entire Track Point.

3 Increase the Track Point's search region (the outer box) so it's about double its original size, and then increase the feature region (the inner box) so it surrounds the number 0 and the black circle below the number. (To change the size of either region, drag any corner handle of the region.)

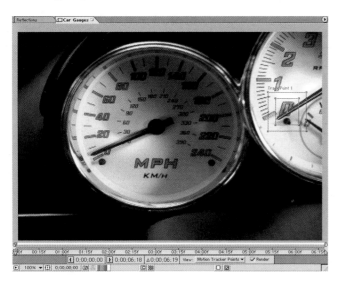

Starting positions for the search and feature regions

The area within the feature region is what the motion tracker will try to stay aligned over as the footage plays. Your objective is to position this region over an area that contains something distinct that the motion tracker won't easily lose sight of. The number 0 and the black circle are clearly defined visual targets for the motion tracker, but they move a great deal; so, you want to make sure the search region is large.

Tip: When you move a Track Point's feature region, the area within the region is magnified by default. You can turn this option off or on by choosing Magnify Feature When Dragging from the Tracker Controls palette menu.

4 Still in the Car Gauges layer window, go to time 5;06 and click the Set Out Point button ▐. At time 5;06, the area you're tracking moves out of the screen and can't be tracked.

Note: You may wonder why you're tracking the RPM gauge on the right instead of the speedometer gauge in the center of the first frame in the footage. Excellent question. The problem with the speedometer is that it leaves the screen much sooner than the gauge you're tracking, so after a few seconds there's nothing to track. In the next few steps, you'll learn how to track something even after it goes offscreen.

5 Turn on the Scale option in the Tracker Controls palette. A second Track Point appears in the Car Gauges layer window.

6   Move the entire Track Point 2 so it's above Track Point 1 and on top of the number 2 in the RPM gauge on the right. Expand the search region of Track Point 2 to give you room to expand the feature region within it, and then expand the feature region to surround the gauge's number 2.

Now, as the gauge becomes larger or smaller, the tracker will record this change in scale by tracking the distance between the two track points.

Tracking the distance between the numbers 0 and 2 on the gauge to track Scale

7   Go to time 0;00 in the Car Gauges layer window, and click the Analyze Forward button in the Tracker Controls palette.

As the footage plays and the motion is tracked, pay attention to the feature region of each Track Point; if a region starts drifting away from the area it was originally tracking, click the Stop button in the Tracker Controls palette, and then click the Analyze 1 Frame Backward button

until you reach the frame where the drifting began. Then adjust the Feature Region (the inner box) so that it's over a better area to track. After adjusting the feature region, click the Analyze Forward button again to resume tracking. After Effects automatically replaces the drifting points in the motion path with new points.

The Analyze Forward button on the Tracker Controls palette

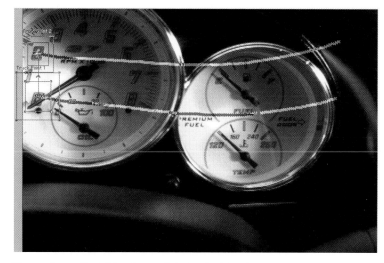

The motion paths of the two points tracked on the gauge

8   To apply the motion path to the Speedometer layer, make sure the Motion Target option in the Tracker Controls palette is set to Speedometer; then click Apply in the palette, choose X And Y in the Motion Tracker Apply Options dialog, and click OK.

Expand the Position, Scale, and Anchor Point of the Speedometer layer in the Timeline. You'll see that the tracking process has created the Scale and Position keyframes needed to mimic the motion in the Car Gauges layer.

Your goal in tracking the motion of the RPM gauge is to make the Speedometer layer mimic the motion of the Car Gauges layer. If you preview the movie, you'll see that it's not quite what you may have expected: The virtual reflection isn't aligned with the speedometer. That's because you have one more adjustment to make:

1   Go to time 0;00, and adjust the Speedometer layer's Anchor Point until the layer is within the gauge on the speedometer. Doing so offsets the image and keeps its motion on track as it goes offscreen.

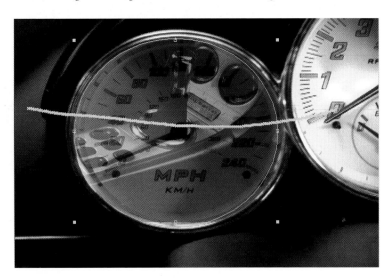

The Speedometer layer in position at time 0;00

2   At time 0;00, add a 0% Opacity keyframe to the Speedometer layer.

3   At time 1;00, change the layer's Opacity to 30%.

4   Change the layer's Blending Mode to Add in the Timeline's Modes column.

Now click the Ram Preview button in the Time Controls palette to see what you've accomplished so far. If you need to fine-tune the reflection's position at any point, you can add Anchor Point keyframes to the Speedometer layer and adjust the Anchor Point value until the reflection is in the right position.

Creating the Second Reflection

Now that you've created the first reflection, creating the second reflection for the RPM gauge should go smoothly. You won't be able to copy and paste the values from the first reflection because, among other things, the duration and image size are different. Instead, you'll use the same process you used to create the first reflection (you'll use a different process for the third reflection later in this chapter):

1   Add the **Model.jpg** file from the Project window to the Reflections Timeline at time 0;00, and set the layer's Opacity to 50%.

2   Go to time 3;00, and position the Model layer so that it's centered over the RPM gauge.

3   Use the Elliptical Mask tool on the Model layer to draw a circle around the white face of the RPM gauge.

4   Set the mask's Mode to Add and Feather to 50, 50.

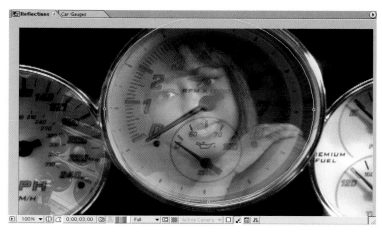

Masking the Model layer over the RPM gauge

Animating the second reflection

You'll animate the second reflection using the same methods you used to
animate the first reflection. This time, though, you'll track different points
on the Car Gauges layer and add a second tracker to the layer:

1   Double-click the Car Gauge layer in the Timeline to open it in a layer.

2   Go to time 0;15, and click the Set In Point button [⟨] in the Car
     Gauges window.

3   Go to time 6;00, and click the Set Out Point button in the Layer
     window. This is the last frame before the image goes past the edge of
     the comp.

4   Choose Animation > Track Motion, and make sure Position and Scale
     are turned on in the Tracker Controls palette.

     Expand the Car Gauges layer and its Motion Trackers group in the
     Timeline and note that the layer has two trackers now: the tracker that
     you used to track motion for the first reflection you created, and the
     tracker you just created for the second reflection.

Tip: To make it easier to distinguish the current tracker from the
tracker you used for the first reflection, rename each tracker in the
Timeline. To rename a tracker, click the tracker's name in the Timeline,
press Enter on your keyboard, and then type a unique name.

5   Move Track Point 1 over the black center dial of the RPM gauge.

6   Place Track Point 2 over the picture of the oil can on the gauge.
     Adjust the search and feature regions of each Track Point as needed.

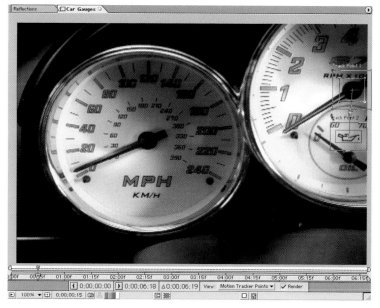

Aligning the tracker for the second reflection

7   Click the Edit Target button in the Tracker Controls palette, choose
     Model.jpg from the Layer menu, and click OK.

8   Click the Analyze Forward button in the Tracker Controls palette.

Just as before, pay attention to the feature region (inner box) of each Track Point; if a Track Point starts drifting away from the area it was originally tracking, click Analyze 1 Frame Backward until you reach the frame where the drifting started, and then adjust the feature region so it's over a better area to track. After adjusting the feature region, click the Analyze Forward button again to replace the drifting points in the motion path.

9   Once you're satisfied with the motion path, click Apply in the Tracker Controls palette, choose X And Y in the options dialog, and then click OK.

If you expand the Model layer in the Timeline, you'll see the Scale and Position keyframes that the motion tracker added.

10 Adjust the Model layer's Anchor Point in the Timeline so that the image lies in the middle of the RPM gauge.

11 To fade in the Model layer, add a 0% Opacity keyframe to the layer at time 0;00, and change the layer's Opacity at time 1;00 to 40%.

12 To fade out the layer, add another 40% Opacity keyframe at time 4;15, and then go to time 6;00 and change the layer's Opacity to 0%.

Click the Ram Preview button in the Time Controls palette to see the results.

Parenting the Third Reflection

Motion tracking is straightforward when you have footage like the Car Gauges layer that contains distinct contrasting visual elements that are easily tracked. However, the process can get a little tedious no matter how accurate the resulting motion path is. This time, you'll use a simpler technique that capitalizes on the motion you've already tracked:

1   Go to time 0;00, and add **Saleen_Car_08.avi** to the top of the Timeline's layer stack.

2   Go to time 5;00, and change the layer's Opacity to 50% and Scale to 60%.

3   Position the image so that it's over the fuel gauge to the right of the RPM gauge.

4   Use the Elliptical Mask tool on the Saleen_Car_08 layer to mask it to the gauge's white face.

5   Set the mask's Mode to Add and Feather to 50 pixels.

6   Set the Saleen_Car_08 layer's Parent value to the Model layer in the Timeline's Parent column. Now the Saleen_Car_08 layer will mimic the motion of the Model layer.

7   To fade the reflection in and out, copy the Model layer's Opacity keyframes, and then paste the keyframes on the Saleen_Car_08 layer at time 0;00.

Housekeeping

You need to do one housekeeping chore. The Reflections comp's Duration can be shortened to 6;00 seconds because there's no animation beyond that point in time (the composition also fades out by that time). There are a few ways to accomplish this task; in this case, you'll use the Work Area bar and a command:

1   Set the Reflections composition's Work Area bar to span from 0;00 to 6;00.

The Work Area bar before trimming the Reflections composition's duration

2   Choose Composition > Trim Comp to Work Area.

Now Try This

You've done the hardest work by creating the first sequence for this chapter's final movie. What's left is to create a master composition that contains the sequence you created and then add the two remaining sequences: the second sequence is a piece of footage of the Saleen car's exterior, and the third is the Saleen logo and slogan. To complete these remaining elements, follow these steps:

1   Create a new Master composition that's 15 seconds long. Add the **Saleen_Car_08.avi** footage to the Master comp starting at time 4;00, fading it in from 0 to 100% Opacity from time 4;00 to time 6;00. Fade the layer out from time 9;00 to time 11;00.

2   Add the **Saleen_logo_layers.psd** footage to the Master Timeline at time 7;00, and animate the layer's Scale from 85, 85% at time 7;00 to 300, 300% at time 14;29. Fade in the layer from 0 to 100% Opacity from time 7;00 to time 8;15.

3   Duplicate the layer. Apply the Box Blur effect to the lower logo layer, and set the effect's Blur Radius to 21.0.

4   Change the Scale of the top logo layer to 100%. Apply the Drop Shadow effect to the layer, and set the effect's Opacity to 85%, Distance to 10, and Softness to 7.

5   To animate the slogan into the scene, create a text layer with Text Size 28px that displays *THE DRIVE OF YOUR LIFE*. Apply the Random Shuffle In text animation preset (from the Animate In category) and the Drop Shadow effect to the layer.

If you'd like to take this project even further, try this:

• Create three small light reflections by using Light layers or Solid layers with the Lens Flare effect. Parent the layers to the motion tracked layers.

• Apply the Hue/Saturation effect to all the video footage, and use the effect's Colorize option to make all the footage monochromatic.

• Apply the Bulge effect to the masked layers to distort the images to suggest the shape of the glass on the car gauges.

CHAPTER 20 | Designer's Corner

I like to watch do-it-yourself home renovation programs and shows that go into detail about crime forensics, such as *CSI* (*Crime Scene Investigation*)—basically, any program in which experts dissect something in order to construct something else. One recurring feature in do-it-yourself home renovation shows is a drawing that transforms into a full-color photograph of the actual final result.

In this chapter's project, you'll create a similar effect by fading a black-and-white pen sketch into a colored pencil sketch and finally into the photo the sketches are based on. You'll also use perspective corner pin motion tracking to map a movie onto a moving TV screen.

It Works Like This

Check out the **Ch20FinalProject.mov** file to see the final results of this chapter's project. The chapter shows you how to make still images of an office come to life. Here's an overview of the steps required to complete the project:

1. Assemble still photos of a room to create an animated sequence for the background that ends the final movie.

2. Animate a still image to create the zooming-out effect that opens the final movie.

3. Add transitions between the sketches, and animate them by assigning a Parent layer.

4. Track the motion in the still image you animated by using a Perspective Corner Pin tracker.

5. Apply the motion you tracked to a movie file, so the file fills the TV screen in the still image.

A close-up view of a sketch of a room zooms out to a full view.

The sketch fades to reveal the original photo.

The title slides into place by following a white path.

Preparing to Work

This chapter's project requires a series of still images that you'll use to build the background sequence and a movie file that you'll use to fill a TV screen, all of which are provided on this book's DVD. Two of the still images in PSD format are digital photographs that were modified with some of the Artistic filters in Photoshop to create the appearance of sketched drawings.

To prepare for this project, do the following:

1   Start with a new project, and save it as Ch20DesignersCorner.

2   Import the **Stills** and **Video** folders from this chapter's folder on the book's DVD.

3   Create a new composition named Master using the NTSC DV, 720 × 480 comp preset, with Duration 15;00.

Assembling the Background Sequence

You'll start this project by building the sequence of still images that plays in the background during the second half of the animation. The Sequence Layers command enables you to quickly lay out the images in time and create transitions between them. Then you can use the Hue/Saturation effect to reduce the images' colors to a single hue. Follow these steps:

1   Go to time 5;00, and place all the JPEG files (**Img_01–12**) from the **Stills** folder into the Master Timeline.

2   Select all the layers in the Timeline, go to time 7;00, and then press Alt (Windows) or Option (Mac OS) and the] key to trim the layers' Out points to the current time.

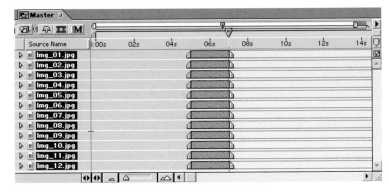

Trimming the layers' duration

3   With all the layers still selected, choose Animation > Keyframe Assistant > Sequence Layers. Select the Overlap option, set Duration to 1;00, set Transition to Dissolve Front Layer, and then click OK.

These options automatically spread the layers out over time and add Opacity keyframes to fade the layers from one to the other.

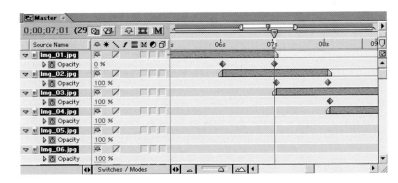

The Timeline after you apply the Sequence Layers command

4   With all the layers still selected, choose Layer > Pre-Compose to combine the layers into a single composition nested in the Master composition. Name the new composition Background.

5   Go to time 5;00, and press Alt (Windows) or Option (Mac OS) and the [key to trim the layer's In point to the current time.

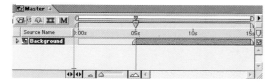

Trimming the Background layer's In point

6   Apply Effect > Adjust > Hue/Saturation to the Background layer. Turn on the effect's Colorize option (under the Master Lightness option), and set Colorize Hue to 0 x +220.0 and Colorize Saturation to 55.

Now every image that makes up the Background layer appears in blue hues.

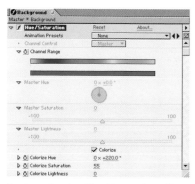

The effect's Colorize option gives the entire sequence a uniform hue.

Settings for the Hue/Saturation effect

If you preview the Master composition, you should briefly see one JPEG image at a time. Each image fades out as a different JPEG image fades in.

Getting the Big Picture

The animation that opens this project's final movie starts with a close-up view of a still image, which then moves away from the viewer on a zigzag path. In this section, you'll create those results by animating a still image's scale and position. You'll animate two other stills by assigning the animated still as their parent:

1   At time 0;00, place **Img_14bigSketch2.psd** into the Master Timeline under the Img_14bigSketch1 layer, and then place **Img_14bigSketch3.psd** under the Img_14bigSketch2 layer.

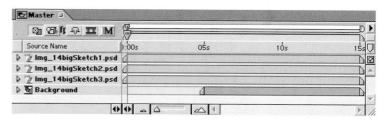

Adding the Sketch layers to the Master composition

2   Set the Parent value of the Img_14bigSketch2 and Img_14bigSketch3 layers to Img_14bigSketch1 in the Timeline's Parent column.

3   Add a 50, 50% Scale keyframe to the Img_14bigSketch1 layer as well as a Position keyframe with values 500, 220.

4   Go to time 4;00, and change the layer's Position to 360, 240.

5   Go to time 6;15, and change the layer's Scale to 12, 12%.

Because you're using parenting, you can modify the animation of all three layers by adjusting the keyframes of a single layer: the Parent layer.

Adding the TV Picture

The Img_14bigSketch images show a big-screen TV that doesn't display anything; in fact, the TV screen is transparent in the source file. Your next task is to fill the TV screen with the **FillMovie.mov** file, which shows a sequence of still images that should look very familiar since several of them are in the background layer you created. This task would be mighty simple if the still image that contains the TV stayed true to itself and remained still! Since you've animated it, though, you need to track the motion of the TV screen with a Perspective Corner Pin tracker and apply that motion data to the movie file. Even though you've animated the Img_14bigSketch1 layer, After Effects won't let you track the layer's motion, since it's a still image. To get around this, you'll pre-compose a duplicate copy of the layer and track the motion in the new composition.

Note: The motion-tracking features are available only in the Professional version of After Effects. If you have the Standard version, you can install a trial version of After Effects Professional from this book's DVD.

Here are the steps:

1   Go to time 0;00 in the Master Timeline, and place **FillMovie.mov** above the other layers in the Timeline.

2   Duplicate the Img_14bigSketch1 layer.

3   Select the duplicate copy (the topmost version), choose Layer > Pre-Compose, and click OK.

4   Select the pre-composed layer you just created, and choose Animation > Track Motion.

5   Set the Track Type option in the Tracker Controls palette to Perspective Corner Pin. Four Track Points appear in the layer window, one for each corner of the area you want to fill with the movie—in this case, the TV screen.

Motion-tracking settings in the Tracker Controls palette

6   Drag one Track Point onto each corner of the big-screen TV, which
    appears as a black rectangle in the left half of the layer window. To
    drag an entire Track Point, hold your mouse pointer anywhere within
    the Track Point except on a line or the attach point (the cross-hairs in
    the center); when your mouse pointer is in position to move the entire
    Track Point, the pointer displays the Move Track Point icon ![icon].

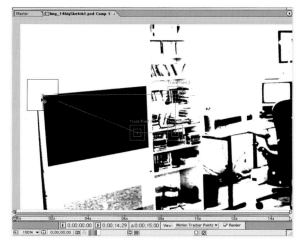

Positioning one of the Track Points

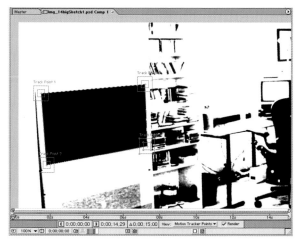

The Track Points in position to start tracking the TV screen's motion

Tracking the still's motion

Now that you've set up the perspective corner pin Track Points on each
corner of the TV screen, you can begin tracking the motion of the still
image. Follow these steps:

1   Go to time 6;15 in the Img_14bigSketch1 Comp 1 layer window, and
    click the Set Out Point button ![icon] at the bottom of the Layer win-
    dow. Clicking this button specifies where you want the motion tracker
    to stop tracking in time. The image stops moving at that point, so you
    don't need track the motion beyond that point in time.

2   Press the Home key on your keyboard to return to time 0;00, and
    click the Analyze Forward button in the Tracker Controls palette
    to track the motion. By default, your tracker is paying attention to
    the luminance within each feature region. Since each region is dis-
    tinctly black and white, the tracker should have no trouble tracking
    the motion of the TV screen. But even a minute amount of drifting
    or jumping can ruin the illusion, so keep a close eye on it and follow
    these guidelines:

    Pay attention to the feature region (the inner box) of each Track Point
    to ensure that none of the Track Points strays from the TV corner it's
    tracking; alternatively, you might find it easier to watch the lines that
    connect the four trackers to check for a line that strays from the shape
    of the TV screen. If any region starts drifting away from the TV screen
    corner it was originally tracking, click the Stop button in the Tracker
    Controls palette and then click the Analyze 1 Frame Backward but-
    ton until you reach the frame where the drifting began. Then, adjust
    the feature region so it's back on track and the lines between it and

the adjacent Track Points lie along the TV screen. After you adjust the feature region, click the Analyze Forward button again to resume tracking. After Effects automatically replaces the drifting points in the motion path with new points.

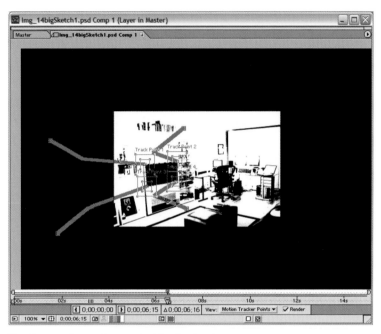

The four motion paths created by the tracker

3   Make sure the Motion Target option in the Tracker Controls palette is set to **Fill Movie.mov**, and then click the Apply button to add the motion data to that layer.

Return to the Master Composition window to preview the results. The FillMovie layer should appear within the TV screen and stay there as the Img_14bigSketch1 Comp 1 layer moves.

The FillMovie layer appears within the TV screen.

Revealing the Photo

You're ready to create a transition from the sketch of the room to the high-res photograph of the room. All the layers are in place, and it's just a matter of adding four well-placed keyframes:

1 Add a 100% Opacity keyframe to the Img_14bigSketch1 layer at time 2;00 in the Master Timeline. Go to time 3;00, and change the Opacity value to 0%.

2 Add a 100% Opacity keyframe to the Img_14bigSketch2 layer at time 3;00. Go to time 4;00, and change the Opacity value to 0%.

3 Go to time 5;00 so you can see the Img_14bigSketch3 layer in the Composition window.

4 To keep FillMovie from just popping on the screen, add a 0% Opacity keyframe to the layer at time 0;00, and then change the Opacity value to 100% at time 1;00.

5 To fade in the Background layer, add a 0% Opacity keyframe at time 5;00; then, go to 6;00 and change the value to 100%.

Now Try This

To design the remaining elements for this project and extend the project further, do the following:

• Add a WEEKDAYS 7PM text layer, and animate the layer into the scene using an Animation Preset from the Effects & Presets palette.

• To fade in the entire project, create a black Solid layer and animate it from 100% Opacity at time 0;00 to 0% Opacity at time 0;10.

• Add the DESIGNER'S CORNER text layer. Animate it into the scene by adding a rectangular mask to the layer, setting the Path property to the mask in the layer's Path Options group, and adding a Tracking animator.

• Apply the Stroke effect to the DESIGNER'S CORNER layer, and set the effect's Path property to the layer's mask to visualize the path that the text runs along.

• Duplicate the DESIGNER'S CORNER layer, and apply the Box Blur effect to the lower copy to add a blue blurred glow behind the main title.

• Apply the Stroke effect to the Img_14bigSketch3 layer to add a white outline to it.

CHAPTER 21 | Animated Filmstrip

This chapter was inspired by a project I created for a client who wanted to portray their company's history chronologically in brief snippets. I used After Effects and Photoshop to create a storyboard that illustrated my idea to animate a filmstrip passing across the screen. The strip speeds by, stops to play a movie within a film frame about some company milestone, speeds up until it reaches the next milestone and its movie, and so on. It's a rich effect and relatively easy to produce with After Effects.

This chapter's project demonstrates how to create a filmstrip that contains video inside each frame instead of still images. You'll animate the filmstrip so it alternates between fast-forwarding in a blur and slowing down to provide glimpses of the videos playing in its frames.

It Works Like This

Check out the **Ch21FinishedProject.mov** file in this chapter's folder on the book's DVD to see the final results of this project. To get those results, you'll do the following:

1. Create a virtual filmstrip by masking out sprocket holes in a solid layer.

2. Add movie files to the strip to create the film frames.

3. Animate the entire filmstrip across the screen, making it slow down and speed up.

4. Create exaggerated motion blurring with—what else?—an effect.

The filmstrip enters the scene from below.

The filmstrip speeds forward in a blur...

...and slows down to give glimpses of the video playing in its frames.

Preparing to Work

This chapter's project requires only a single piece of video that you'll use to fill the frames of the filmstrip you'll build. You'll use the finished movie from Chapter 19, "Tracking Reflections" (found on the book's DVD), as your source footage. Your first composition will contain only the filmstrip, so naturally the composition will be long and skinny.

To prepare for this project, do the following:

1   Start with a new project, and save it as Ch21AnimatedFilmstrip.

2   Import the **Ch19FinishedProject.mov** file from the Chapter 19 folder on the book's DVD—yes, the Chapter 19 folder, not this chapter's folder (Chapter 21). You'll use that chapter's finished movie to create the filmstrip's frames.

3   Create a new composition named Film Strip with Width 320, Height 2000, Frame Rate 30, and Duration 15:00.

4   Choose Composition > Background Color, and set the color swatch to white (RGB: 255, 255, 255).

The Film Strip composition

Creating the Filmstrip

The Film Strip composition is so long that manipulating your layers and masks may be challenging if you're using only one monitor to display After Effects. Several techniques may help make the process a little easier; look for tips throughout the sections on creating the filmstrip.

You'll create the filmstrip from a Solid layer by masking out sprocket holes along each length of the solid. To help you judge the size you need to make your sprockets' masks, you'll add the first frame of the filmstrip for reference.

Follow these steps:

1   Create a comp-size Solid layer named Film Strip, colored black (RGB: 0, 0, 0), in the Film Strip composition.

2   Drag the **Ch19FinishedProject.mov** file to the top of the Film Strip Timeline starting at time 0:00.

3   Set the Ch19FinishedProject layer's Scale to 50, 50% and Position to 160, 100, which puts the layer near the top edge of the composition.

4   Use the Rectangular Mask tool to draw a small rectangle in the upper-left corner of the Film Strip layer. Make the mask a size that looks appropriate for a single sprocket hole in a filmstrip, and position it between the left edge of the solid and the left edge of the video layer.

Tip: To quickly zoom in toward the center of the composition for a closer view, slide the scroll wheel forward on your mouse. To zoom in to the area that lies under your mouse pointer, press Alt (Windows) or Option (Mac OS) as you slide the scroll wheel forward. Slide the mouse wheel backward to zoom outward. (These are new features in version 6.5 of After Effects.)

Your black solid should now appear with a small black sprocket hole, since the mask is set to Add by default; this looks essentially like a negative version of an actual filmstrip. You'll flip the colors in the next step.

5 Select the Film Strip layer, and press M on your keyboard to reveal the layer's mask group. Set the mask mode to Subtract in the Timeline's Switches/Modes column.

Now you have a black strip with a white sprocket hole in the upper-left corner. The hole is actually transparent and displays whatever is underneath the layer—in this case, the composition's background color.

A Subtract mask creates the first sprocket hole.

One sprocket hole isn't enough for a filmstrip, so next you'll clone your sprocket to create the lines of sprockets that would appear on a strip of film. (What comes to mind when you see the word *sprockets*? How about a TV host named Dieter—German pronunciation, as in "Deeter"—and a touchable monkey? But I digress…)

Duplicating the sprockets

The hardest part of creating your filmstrip is over now that you've created the first mask. Next, you need to duplicate the mask enough times to create the other sprockets:

Tip: To make it easier to position your sprocket-shaped masks, increase the Composition window's magnification and use the Hand tool to navigate around the window. You can press the Shift key to temporarily switch to the Hand tool.

---

1 Expand the Film Strip layer in the Timeline, highlight the Mask 1 name to select the mask, and then choose Edit > Duplicate to duplicate the mask. At this point you should duplicate the mask only once in order to establish the spacing between your sprockets.

2 With Mask 2 still selected in the Timeline, press the Down Arrow key on your keyboard until the mask is lower than the first mask and there's black space between it and the other film sprocket.

Tip: For more visual guidance as you lay out your masks, you can display a grid or rulers in the Composition window by choosing one or the other from the View menu.

Now that you've decided on the spacing between the sprockets, you can duplicate the two masks to create the next set of sprockets.

3 Hold down the Shift key, and select both masks in the Timeline.

4 Choose Edit > Duplicate, and then press the Down Arrow key until the selected masks are below the other masks and all the masks appear evenly distributed relative to one another in the Composition window.

Tip: Press the Shift key with the Down Arrow button to move the masks a larger distance than pressing Shift alone.

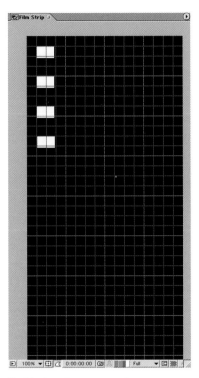

Positioning the new masks

5   You may have guessed that you should now select all four masks, duplicate them, and move the new masks below the others.

6   Repeat the duplication until you've created enough sprocket holes to spread across the left side of the composition.

The masks subtract from the solid layer to create the appearance of film sprockets.

7   To create the sprockets holes that should appear on the right side of the filmstrip, duplicate all the masks, and press the Right Arrow and Shift keys until the new masks are in position between the right edge of the movie layer and the right edge of the solid layer.

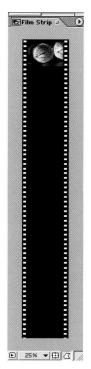

Adding sprocket holes to the right side of the layer

Adding More Film Frames

To create the remaining film frames for your filmstrip, you'll use the same technique you've been using thus far: duplication. This time, though, you'll use a simpler method to lay the videos out across the filmstrip than you used to position the sprockets. Instead of saying, "Your procedures have become tiresome," you'll say, "I am as happy as a little girl!" (sorry— I can't resist including these *Saturday Night Live* references whenever the term *sprockets* appears).

Here are the steps:

1   Duplicate the Ch19FinishedProject layer nine times in the Film Strip composition so you have a total of ten copies.

2   Set the Position of the topmost video layer in the Timeline to 160, 1900 to place it near the bottom edge of the composition.

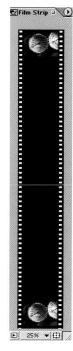

You can distribute the remaining videos between two strategically positioned videos.

3   Select all ten video layers, and click the first Distribute Layers button in the Align palette—in other words, the first button in the second row of buttons in the palette. (Wouldn't it have been nice if you could have used this feature to distribute the sprocket masks evenly across the solid layer? Unfortunately, this feature only works with layers at this time.)

The Align palette

The Distribute Layers buttons instantly position layers evenly between the two layers that are most distant from one another.

4   With all the video layers still selected, turn off each layer's Audio switch.

Creating the Master Comp

You've created your filmstrip, and it's almost time to animate it. First, though, you must create an environment for it to run through:

1   Create a new composition named Master using the Medium, 230 × 240 composition preset with Duration 10:00 seconds.

2   Place the Film Strip composition into the Master Timeline starting at time 0:00.

3   Set the Film Strip layer's Scale to 70, 70%.

4   To change the duration of the Film Strip layer, select the layer and choose Layer > Time Stretch. Set Duration to 9:29, and click OK.

5   Still at time 0:00, add the **Ch19FinishedProject.mov** file to the Master Timeline under the Film Strip layer.

6   Apply Effect > Blur & Sharpen > Fast Blur to the Ch19FinishedProject layer. Set the effect's Blurriness to 30.

7   Apply Effect > Adjust > Levels to the Ch19FinishedProject layer. Set the effect's Input White value to 200; this value blows out many of the layer's highlights and helps stylize the video's content.

Animating the Filmstrip

"Now is the time on Sprockets when we dance!" In other words, it's time to animate the strip of film to run across the screen. The film will go across the screen at different speeds, slowing down so the viewer can see particular sequences playing within the filmstrip frames and appreciate all your hard work, and then speeding up to fast-forward through some sequences. In addition, you'll animate the filmstrip's Scale to add a sense of space around the filmstrip as it appears to move closer to the user.

Follow these steps:

1   Add a Position keyframe to the Film Strip layer at time 0:00, and set the Position to 160, 940; this value moves the entire layer offscreen and just below the composition's bottom edge.

2   Go to time 2:00, and change the Film Strip layer's Position to 160, 600. This moves the filmstrip upward and across the Comp window.

3   Go to time 2:15, and change the Film Strip layer's Position to 160, 150.

4   Go to time 3:00, and change the layer's Position to 160, 340.

5   To make the filmstrip hold its current position from time 3:00 to 4:15, go to time 4:15 and put a checkmark next to the Film Strip layer's Position property in the Timeline's A/V Features column. Doing so adds another Position keyframe with the same value as the previous one.

6   Go to time 5:00, and change the layer's Position to 160, 0.

7   Go to time 6:00, and change the Position value to 160, 340.

8   Still at time 6:00, add a Scale keyframe with a value of 70, 70%.

9   Go to time 8:00, and change the layer's Scale to 100, 100% and Position to 160, 630.

Simulating motion blur

To make your animated filmstrip even more convincing, it should appear blurred when it's zipping by at its faster speeds. To exaggerate the motion blurring, you'll use a blurring effect and animate the blurriness so that the filmstrip goes in and out of focus as it slows down and speeds up:

1   Apply Effect > Blur & Sharpen > Box Blur to the Film Strip layer. Set the effect's Iterations to 3 and Blur Dimensions to Vertical.

2   Go time 2:00, and add a Blur Radius keyframe with a value of 0 to the effect. This value leaves the movie in focus; no blurring occurs.

3   Go to time 2:10, and change the effect's Blur Radius to 30.

4   Go to time 3:00, and change the effect's Blur Radius to 0 to bring the movie into focus again.

5   Go to time 4:15, expand the Box Blur effect in the Film Strip layer, and put a checkmark next to the Blur Radius property in the A/V Features column to create another Blur Radius keyframe with a value of 0.

6   Go to time 4:20, and set the effect's Blur Radius to 30.

7   Go to time 5:00, and change the Blur Radius to 0.

Now Try This

This chapter's project can serve as a great foundation for other variations. For example, imagine adding five more filmstrips, each showing a different movie, and placing the strips in 3D space with different Z-axis Property values. But before you take this project out and run with it, you need to complete a few finishing touches to complete the final look of this chapter's finished movie:

• To give the filmstrip more of an organic feel, like that of a real filmstrip, apply the Turbulent Displace effect to the Film Strip layer.

• To give the filmstrip the texture of film grain, apply the Add Grain effect (new in After Effects 6.5) to the Film Strip layer. If you're feeling really ambitious, you can use an image scanned from film, and apply the new Match Grain effect to the Film Strip layer to give it the same appearance of grain.

CHAPTER 22 | Video Cubes

The 3D features in After Effects let you change the position and rotation of any layer along the layer's X, Y, and Z axes, essentially like moving around pieces of paper that vanish from view when perpendicular to the camera. But you can't make a layer truly 3D with depth and volume. Instead, you can assemble multiple items together so they look like a single 3D object with a shape that you can view from any angle and which you can animate as a whole.

This chapter shows you how to assemble a 3D cube made of videos and stills and then animate the cube so it implodes into the scene, spins fast, pauses to show off a video on its side, and repeats that cycle until it explodes out of the scene. You can use the same techniques to create a variety of very dynamic moves and transitions with any other virtual 3D object you design.

In addition, you'll learn how to design a blinking cursor that discloses words onscreen and a unique logo reveal that fits the style of the entire project.

It Works Like This

Check out the **Ch22FinishedProject.mov** file in this chapter's folder on the book's DVD. This project shows you how to create and animate a 3D cube that's formed from a circle of movies that fly in from behind the viewer to become the top, bottom, and sides. The cube spins, pauses to reveal a movie on one side, and then spins fast to reveal a different side. You'll use these techniques:

1. Position a movie and still layers to form a 3D cube.

2. Use a Null Object layer to animate the cube's sides so they implode into the scene, forming the cube; spin at different rates of speed; and then explode out of the scene.

3. Create a background made of words that crisscross the screen and recede into the distance.

4. Create a virtual command line, complete with blinking cursor and letters typed onscreen.

5. Gradually reveal the logo, strip by animated strip.

Words scroll in both directions as walls of video and a logo fly in.

The cube spins and pauses at each side's video while a blinking cursor types out titles.

Invisible stripes wipe the logo in as the cube explodes.

Preparing to Work

The six sides of the video cube you'll build are made with four movies and two copies of an Illustrator file. You'll import these files and create your first set of compositions next.

To prepare for this project, do the following:

1   Start with a new project, and save it as Ch22VideoCubes.

2   Import the **MovieClips** and **Stills** folders from this chapter's folder on the DVD into the Project window.

3   To create a new composition for each of the movie clips all at once, select all four movie files in the project window, and then drag them simultaneously onto the Create A New Composition button located at the bottom of the window.

4   In the resulting dialog, set the Create option to Multiple Compositions, and click OK. Four new compositions named for each movie appear in the Project window. You'll work with these in the next section.

5   Create a new composition named Main, using the NTSC D1 Square Pix, 720 × 540 comp preset.

6   If the composition's background isn't already colored black, choose Composition > Background Color and set it to RGB: 0, 0, 0.

Creating the Cube

The first task in designing your animated video cube is to form the cube by positioning your movie compositions (the cube's sides) in 3D space. To make it easier to then animate your cube, you'll create a Null Object layer and assign it as the parent to the movie compositions. By parenting the movie comps to the Null Object layer, you can rotate and move all the movies together while only creating and managing the keyframes for one layer: the null object. Follow these steps:

1   Drag the four Clip compositions into the Main Timeline starting at time 0;00.

2   Turn on the 3D switch in the Timeline's Switches column for all the layers.

3   Create a new Null Object layer (Layer > New > Null Object) starting at time 0;00. You'll use this layer to animate the cube in a later section.

4   Turn on the Null 1 layer's 3D switch.

5   Set the Null 1 layer's Anchor Point to 50.0, 50.0, 0.

6   Select all the layers except the Null 1 layer, and then set each layer's Parent value to Null 1 in the Timeline's Parent column.

7   Choose View > New View to open another Composition window for the Main comp.

8   Choose Top from the new view's 3D View pop-up menu at the bottom of the Composition window. The Top view lets you see the cube's shape from above as you build it.

9   Select the four Clip layers in the Timeline, press R on your keyboard to display their Rotation and Orientation properties, and then press Shift+P to also display their Position properties.

10 Set the following values for the Y Rotation properties of the Clip layers that are listed here:

    Clip 02 Comp 1: 0 x +90.0

    Clip 03 Comp 1: to 0 x +180.0

    Clip 04 Comp 1: 0 x +270.0

11 Set the following values for the Z-axis Position property of these Clip layers:

    Clip 01 Comp 1: -160.0

    Clip 03 Comp 1: 160

12 Set the following values for the X-axis Position property of the Clip layers that are listed here:

Clip 02 Comp 1: −110.0

Clip 04 Comp 1: 210

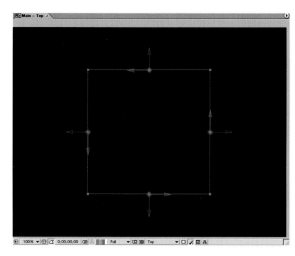

The video cube seen from the comp's Top view

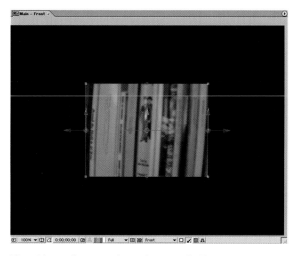

The video cube seen from the comp's Front view

Capping the cube

You've created the four sides of your cube, and now you need to add a top and bottom to it. This time you'll use a still image of a logo to form each side, instead of video:

1 Add the **a2d_designlogo.ai** file from the Project window to the bottom of the Main Timeline starting at time 0;00.

2 Duplicate (Edit > Duplicate) the a2d_designlogo layer once.

3 Move one of the a2d_designlogo layers in the Main Timeline's layer stack so it's layer 2 below the Null 1 layer.

4 Set the X Rotation of the a2d_designlogo layer that's layer 2 to 0 x +270.0 and its Y position to −70.

5 Set the X Rotation of the bottommost a2d_designlogo layer 7 to 90 and its Y position to 170.

The cube's top and bottom caps

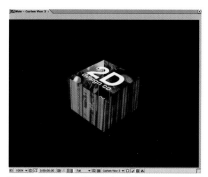

The cube seen from the View 3 comp view

Imploding the Cube

The video cube in the finished animation starts with all its sides separated and offscreen. The sides then quickly come in from all directions until they meet and form the spinning cube.

Your first task is to create the keyframes for the starting position of each side before they implode and come together:

1   Select all the layers in the Main Timeline, and press the P key to display only the Position properties in the Timeline.

2   Go to time 2;00, and add a Position keyframe to every layer except Null 1.

3   Press Home on your keyboard to go to time 0;00, and then set the following Position values for the listed layers:

   a2d_designlogo, layer 2: 50, -490, 0

   Clip 01 Comp 1: 50, 50, -580

   Clip 02 Comp 1: -530, 50, 0

   Clip 03 Comp 1: 50, 50, 580

   Clip 04 Comp 1: 630, 50, 0

   a2d_designlogo, layer 7: 50, 590, 0

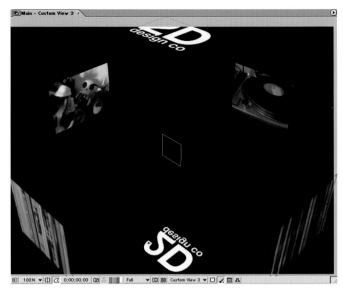

The cube viewed in Custom View 3 before it implodes

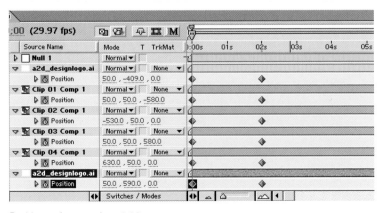

Position values at time 0;00

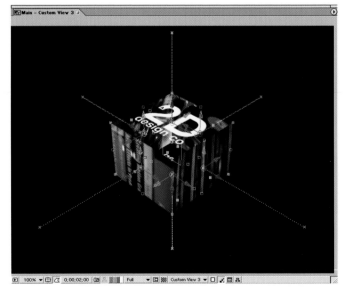

The cube with motion paths that illustrate the path each side travels on

The cube's sides currently come in at full Opacity. To give them more nuances, you can fade them into the scene by animating their Opacity:

1   Select all the layers except Null 1 in the Main Timeline, and press T on your keyboard to display their Opacity properties.

2   Go to time 0;15, and click any selected layer's Opacity stopwatch in the Timeline to add a 100% Opacity keyframe to every selected layer.

3   Press Home to go to time 0;00, and set the Opacity of any selected layer to 0% to change the value for all the selected layers.

Now the video sides appear translucent when they're in the distance and become more opaque and distinct as they come together.

Exploding the Cube

You've done all the work of animating the cube so it comes together. Now you'll reverse the animation so the cube explodes out of the comp at the end of the animation. Instead of repeating the steps you performed to create the first half of the video cube's animation, you'll duplicate the existing Position keyframes and reverse them in time. Here are the steps:

1   Select all the layers except Null 1 in the Main Timeline, and press P to display their Position properties.

2   Deselect the layers.

3   Click the first Position property's name to select all of that layer's Position keyframes, and then copy (Edit > Copy) the layer's keyframes.

4   Go to time 13;00, and paste (Edit > Paste) the keyframes onto the same layer.

5   Repeat steps 3 and 4 for the remaining layers.

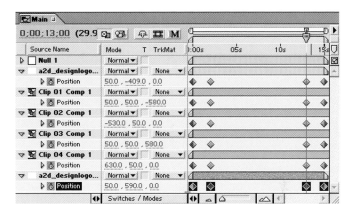

Duplicating the first pair of keyframes on each layer

6   Use the Selection tool to drag a marquee around (appears as a dotted line as you drag) and select all the Position keyframes that appear starting at time 13;00 and later in the Timeline. To create a selection marquee, make sure you click somewhere other than on a keyframe or a duration bar.

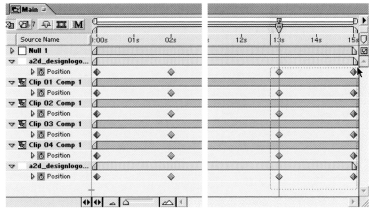

Dragging a selection marquee around the layers' last pair of keyframes

7   With all the layers' last two Position keyframes selected, choose Animation > Keyframe Assistant > Time-Reverse Keyframes. As a result, the box appears intact at time 13;00, just as it does at time 2;00, and it appears exploded at time 15;00.

8   To increase the speed of the box's explosion, use the Selection tool to select all the Position keyframes at time 13;00.

9   Go to time 14;00, start dragging the selected keyframes, and then press Shift to snap the keyframes to the current time (14;00 seconds).

If you press Shift before you begin dragging a selected keyframe, you'll deselect whatever keyframe you clicked on instead of snapping all the selected keyframes to the current time.

If you expand the Null 1 layer's Transform group in the Timeline and change the values of its Orientation, you'll notice that the box sides remain in cube-formation whether the box is exploded or intact and that the box faces a different point in space according to the Orientation values you specified.

The box at time 11;03 with the Null Object layer's Orientation set to 92, 179, 183

Make these final adjustments:

1   Set the Spinning Cube Pre-comp layer's Scale to 75, 75% and Position to 360, 208.

2   Turn on the layer's Continuously Rasterize switch in the Timeline's Switches column.

Spinning the Box

Currently, the cube's sides come together to form the cube, time passes, and then the cube explodes out of view. Your next task is to make the video cube spin in place really fast at certain times and slowly at other times. To do this, you'll animate the Null 1 layer, which you've already assigned as the parent to every cube side at the start of this chapter. As a result, the cube sides will inherit the Null 1 layer's keyframes (although no new keyframes appear in the Timeline for the cube sides' layers) and animate as one without disturbing the cube shape they form.

Follow these steps:

1   Select the Null 1 layer, and press R on your keyboard to display its Rotation and Orientation values.

2   Make sure the Null 1 layer's Orientation is 0, 0, 0 in the Main Timeline.

3   Create a keyframe for Y Rotation at time 0;00 with a value of 0 x +0.0.

4   Press End on your keyboard to go to the end of the Timeline at time 14;29, and change the Y Rotation to 10 x +0.0.

The keyframes you just created rotate the box ten times from the start of the animation to the end. Next you'll add keyframes so the box spins quickly and then slows down at various times:

1 Set the Null 1 layer's Y Rotation property to the following values at the specified times:

>   2;00: 5 x 0
>
>   2;20: 5 x 70
>
>   4;20: 5 x 110
>
>   4;25: 5 x 235
>
>   6;25: 5 x 290
>
>   7;00: 6 x 165
>
>   9;00: 6 x 205
>
>   9;05: 6 x 340
>
>   11;05: 7 x 20
>
>   11;10: 8 x 50

2 At time 0;00, add an X Rotation keyframe with a value of 0 x -90.

3 Go to time 2;00, and set the X Rotation value to 0 x +30;00.

4 Press End to go to time 14;29, and change the X Rotation value to 0 x 0;00.

5 Select all the layers in the Main Timeline, choose Layer > Pre-Compose, and name the nested comp Spinning Cube Pre-comp.

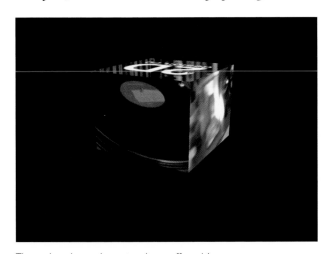

The cube slows down to show off a video.

Adding Reading Material

Your next task is to create the background of words crisscrossing the screen behind the video cube. You'll create a line of text and stagger copies of it in time with the help of layer markers, to create a loop of words sliding across the screen in a single line:

1 Create a new composition named "letters 1 row Forward", using the NTSC D1 Square Pix, 720 × 540 composition preset, with Duration 59;28.

2 Go to time 0;00, and create a Text layer that displays the following text on a single line with Font Family set to Arial or Helvetica Neue and Text Size set to 26:

hard working · ambitious · creative · problem solvers · authors · parents · people like you · musicians · painters · geeks · lovers ·

Most of this text appears offscreen because of the length of the layer.

3 With the text layer still selected in the Timeline, go to time 8;00, and then press Alt (Windows) or Option (Mac OS) and the] key to change the layer's Out point to the current time. This shortens the layer to 8 seconds.

4 Still at time 8;00, add a Position keyframe to the text layer and set its value to -1108, 270. This puts the text completely offscreen.

5 Go to time 0;00, and change the layer's Position to 1832, 270. The text is still offscreen, but now you should see the dots of the layer's motion path going horizontally across the middle of the comp.

6 Go to time 6;02, and choose Layer > Add Marker to add a layer marker at the current time. You'll use this marker to make the words travel continuously across the screen.

7 Duplicate the text layer 10 times so you have a total of 11 copies. Notice that the duplicate layers retain the layer marker you added to the original.

8   To go to time –6;02, click the Current Time Marker in the upper-left corner of the Timeline. In the Go To Time dialog, enter **–6;02** (that's *negative* 6;02). The Current Time Indicator disappears, since you're currently outside the duration of the Timeline.

9   Still at time –6;02, select the bottommost text layer in the Timeline, and then press [on your keyboard to move the layer to start at the current time. Note that the layer above starts where the bottommost layer's layer marker appears in time.

![Timeline window showing letters 1 row Forward with 11 layers of "hard working" text aligned at start]

The selected layer's In point is off the Timeline.

10 Leave the bottom two layers where they are in time, and line up all other layers so that each starts where the layer marker of the layer below it appears in time. The easiest method is to go the point in time where the lower layer's marker appears and then Shift+drag the layer above to snap the start of the layer's duration bar to the current time at the layer marker.

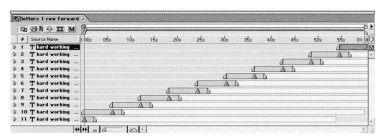

Staggering the layers in time so each starts at the layer marker of the layer below it

If you preview the comp, the line of text travels across the screen from right to left and looks like it never ends.

Changing directions

To make the background more dynamic, it also needs lines of text going in the opposite direction of the text you just created. Luckily for you, this part is far simpler than before. You'll duplicate the "letters 1 row Forward" composition and reverse its keyframes in time:

1   Duplicate the "letters 1 row Forward" composition in the Project window. Name the duplicate "letters 1 row Reverse".

2   Open the new composition, and select all of its layers in the Timeline.

3   Press P to display the Position properties of all the layers.

4   Hold down the Shift key as you click each layer's Position property name to select all of the Position properties.

5   Choose Animation > Keyframe Assistant > Time-Reverse Keyframes. As a result, both keyframes in each layer switch positions in time, causing the words to travel from left to right instead of right to left.

Adding rows and rows

All that work, and you've got only two lines of continuous text! Now you'll duplicate those compositions and position them up and down the Main composition:

1   Open the Main composition, and close all other comps.

2   Go to time 0;00, and add both the "letters 1 row Forward" and "letters 1 row Reverse" compositions to the Main Timeline below the Spinning Cube Pre-comp layer.

3   Duplicate both "letters…" layers once, and set the resulting four
    layers' Position properties as follows (the layers' stacking order doesn't
    matter):

    letters 1 row Reverse: 325, 255

    letters 1 row Reverse: 345, 315

    letters 1 row Forward: 355, 345

    letters 1 row Forward: 245, 285

The Main composition at time 0;00

4   Select the four "letters…" layers, and turn on the Continuously
    Rasterize switch in the Timeline's Switches column.

5   With the four text layers still selected, choose Layer > Pre-Compose,
    and name the new composition "letters 4 rows".

6   Duplicate the "letters 4 rows" layer four times so you have a total of
    five copies. Select all five, press P to display their Position properties,
    and set their values as follows:

    1 letters 4 rows: 360, –10

    2 letters 4 rows: 360, 110

    3 letters 4 rows: 360, 230

    4 letters 4 rows: 360, 350

    5 letters 4 rows: 360, 470

7   Select the five "letters…" layers, and turn on the Continuously
    Rasterize switch for each.

8   With the five "letters…" layers still selected, choose Layer > Pre-
    Compose, and name the new composition Letters Background.

When you play back the animation, the background should be filled with
rows of words traveling horizontally in both directions.

The Main comp at time 2;09

Adding some dimension

You've created your background of words crisscrossing the screen behind
your video cube, but you could argue that the background seems to flatten
the cube. A drop shadow (yawn…) might help, but in this case you'll use a
different technique to add some depth to the scene: You'll make the background appear to fade away into the depths of space behind the video cube.
Here are the steps:

1   Press the Home key to go to time 0;00, and then add the **gradient.tif**
    file to the Main Timeline above the Letters Background layer.

2 Set the Track Matte of the Letters Background layer to Luma Matte "gradient.tif" in the Timeline's Modes column. The background of words now fades in from the top to the bottom of the Comp window.

The luminosity of the Letters Background layer matted by the gradient layer

3 Go to time 11;00, and add a Position keyframe to the gradient layer. Set the Position to 360, 270.

4 Go to time 13;00, and change the layer's Position to 360, 680.

These keyframes move the gradient layer from the center of the composition window downward until it's offscreen. The background of words disappears from view as a result.

Now, compare the illustration of the frame at time 2;09 to the same illustration of this frame in the previous section. Even though you and I know that the background of words has no depth, the user will focus on the cube's shape, and the background will seem like a landscape receding into the distance. It's a nice effect without having to skew the lines of text into perspective.

The Main composition at time 2;09

Adding the Command Line

The finished animation includes a blinking white cursor that appears in the lower-left area of the comp. The cursor moves from left to right to reveal a word as if the word is being typed onscreen. To create this component, you'll animate a solid to create the blinking cursor and animate another solid's scale to matte and reveal underlying words.

Your first task is to create the Text layers:

1 Create a new Text layer for each line of text that follows (four text layers total), with Font Family set to Arial Black or Helvetica Neue, Text Size set to 26px, Fill Color set to white (RGB: 255, 255, 255), and Alignment set to Justify Last Left:

    ad campaigns

    posters

    promotions

    trailers

2 Select the four new text layers in the Timeline, press P to display their Position properties, and set all their Positions to 100, 440.

This puts all four words toward the lower-left corner of the composition. The words are unreadable at this point, since they're stacked on top of one another in a jumble of white characters.

Creating the blinking cursor

The blinking cursor is actually a Solid layer that continuously cycles from 100%, to 66%, to 33%, to 0% Opacity over time. You'll also make the cursor move across the screen so it looks like someone's typing the underlying words:

1 Go to time 0;00, and create a Solid layer named "cursor" with Width 10 and Height 50, colored white (RGB: 255, 255, 255).

2 Go to time 2;00, make sure the cursor layer is selected, and then press Alt (Windows) or Option (Mac OS) and the] key to trim the layer's Out point to 2 seconds.

3 Go to time 0;10, and add a Position keyframe with a value of 100, 430. This puts the cursor at the start of the four words.

4 Go forward 1 second to time 1;10, and change the layer's Position to 430, 430.

5 Press Home to go to time 0;00, and press T to display the cursor layer's Opacity property.

6 Still at time 0;00, add a 100% Opacity keyframe to the cursor layer.

7 Go forward three frames, and change the layer's Opacity to 0%.

8 Go forward three frames, and change the layer's Opacity to 33%.

9 Go forward three frames, and change the layer's Opacity to 66%.

10 Click the Opacity property name to select all of its keyframes, and then copy them (Edit > Copy).

11 Go forward three frames from the last Opacity keyframe in the layer, and paste the keyframes. Repeat this step until the cursor layer has Opacity keyframes spanning its entire length of time, as marked by its duration bar.

12 Duplicate the cursor layer three times so you have four copies, one for each word.

13 Place one cursor layer above each of the text layers (trailers, promotions, posters, ad campaigns) in the Timeline's layer stack.

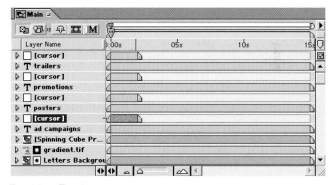

The Main Timeline

Wiping the words

The final component of your virtual command line gradually reveals a word one character at a time after the blinking cursor has passed the character. You'll create this effect by animating the scale of a Solid layer and using the solid as a track matte for the word. Your first step is to set up and animate the solid:

1 At time 0;00, create a new Solid layer named Wipe with Width 380 and Height 50, colored white (RGB: 255, 255, 255).

2 Set the Wipe layer's Anchor Point to 0, 25 (the middle of the left edge of the Solid layer) and Position to 50, 430. The Solid layer now overlaps the four stacked words and the blinking cursor.

3 Go to time 0;10, and add a Scale keyframe to the Wipe layer with a value of 4, 100. The Wipe layer is now just slightly wider than the blinking cursor.

4   Go to time 1;10, and change the layer's Scale to 100, 100. Now the Wipe layer grows in length from left to right over time.

5   Duplicate the Wipe layer three times so you have four copies, one for each word you need to reveal.

6   Place one Wipe layer under each cursor layer in the Timeline's layer stack.

Your Timeline should have layers in the following order: cursor, Wipe, trailers, cursor, Wipe, promotions, cursor, Wipe, posters, cursor, Wipe, ad campaigns, Spinning Cube Pre-comp, Letters Background.

The Main Timeline

Animating the words

Your final tasks to complete the virtual command line are to assign each word a Wipe layer for the word's track matte and then stagger the words in time along with each word's associated cursor and solid layer. Follow these steps:

1   Set the Track Matte of each text layer (trailers, promotions, posters, ad campaigns) to Alpha Matte "[Wipe]" in the Timeline's Modes column. Now the Wipe layer that's above each text layer serves as a matte to the word.

2   Select all the layers except Letters Background and Spinning Cube Pre-comp in the Main Timeline.

3   Go to time 2;00, and press Alt+] (Windows) or Option+] (Mac OS) to trim the selected layers' Out points to the current time.

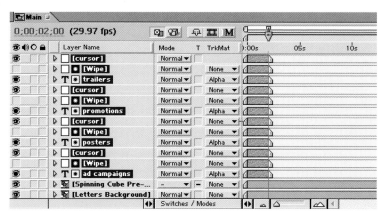

Trimming the command line's layers

4   Select the top three layers (cursor, Wipe, trailers) in the Main Timeline.

5   Go to time 2;20, and press the [key to move the selected layers so they start at the current time. The cube has already come together at this point, so you want each set of command-line layers to start at this point in time or later.

You'll move the remaining cursor/wipe/word groups in time next.

6   Select the next three layers (cursor, Wipe, promotions) in the Timeline.

7   Go to time 4;25, and press the [key to move the selected layers in time.

8   Select the next three layers (cursor, Wipe, posters) in the Timeline.

9   Go to time 7;00, and press the [key.

10 Select the next three layers (cursor, Wipe, ad campaigns).

11   Go to time 9;05, and press [.

Staggering the words and their associated cursor and wipe layers in the Main Timeline

12   Select all the layers except Spinning Cube and Letters Background, and then choose Layer > Pre-Compose. Name the new composition what_we_do. Make sure the what_we_do comp layer is above the Spinning Cube Pre-comp layer in the Timeline.

At time 5;15, the blinking cursor reveals the word *promotions*.

Revealing the Logo in Stripes

Your video cube uses a company logo for its top and bottom sides, but the videos in the cube sides get the most exposure as the cube whirls and spins. To give the logo the attention it deserves, you'll put it in the spotlight near the end of the animation and fully reveal it as the cube explodes in the background. To do so, you'll create a unique reveal for the logo by animating a bunch of solids in the shape of vertical stripes. Then you'll use the solids as a track matte for the logo so only strips of the logo appear wherever a solid's invisible stripe appears:

1   Create a new composition named Line Wipe using the NTSC D1 Square Pix, 720 × 540 composition preset, with Duration 15;00 seconds.

2   Create a white (RGB: 255, 255, 255) Solid layer starting at time 0;00 in the Line Wipe Timeline, with Height 540 (the same as the Main comp) and Width 172.

3   With the Solid layer selected in the Timeline, press Enter or Return and type Square 1.

4   Duplicate the Solid layer nine times so you have ten copies total. The new layers are automatically renamed Square 2, Square 3, and so on (new in After Effects 6.5).

Note: If you had duplicated the layer without first changing the layer name in the Timeline, the names of the new layers wouldn't be automatically renumbered as they are in the previous step. That's because the name you set in the Solid Footage Settings dialog is actually the Source Name, which appears in the Project window and the Timeline's Source Name column.

---

5   To change the width of the new Solid layers, select a layer in the Timeline and press Ctrl (Windows) or Command (Mac OS) and Shift+Y to open the Solid Footage Settings dialog. Set the Width of the new Solid layers as follows:

Square layers 10 and 9: 20

Square layers 8 and 7: 100

Square layers 6 and 5: 50

Square 4: 120

Square 3: 35

Square 2: 65

6   Select all the layers, and press P to display their Position properties.

7   Add a Position keyframe at time 0;00 to all the layers.

8   Deselect the layers, and scrub only the X value (the first value) of each layer's Position property so every layer is offscreen with some to the left and some to the right of the composition area. You want the value for each layer to be unique from the other layers so the solids come in seemingly randomly after you set their landing Position keyframe in the next step.

These are the Position values used for this chapter's finished project movie:

Square 10: -18, 270	Square 5: 750, 270
Square 9: 740, 270	Square 4: -68, 270
Square 8: -56, 270	Square 3: -22, 270
Square 7: 776, 270	Square 2: 752, 270
Square 6: -38, 270	Square 1: 806, 270

9   Go to time 2;00, and change the X value of each layer's Position property so that the white blocks line up edge to edge (in no particular order) and fill the entire Comp window. Make sure you see nothing but white across the whole screen.

These are the Position values for the layers at time 2;00 in the chapter's finished project's movie:

Square 10: 562	Square 5: 140
Square 9: 10	Square 4: 492
Square 8: 670	Square 3: 182
Square 7: 66	Square 2: 230
Square 6: 596	Square 1: 348

10 Choose Window > The Wiggler to display that palette.

11 Click the Position property name of the Square 1 layer, and set the following values in The Wiggler palette:

Apply to: Spatial Path

Noise Type: Jagged

Dimension: One Dimension X

Frequency: 5

Magnitude: 500

If you play back the animation, that block moves more frenetically across the screen.

12 Select the Position property name of the next layer in the Timeline, and click Apply in The Wiggler palette.

13 Repeat step 12 for the rest of the Solid layers.

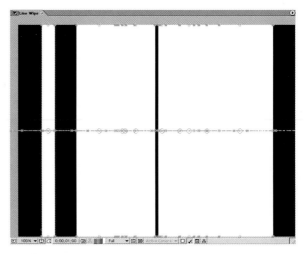

The Solid layers slide in horizontally to fill the composition with white color.

When you play back the animation, all the blocks move across the screen more madly than before you applied the Wiggler. The layers stop after 2 seconds and fill the screen with white color.

Adding the logo

To reveal the logo as animated stripes, you'll use the Line Wipe composition as the logo's track matte. As a result, the solids in the Line Wipe comp won't be visible, and the logo will only appear through the animated shapes of the solids:

1 Open the Main composition, and close any other open compositions.

2 Go to time 10;25, and add the Line Wipe composition to the top of the Main Timeline's layer stack.

3 Add the **a2d_designlogo.ai** file below the Line Wipe composition in the Timeline.

4 Set the a2d_designlogo layer's Scale to 145, 145% to enlarge it.

5 Set the a2d_designlogo layer's Track Matte to Alpha Matte "Line Wipe" in the Timeline's Modes column. The Line Wipe layer now reveals the logo when it plays.

Strips of the logo appear wherever an invisible solid overlaps the logo.

Now Try This

To add the finishing touches to the project, do the following:

• Double the length of the Main composition's duration, and then hide and reveal the logo multiple times. Fade out the logo at the end.

• Add a street address, phone number, and Web address to the Main composition. Animate them in with a Text Animation preset from the Effects & Presets palette.

• Experiment with The Wiggler palette to make the motion paths of the video cube's sides more dynamic and chaotic as they implode and explode.

INDEX